AWAKENING GODS

Teachings From Beyond The Veil
Volume II

T0105548

Also by Jack Bentley

The Last Enemy
Teachings From Beyond the Veil

AWAKENING GODS

Teachings From Beyond The Veil
Volume II

Jack Bentley

Order this book online at www.trafford.com
or email orders@trafford.com

Most Trafford titles are also available at major online book retailers.

Printed in Victoria, BC, Canada.

ISBN: 978-1-4269-2965-6 (sc)

ISBN: 978-1-4269-2966-3 (e-book)

*Our mission is to efficiently provide the world's finest, most comprehensive book publishing
service, enabling every author to experience success. To find out how to publish your book, your
way, and have it available worldwide, visit us online at www.trafford.com*

Trafford rev. 5/18/2010

 www.trafford.com

North America & international
toll-free: 1 888 232 4444 (USA & Canada)
phone: 250 383 6864 ♦ fax: 812 355 4082

Cover Drawing

In the center eye of the cover scene of this book is a depiction of two visions I received on the mornings of August third and forth, 2004, which are reprinted below. I have to apologize to the reader for the feeble attempt to depict something that is indescribable and totally beyond reproducible even with our vast computer graphic technology; however, I felt I must try to produce some type of illustration of what I observed.

The reason I felt I should put this particular drawing on the cover in vivid color is that some of my readers might, on a deeply subconscious level, recognize it and understand that they and I are on the same page spiritually. This could give us the opportunity to realize our spiritual kinship and encourage further communication. This awesome scene is eternally imprinted in my memory.

This drawing shows a swirling universe with the individual consciousnesses of the children of the Most High progressively awakening from their semi- consciousness in this physical realm. Over millenniums these individuals have progressed from spiritual slumber into ever greater states of love and awakening until they achieve total enlightenment and ascend as one with the Most High, the Source of All-That-Is. I present the two visions below in order that you might consider these as you proceed to read the book.

2004 8/3 – This morning during my meditations, **I saw what I believe was the spiritual essence of our Father expressed in light-energy**.

I was praising Him when, suddenly, I saw an awesome scene. In my dark study, with my eyes open and/or closed, I saw a cluster (ring) of bright golden/reddish lights appear around a circular center network of flashing violet lightning strings. The violet lightening strings looked like a nearly solid web of violet light in the space at the center of the golden/reddish light ring. The violet lightning strings seemed to be originating at a center point and flashing out in all directions to the golden/reddish ring. The golden/reddish light ring and the inner violet web resembled a round eye—the iris and pupil. Then, all around the golden light ring in the black background were many tiny white lights brightly flickering on and off and darting about. It was breathtaking to watch.

I believe I was seeing here displayed in light-energy, the essence of our Father's consciousness. It was incredible!

2004 8/4 – This morning during my meditations, I saw the same scene as yesterday morning. This time, however, the intensity became even brighter, and the scene began to change. The golden/reddish light ring began changing colors. The golden/reddish ring changed to bright yellow, but the violet web-work in the center remained. Then, between the yellow light ring and the violet web network, a bright red ring formed. The bright flickering lights outside the yellow light ring were even bigger and brighter this morning. As I watched, the black background beyond the flickering lights, turned from black to foggy grey, and in the background beyond the fog, I became aware of something whirling like helicopter blades, spinning slowly just out of sight. These whirling images were turning both clockwise and counter-clockwise. This scene lasted through my entire meditation.

Preface

Why should you read this book or any other that concerns spiritual ascension? You must do so because you realize you have not yet learned, or you are not yet totally convinced that **you must seek your truth from within your deeper self directly from the Source of All-That-Is**. Probably you are not yet convinced, because you have not yet realized that **your spirit mind can only, ultimately, believe what you receive inwardly from the Father, the Source of All-That-Is**. Until that time, you will be seeking your truth from some modern scientific academia, ancient religious orders, or some current prominent guru. But, they cannot impart truth to your heart—they can only impart words to your mind, words that will be meaningless to you if not confirmed by your deeper self. **All truth comes from within, from the Source of All-That-Is.**

I am a messenger—nothing more. If I completely understood all that has been revealed to me, I would have already ascended. I know that much of what I have been given is for others, and I know we must all realize deeper truths together.

See if these messages resonate with you. Forget the messenger. He is still stumbling along trying to find his way home, but the journey becoming clearer and more exciting every day.

I quote many spiritual masters and other sources in my writings, and usually try to remember, or find, and reference the source of the words. You will notice that I quite often make *exact* quotations from the King James Version of the Bible. This is because, over the years, I have read it so many times that much of it is memorized. You can find great truth in the Bible, but you can also find much religious myth and also outright error. Many dirty hands have handled the translation and editing of those pages—be careful when you read them.

You must learn to glean the truth wherever it is presented. This can only be done by asking your inner, deeper, self if what I am being told or reading is truth. Your inner self knows and will respond; you will feel the truth!

As in my first book, *The Last Enemy*, the messages I have been given do not always follow the same subject from day to day. Most of the time, in fact, I receive totally different messages each time the spirit world speaks to me. I have however, compiled some related messages in the addendum to this book concerning fasting and light ingestion.

Sometimes, as I am writing my comments on a message, I begin to receive further, deeper insights to the original message. You will probably notice the changes in authority and depth as this occurs, and usually, I will record these words in bold italics. The lighter, normal print are my words and comments.

You probably realized after reading my first book that my spiritual journey has now lasted over fifty years. This might be of some concern to some of you. You might think, based on the time it has taken me to see the truth I am now aware of that you don't have enough time left in your life to achieve enlightenment—until you reach a place where you know union with our Father. Not so! Let me remind you of a great truth Jesus gave us concerning spiritual growth. In Matthew 20:16, He said, "*The last shall be first, and the first last.*" **Already, I have watched some of you mature astoundingly fast as you apply yourselves to listening to our Father's voice within.**

A special note about advice from my attorney: You should all know by now that I am not a medical doctor. Some of my book's words have to do with healing, fasting, and light-energy ingestion and probably do not coincide with the opinion of most of the medical profession. Even so, you should seek medical advice before following the instructions given to me by the spirit world or before going on any restricted diet.

You will notice various references to Mother Earth in my writings. Sometimes I call her by the Greek name of Gaia. I think that in the future, I shall probably call her by the far-ancient name of Tiamat as inscribed on the ancient clay and lapis records from Egypt and the Middle East as translated by Zecharia Sitchin.

There will be very little in the Table of Contents in this book because the Spirit World Teachers do not dwell on the same subject day after day, and I am inclined to keep the messages in their chronological order. I believe there is sound reason for the messages being given in this particular order, and I believe that is the way they want it published.

When I refer back to messages recorded in my first book, *The Last Enemy Teachings From Beyond the Veil*, I will refer to the book only as *The Last Enemy*. When I cite references to messages in this present book *Awakening Gods*, only the date will be shown.

Acknowledgements

My Father, my Spirit Guides, Helpers, and Guardians never stop talking to me and sharing my Father's wisdom from beyond the veil. The more often I pause before my Father in praise and silence, the more wisdom He pours out on me. In spite of me, He continues to enrich my mind with His knowledge and truth. He sends his precious emissaries as guides, guardians, healers and helpers. For them, too, I am eternally grateful. I am sure I have kept them all busy since I was a child, especially, my guardians.

I have to acknowledge and praise my dear wife, Jonnie Ann for her constant support and encouragement, without which, it would have been exceedingly difficult for me to write this book. My appreciation also must go to my excellent proofreaders: my wife Jonnie Ann; my sister, Sandra Perl; Margaret Burroughs of Erie, Colorado; and Geoff Cutler of Hornsby, Australia.

The photographic illustrations are my own, but all the drawings were prepared by Drew Mannie of Dropshadow Studios in Denver, Colorado. If you would like to contact Drew, his e-mail address is: <u>dropshadow802@ aol.com</u>.

Contents

IMAGE INDEX

Introduction

We can exist above the toil, trickery, and terror of this planet. We do not have to be influenced by the violence, sickness, war, fear, envy, lies, and deceptions of this 21ˢᵗ century world. We can live in peace and joy, with great health, wealth, and spiritual insight. We each deserve a great life experience and we can have it.

We do not have to face the fear of death from every side day and night. We can live free of fear and even free from death.

This book is a continuation of the wisdom and revelations I received and shared in my first book, *The Last Enemy,* It seems our Father wanted these two books separated by a time span so the words in the earlier book could be assimilated into the many hearts that have read and will read and accepts them.

I'm taking for granted that you, the reader, have already read my first book, but if you have not, you probably should get a copy and read it in order to understand where I am coming from spiritually. The first half of that book tells my personal story and how I came to hear the teachings from the spirit world. The earlier foundational truths given to me in those pages are further built upon in this volume.

The messages recorded in this book, as in my first, are as clear a representation of what I heard as I can make them. At times, after I had recorded a message, the voice would again speak to me, saying, "That is not quite what I was saying. Let's go over it again." At those times I would look at the recorded message and change it as instructed. At times, even weeks later, as I was typing up my notes; a voice would caution me that something was still wrong with what I wrote. Again, I am always obedient when I am instructed to correct or perfect the messages. This reminds me of the Apostle Paul's message in the book of First Corinthians, 13: 9-12. He wrote: *"For we know in part, and we prophesy in part. But when that which is perfect is come, then that which is in part shall be done away. When I was a child, I spake as a child, I understood as a child, I thought as a child; but when I became a man, I put away childish things. For now we see through a glass darkly; but then face to face; now I know in part; but then shall I know even as also I am known."* The Apostle Paul was trying to tell us to not take everything he (Paul) wrote as The Last Word on a subject, because it was "in part" and not the total package of truth.

Each of us has the responsibility to listen, read, observe, then compare, and confirm every word or idea presented with that "witness" within us, our deeper self—the Source of All-That-Is. We will all finally come to realize that we cannot continuously follow other men and their firmly-held beliefs no matter how prominent, educated, or spiritual they may seem to be. We must come to that time in life when we believe only what is spoken or confirmed to us internally, from the Source of all truth.

The ***bold italicized*** words are those messages spoken to me from the spirit world from my Father directly, or through my unseen spiritual guides and teachers. The regular lighter print is my comments on the messages. When I reprint a message from my first book, *The Last Enemy*, it will be indented and presented in smaller print.

Awakening Gods

TEACHINGS FROM BEYOND THE VEIL
VOLUME II

Recently, a lady friend of mine said to me, "Jack, my ten year old daughter asked me, 'Where did God come from?'"

She said, "I told her; 'I will ask Jack.'"

I said, "This is the perfect question people of any age should be asking in order to begin to grow spiritually. They must first recognize their limitations. Tell your daughter that she must grasp the truth that she exists in a <u>sealed mental sphere</u>, or <u>behind a veil</u>, where only a small part of truth may be known. She will remain there until she learns to penetrate the veil, and reach for her truth. For example, we cannot grasp the "*beginning.*" Everything we know in physicality must have a beginning—because it is here! But, how can a rock actually exist if, in the beginning, there was nothing? The rock is here now. I can see it—I can feel it. But, I cannot understand how it got here originally if there was nothing but empty space, and it had to be empty space if there was a beginning (?) The scientific community tells us that it was all formed from cosmic dust coagulating together and forming physical stuff. But, then we ask, 'Where did the physical, cosmic, dust come from?' Others say there was a big bang—a big bang of what? What terrible fuel source was out there that exploded, and formed billions of universes, galaxies, suns, and planets? The religious community tells us that God created it all in six days, so we ask, where did God come from? It just doesn't register, does it? It just does not make sense to us. It does, however, make sense to some."

"In order to make sense of it all, we must come to understand that there is a mental sphere above us, or veil between us and a deeper knowledge, which presently hides the truth from us. We must find a way to penetrate this veil and get to the deeper truth. This can be done only from within our deeper self—that all-knowing genius that resides within, our Father, the Source of All-That-Is."

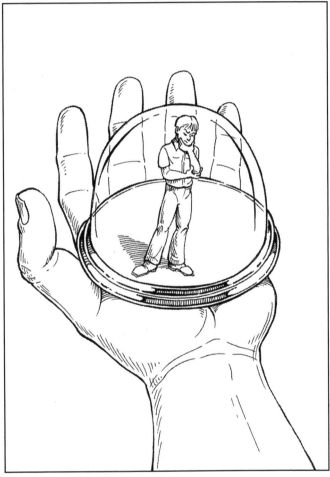

A Sphere Over Our Understanding

The pathway to the Source within is what my books are all about. This pathway has never been hidden from us, so if we come to a time in our lives when we earnestly desire to find truth, it will be opened to us. Our Father does not show partiality. He does not love one of us more than another. He anxiously awaits everyone's response to His moving in their consciousness. He is always drawing each of us to Himself. All we need to do is open up to Him from within.

2002 11/13 - *"Our struggle is not against people, for we only fight against negative thoughts, ideas, precepts and attitudes; <u>but first those apparent in ourselves.</u>"*

<u>"First in Ourselves"</u> are the key and fundamental words here. Our struggle, as we awaken, is seemingly impossible at times as we confront our own habitual thoughts, our global-thought-forms, our appetites, our darker tendencies, our *perceptions* of ourselves and this world around us. It seems like a never-ending battle against countless foes for dominance of our own human mind. How can we ever possibly engage these perceptions and habitual thought forms and win? Let's find out!

A review of a truth taught in my first book, *The Last Enemy,* will help here. Reference 2000 8/16:

> *"When you pray for, or send light-energy to others, empower their quest! They are where they are supposed to be."*

We need to remind ourselves daily that everyone, including ourselves, are exactly where we are supposed to be spiritually right now. It doesn't matter what behavior a person is manifesting presently; that person is doing what he or she <u>must</u> be doing, and what he or she and our Father agreed he or she must be doing to grow spiritually through this present physical manifestation. <u>Our only problem is our judging the actions of ourselves or other people.</u> This shows a lack of understanding of the truth stated above. I am, and he or she is, exactly where we are supposed to be. Our judging of ourselves and others shows our lack of love which would allow us and other people the room to grow through these experiences, no matter how long it must be endured. According to the words given in, *The Last Enemy,* 2000 8/30:

"If you were not capable of doing anything that is happening on this Earth today, it would not be happening at all! It is all part of you doing all that is going on. It is not positive or negative; it just is! Don't judge."

We must allow it all. Within each of us are the answers to every question or situation we face. We have the mind (consciousness-awareness-wisdom-knowledge) of our Father, the omnipotent source, creator, sustainer, of all that is. We need to learn to TUNE IN to His mind (our deeper consciousness) in order to face and overcome any and all situations that we face. We need to learn to stay tuned in to this inner consciousness to keep the truth flowing to us. Discovering how to do this on a continuous basis is why we are here.

One simple method of learning to tune-in is just ask, "What would our Father do in this situation?" Some of us, during our days in denominational religion learned to ask, "What would Jesus do?" We found it worked. There was always an obvious answer to any situation or problem. We seemed to know instinctively and instantly, exactly what Jesus would do, even though, a moment before we didn't have a clue of what to do. Why? We knew what to do because we tuned in to His consciousness within our own mind. We did this before we knew the truth of who we really are and that we have the mind of our Father within us. We must come to know that the consciousness of our Father abides in each of us, and thereby everyone living in physicality or the spirit world, present or past, is a part of that consciousness. We can tune in to any entity living in any realm at any time. Therefore, we are really always turned in. On 10/24 2000, *The Last Enemy*, I was taught that Yeshuah Ben Joseph (Jesus); Michael, the archangel; Gandhi; Enoch; Isaiah: Elijah: Buddha, Mohamed, and all other teachers are available to me—in my own consciousness. We are all one being. We are already connected, so just tune in; ask and let them speak. Remember what happens when we asked, "What would Jesus do?" It works! All we need to do is ask, "What would Gandhi do?" or "What would Elijah do?" We share our Father's mind and therefore, every other mind that has ever existed. There is no limit in this—we are free agents to communicate with whomever we choose from any date in time, before time began, *"or in any future realm."* I don't know where that last phrase came from. I guess He will talk more about the inference here later.

2002 11/13 - *"Global-thought-forms are living spirits created by us, the sons of God. Yes, we are omnipotent beings, ever able to create eternal spirits like ourselves, just as the Father created us. Negative spirits or negative global-thought-forms, must be CONVERTED (re-polarized) to become positive. There are only <u>love</u> (Positive), or <u>fear</u> (Negative) thought-forms. Knowing this, you can lovingly deal with every negative spirit. Love (passionate compassion) is the only force that can effect that change."*

There you have it! We are one with our Father (omnipotent creators). Our thoughts (imaginations) are creating **as-we-go**. We can be our own greatest enemy, or our own deliverer. We must guard our minds and our thoughts.

Our personal thought-forms become global-thought-forms as more and more people accept them. Our minds are always broadcasting thought-forms and these are being received by people all over the world. If these thought-forms appeal to them and are not out-rightly rejected by them, then these thought-forms become part of their subconscious thought-form reservoir. At the same time, we are receiving their emotional thought-forms. The natural flow of so many of us dwelling on a particular thought-form gives it local, then regional and finally global power through global acceptance, hence, a global-thought-form.

These words are loaded with wisdom and victory. We create both positive (love) thought-forms and negative (fear) thought-forms every day as we go about our daily living. Our accompanying emotion is what seals these thought-forms in our consciousness.

We are aggravated by many of the negative spirits (thought-forms) that torment us because we accepted these negative global-thought-forms. These negative spirits or thought-forms infiltrate the consciousness of our body cells and create illness and physical disorders. Cancer and heart disease are examples of this.

We accept a negative thought-form or concept and begin to worry that such and such a disease might manifest in our body. By dwelling on the possibility we might have or might contract such a disease, we eventually program our minds with these negative thought-forms. Then, we must deal with them. Over a period of time, we **program** related body cells to manifest the disease by our constantly dwelling on the fear of its manifestation. We subconsciously direct our body to produce the illness that could destroy our body. Our body cells are absolutely faithful and will produce the disease they believe we desire by our thought creation process. The cells of our bodies love us with a compassion that will even allow them to destroy themselves in order to be obedient to our wishes.

Thank God, they also can be redirected, or reprogrammed to heal any illness, infirmity, or disease we might have created or allowed to be created. We certainly do "reap what we sow." If we sow the seeds of negativism, we will surely reap the fruit of fear, disease and death. If we sow the seeds of love, joy and peace, we will re-polarize the negative thought forms in our minds to be positive, and begin to live victoriously every day. Our victory will be evidenced by a greater love, joy, peace, and health in our lives. We will see victory over illness, aging, and the calamities of this Earth experience.

2002 11/14 – *"Look past the evil that men do and engage that spirit that is plaguing the individual. Deal with that spirit in love and kindness. The CORE of every being is the Father—Love."*

We are seeing people today, even heads of nations, who seem to be obsessed with religious and/or political perceptions and ambitions that are contrary to love and peace. Some of these people are in a state of manic depression (fear) over paranoid ideas (perceptions of persecution) and feel alienation at the hands of others, which means "I must kill the infidels or be killed!" Usually this kind of obsession is the result of a lifetime of systematic teachings of paranoia, hatred and persecution.

Yet, the people perpetrating these kinds of evil teachings and the recipients are entities whose core is love. It is not from love that this evil is manifesting—it is in spite of that love. The core love entity in the people is being pressed into silence by the dominate obsession with negative thought-forms. The Bible states in 1Timothy 4:2: *"…having their conscience seared with a hot iron."* The Apostle realized that it is possible to completely turn off our conscience by our willful pushing aside the voice of the Source of love that dwells within each of us.

Look past the outward manifestation of these obsessed people and realize you are engaging alien negative thought-forms or spirits. Deal with these spirits in love.

Father spoke again: *"Be sure of this: Every spirit longs to be positive and to manifest love and harmony—that is their primary quest."*

This means also that we must look past <u>our own</u> negative thoughts and actions and engage those entities who are oppressing us—the thought-forms we are negatively obsessing about—our own self-created negative thought-forms. We must engage these spirits and love them into positive energy. Our core being is love (our Father), so we must be what we really are—LOVE. Remember, we are omnipotent beings. Therefore our thoughts are creating constantly—that is our nature. Only our time-delay agreement prevents our thought generated creations from instantly manifesting before us.

2002 11/14 - *"Your mission is to heal those spirits throughout the universe who are not manifesting their love. You do this by seeing them* <u>as they will be</u> *and not as what they are presently manifesting. THEY COULD NOT PREVENT THEIR CREATION INTO NEGATIVITY. They all LONG FOR FREEDOM from negativity that they might live and serve us all in great love, peace and harmony with All-That-Is."*

First, are there other people in this universe? Father, would not have said our mission is to heal them throughout the universe if they do not exist. However, He does not say what, if any, physical form they might be.

Every person and spirit entity longs for a life of love, joy, peace and harmony with others, and longs to dispel the fear that causes them to be less than they could be. *Every individual person has an irresistible love alive inside him or her* which is the real individual. This love cries out for release that it might manifest in their present body. We must help, but first we must help our own selves. We heal ourselves, not by judging ourselves, but by seeing ourselves as we will be—a gloriously ascended expression of love, and not as what we are presently manifesting both mentally and physically. Physician, heal thyself! Then you will be able to help others.

2002 11/14 - *"You asked, 'Can these negative spirits be embodied?' Yes, they can and many are embodied on Earth today. Many are living among us on Earth and only mature spiritual beings can help them. Keep your mind open about this. You have been resisting this teaching."*

I pleaded, "Lord, I am not even aware of how I am resisting, or what I am resisting. Please show me!"

These negative spirits **we** have created anxiously await our spiritual awakening, that we might free them from doubt, fear and the terror of living constantly opposed to themselves, and constantly having to fight the demands and attacks of everyday life. They want to wake up from this hell that binds them. Some of these negative spirits are busy destroying our bodies which they love with a passion, but they are absolutely diligent to perform the task we have assigned them with our negative thought-forms. Help them! And, help yourself to perfect health.

2002 11/14 - *"Those the Father created in the beginning were beings (spirits) created in His own image, LOVE. Likewise, we are omnipotent beings and are creating beings/spirits after our own images (imaginations). However, unlike the Father, we are creating both positive (love) spirits, and negative (fear) spirits. Now you can understand why we have to guard our thoughts and words. We are creating and empowering all the time."*

We need to learn and be constantly aware that **we are omnipotent**, "creating" every minute by every emotional thought we think. We cannot stop creating. Creating is our nature. We are omnipotent creators. No wonder the world is full of chaos! I'm responsible for some of it. I still, many times, indulge in emotional negative thinking, accusing, blaming, judging and doubting. We must stop this! *Everyone is exactly where he or she are supposed to be* in his or her individual spiritual evolution, and <u>so are the nations of this planet exactly where they are supposed to be.</u> Let them evolve.

2002 12/04 - I asked in meditation this morning, "Father, I want to love and adore you as you love and adore me. Show me how."

A voice answered, *"Love Me in them! Hidden in each one of them is a unique part of Me. Find it and you will find another adorable part of Me and of yourself. Think of the pearl hidden in the oyster. I'm there, find Me!"*

Pearl in the Oyster

"Them," means both people and the spirits troubling other people and ourselves. Every troubling spirit is another fearful entity that must be freed from fear. Once that fear and negativity is converted to love, an irresistible, unique, eternal and compassionate entity will be revealed. Also, *"loving Me in them,"* means all entities, including the less conscious animal kingdom and even the quietly conscious element/ Earth kingdom. It is all alive, and its life is our Father.

If you are critically ill, do remember dear friend, the cells that are producing the illness in your body believe they are honoring your deepest desire to destroy the body, because that is what you are fearfully dwelling on; and that may be your earnest destiny, and that is all right. But, if you really don't believe you want to die and leave this body, then love your body cells for their diligence on your behalf and redirect their efforts toward wellness of your body. They will obey! They desperately want to serve you. Just do the redirecting over and over again day after day **until you believe it**, and you will see they get the message too.

2002 12/11 - *"See the uniqueness in others. Look past your judgment of their good or evil and see the uniqueness that is Me. It is also a unique part of you. It is all together lovely and good."*

The method you use to implement another's recovery from negativism (fear/evil) is love. Look past the facade people put up and engage that uniqueness that is the real person, the irresistible one. If we can discover and receive this truth and understand that every person, animal, and even every rock, is a unique part of our Father—**is a part of His consciousness, love and softness, His strength and certainty, that is manifested nowhere else in all creation**, then, <u>we can finally see the irresistible One everywhere</u>; Then, we are home!

2002 12/16 - *"When you judge another, you are judging another part of Me. You are judging a part of yourself. Remember what Jesus said: 'Judge not that ye be not judged.'* (Matthew 7:1) *Now you know His deeper meaning."*

I have received this message before, but evidently, I needed to hear it again. I keep forgetting all these people who sometimes disgust and offend me, are manifestations of my Father and of myself!

Take time to reflect on this message. Don't you want to see and understand more about yourself? Look into the eyes of those around you! See the positive and negative manifestations of yourself—it is all you. It is all me. We really are all various manifestations of each other.

Would you take the time to look into the eyes of the next person you meet—seeking a glimmer of that real, eternal, irresistible brother or sister, a part of the Source of all that is, that is manifested nowhere else in the universe? You may never again in this life be permitted to view this facet of our Father.

Take time also to look into the eyes of any dog you meet. Dogs were created to teach man the art of unconditional love. You will find first, that dogs prefer to live with people more than with their own species. They _feel_ their mission to teach us love more than they understand it. They feel deeply that their mission is to teach us unconditional love. They will take our constant abuse and still lie down before us, lick our hands and wait for more abuse. They will stand by us when all others forsake us, and as much as is in their power, they will protect us with their own lives. They will always let us know we are loved. They will greet us when we arrive home from work with tremendous joy and welcome us back into their world with joy and kisses. They never judge us as doing wrong when we carelessly mistreat or disappoint them. Like our Father, they love us unconditionally, and eternally. They are definitely an expression of His love.

2002 12/16 - _"Each person you encounter is another part of yourself. Are you seeing them? Are you seeing yourself? Observe! Learn of yourself."_

I know this is hard! It is hard to try to find myself in some of the folks we meet. I'd rather not consider the possibility that some of them could be manifesting a part of me, but they are, and I need to know this part of me, too. I must learn of myself.

I need to remember the message I received on 2000 8/30, *The Last Enemy*.

> *"If you were not capable of doing anything that is happening on this Earth today, it would not be happening at all. It is all part of you doing all that is going on. It is not positive or negative; it just is! Don't judge."*

Again, on 2000 8/30, He said:

> *You are here to find out who and what you are; to find out what you are capable of. You have to know yourself before you awaken to the omnipotent power that you are."*

We must remember that everyone, every-last-one, is here under the same conditions and restrictions that we are: They don't know who they are. They don't know that they are omnipotent. They don't know they can speak universes into existence. They all agreed to this linear time-delay existence that they might grow thereby. They have not been given rules to live by. **They don't know how to act here on Earth because their memory has been erased!** They have been placed in this wilderness and told to find their own way home. But, they don't even know what or where home is. Each one, not only allowed this experience, they ordered it! Most don't know what to believe or how to behave. Most live out their lives in fear and disbelief, even in the churches. (Hosea 4:6) *"My people are destroyed for the lack of knowledge."* The knowledge they lack is, knowing that they can gain wisdom and understanding to live by simply going inward until they link up with their inner self, our Father's consciousness. We will return to this Earth or some other hostile environment again and again until we find this truth.

Actually, every entity you encounter be they human, animal, vegetable or mineral is another part of yourself. Observe. They are each an individual entity. They are every single one, a living spirit. You can know them! You must learn to know them!

2002 12/27 - *"You must learn to rest in Me, even in the most desperate and serious situations. This is why you continuously face new disturbing events. You must learn to ALLOW EVERYTHING. You, yourself, have written the script for your own life's situations and events. Rest in this truth!"*

How could I ever doubt this? During every desperate situation in my life, my Father has been there to protect, comfort and deliver me. How could I ever not be cognizant of His presence?

Have I really pre-written the script for all these desperate and disturbing events I face? Sometimes, in reply to this utterance, I think I may have overestimated my spiritual ability and depth when I set up my life's script. I find it hard sometimes to REST, ALLOW and believe it will be a victorious experience, but deep down I am aware of ultimate victory.

2002 12/29 - *"Remember, I told you:* (1988 11/8) *'Your financial success is unavoidable?' Do as you will. I cannot, and will not change that promise.'"*

At this time, the fall and winter of 2002, things were not looking very promising for our lawn irrigation equipment supply business in the Colorado Front Range with a three-year drought in progress, water restrictions, and no relief in sight. Actually, some meteorologists are predicting five to <u>thirty</u> more years of this drought in the Colorado Front Range.

I pondered, "Am I going to have to lead this company into other business ventures, or is adequate moisture going to return to the Front Range?"

Another thought crosses my mind concerning the above words. "Why do we constantly and unquestionably take the words of these self-proclaimed experts as the last truth on a given situation?" This particular meteorologist made his prediction of gloom and doom just as our local and national media always love to do: dwell on the most negative, hurtful, fearful, debilitating, annoying words possible, but never predict the positive, delightful, uplifting and helpful future. It is anathema in the news publishing business to say anything positive and helpful. Why is this so? Is it because we are so full of fear that fears and tragedy are all we want to hear? Is fear all that sells? Or, is it that the experts and publishers are so full of fear themselves that fear is all they think about, talk about, listen to and agree with? I think that is it. They all live in fear and feed on fear so fear is all they see and know. What else could they publish?

2002 12/30 - *"You must face desperate situations until you learn to allow them and rest in them, or until you decide to cure them by your own creative energy."*

I am certainly feeling desperation now that there is only twenty percent of normal mountain snowfall in the Rocky Mountains. The Colorado Front Range receives its water from the mountain snow-melt run-off each year into its reservoirs. My business is the wholesale distribution of lawn irrigation products. Sales were down twenty percent, and looking as if they could fall to as much as fifty percent.

I am additionally concerned because I have just recently purchased a new home, and my former home has not yet sold. Everything in Colorado has slowed down, including home sales.

Three years ago, Jonnie Ann and I purchased a mountain getaway home. So we are presently making two house payments and, on top of that, an equity loan payment we arranged on our old house to pay down the balance on the new home.

Now, He is telling me I can "cure" the desperate drought situation by my own creative energy. How do I cure a drought? I know He will show me very soon.

As you can see from my thoughts above, I certainly hadn't yet fully learned to rest in these desperate situations. Thank God, I have been given so many miracles in my life to know I can, if I will, sit back and rest in Him and His words. It is out of my hands and in His. Lord, teach me to rest completely in You!

2003 1/8 - I was awakened at 4:00a.m. by someone calling urgently, *"Jack!"*

I rose up and asked, "What?"

The voice again called, *"Jack!"*

Again, I answered, but no one was there. My wife was still asleep beside me and was not awakened by the voice or my reply. I realized it was time to get up for meditation.

We must keep our appointments with our Father, angels, healers, helpers, guides and guardians. We need them a lot more than they need us. Yet, some have dedicated their existence to serving us.

2003 2/1 - *"I am your soul's mate. Rest in Me! Rest in Me!"*

I responded, "Lord, I'm trying to rest in you, but the situation around me hasn't changed, no matter how much I pray about it. Like they used to say in the South, 'It's hard to drain the swamp when you are up to your hips in alligators.' I know you are saying, 'Like a soul-mate I am always with you.' But, sometimes I'm unaware of your presence when I see the chaos around me. Help me rest in You, Father."

2003 2/5 – *"Remember in 1998, I told you to 'Avoid emotional distractions that might effect your meditations?' This is one of those distractions, as is the mountain house."*

OK, just three years ago, we purchased a house in Big Elk Meadows near Estes Park, for a mountain getaway. It is a beautiful mountain house, and we were really enjoying fixing it up and spending most of our spare time up there. Yes, I let it become a distraction, a big one.

Our Mountain House in Big Elk Meadows

During the drought in the spring and summer of 2002 a mountain forest wild-fire (The Big Elk Fire) swept through the mountains behind our mountain home. It came down the mountain behind our house to within forty feet of the house.

Our mountain community fire department had covered our house with fire-retardant foam as the fire approached in hope this would save our house. There is a lake in front of our house, and as the raging inferno raced down the mountain, the fire fighters fled across the dam to the other side of the lake, and standing on the other side of the lake from our house, they said their faces were burning from the heat of the fire behind our house. The foam is supposed to withstand 3000 degrees for at least an hour. It did!

The fire retardant foam saved our house and other houses in Big Elk Meadows that were backed up to the mountain, but then we were advised of another problem. The burning of the pine needles in the trees on the mountain behind our house during the forest fire will cause a substance like wax to drip on the ground, covering it with a plastic-like sheet. The Forrest Service told us we could expect the ravine running down the mountain behind our house to be flowing full of water when the fall monsoon rains came—if they came. We were told by the Forest Service that we needed to widen and deepen the ditch behind our house and redirect the water away from the back of the house.

I rented a backhoe and bobcat and cut the ditches as the Forrest Service advised. Then I dammed up and turned the old ravine to re-direct the mountain runoff water to a new ditch. I then lined my new ditch, and the dam, with landscape fabric and cobblestone which made it very pleasing to the eyes.

Later, the rains finally came with a vengeance, much longer and much harder than folks up there had seen in their lives; the water came rushing down the ravine three feet deep washing away the cobblestones and ignoring my beautiful new ditch, but cut its own new ditch next to my garage. I spent the summer of 2003, constantly repairing my ditch. Presently, I am digging out and deepening the new ditch where the water seems to want to go beside my garage. I am lining it with rubber and then with three inches of concrete. As we pour the concrete, I am pressing the rescued cobblestones into the wet cement. Hopefully, the ditch will hold now, and the cobblestone liner will remain in the ditch. (Note: In 2004, it held up wonderfully all year.)

2003 2/6 - *"Do not resist. Rest in Me. Be like a leaf floating on water; it delightfully goes wherever the water takes it. <u>Water</u> is taking you where you need to be."*

I love these words! My first thought was, "Have you ever tried to rest in a desert that you know is crawling with scorpions? Lord, I'm trying to rest, but these problems wake me up at night. How do I rest?"

I was reminded of the words given to me on 2000 8/16, *The Last Enemy*.

"They are where they are supposed to be."

I related how I was taught that water is a type and shadow of the words of the Father; His divine plan is guiding my steps and the events in my life. I do need to rest in the water. I need to rest in the words I have received. I need to realize my life is being directed by Him with my best interests at heart. He knows what is best for me, and right now what is best for me is to learn the lesson of resting in Him, trusting His judgment and plan for my life, no matter what the outward situation. He knows what experiences I need and is throwing those situations at me that will most quickly shape my thinking and advance my enlightenment.

I must learn this lesson or endure endless tests and trying situations that are used to force me to give up and give in to my own life's plan; then rest in it, knowing it will happen exactly as my Father and I planned for my spiritual growth evolution. I will Rest!

2003 2/20 - *"Know who you are. You are that consciousness that pervades all that is."*

He is pressing on my mind that the water and weather share my consciousness—my consciousness is in every drop of water on Earth. I believe this truth will be of utmost significance in other activities later in my life's mission.

I believe He is telling me that the water that is resting in the Pacific Ocean is a part of me, waiting for me to call it forth into the clouds; that I am also the winds awaiting my commands to bring the clouds to the Rocky Mountains so the rains will end this drought.

2003 2/21 - *"Remember seeing the creation of the Sun? That light beam was focused consciousness. Consider this and learn to focus your consciousness on what you desire."*

"You Are Seeing the Sun's Creation."

After struggling a month or two with this focusing technique, I said, "All right Lord, **with high emotion** and with as much focus as I can muster, I will command the rains to come." With this, I went out into a field in the foothills and faced west toward the Rocky Mountains and the Pacific Ocean. I wanted my eyes to be fixed on raw nature as I prayed and created this weather system.

I commanded, "Let the rains come! Let them come gently but plentiful so as not to flood the farmers' fields and the cities. Let there be an abundance of water in the Front Range."

The plentiful rains began within a few days. Water restrictions were eventually reduced or cancelled throughout the state.

Do I take credit for ending the Colorado drought? What do you think?

This truth and teaching was not just about bringing back the rain, but a life-long admonition about creativity. We must learn to focus our consciousness, our awareness, and attention on what we want to create, change, stop, cure, receive, or desire but without causing a negative or harmful effect on others.

This "Focusing of Consciousness" is a technique that must be practiced until it becomes a part of our everyday life; it must become evident that we are able to affect changes at any time, not only in the atmosphere, but anywhere, on any object or situation on Earth.

At first it seems impossible to concentrate and focus intently because of the way the mind wanders and resists. This is because our habitual method of thinking is haphazard, and wandering, not concentrated. It takes much practice and dedication. (Later on in relating some words I received in 2008, I will reveal a technique of ALWAYS being able to quiet the mind.)

Warning: Trying to use this focused creativity to negatively affect others will bring disaster to one's self. Don't even think about using this technique to hurt or gain control over another person, even for what you feel would be beneficial to them. ("*They are exactly where they are supposed to be.*") Leave them alone! Use this technique on others only when they **personally** ask for help. Otherwise, there will be deep conflict between you and that other person's prearranged life's script, and you will experience a crushing set-back in your spiritual growth.

2003 3/26 - *"The reason you have been so hungry lately and so dissatisfied when you eat is that your whole being is hungering for the Words of Life. Remember, I told you, (2002 1/18) 'When you are hungry, feed on the words you have been given.' Eventually, you will be able to distinguish between physical and spiritual hunger. You have been so busy and distracted relocating that you have not been as frequently feeding on the words. Hence you hunger."*

I have learned when He speaks to listen, and write the words down. Then read them and re-read them every day until they are a part of my being. I find rest and peace in His words.

There will come a day when each of us will hunger and thirst for His word and companionship. We will develop an insatiable appetite for our Father. We will realize this appetite can be satisfied by nothing else but the ecstasy of His presence.

2003 4/16 - *"Your bank account is in the spirit world and is always full. You have the freedom to withdraw any amount, anytime and purchase anything you desire. Wouldn't you rather have it in your unlimited spiritual account than in your local Wells Fargo Bank?"*

Yes, He is talking about earthly, physical purchasing power, too. Most of us think we are limited by the money we have on deposit in our local bank. That is not so! We are **unlimited** in what we may have. All that exists is created from spirit energy, so we may have all and anything we want, if we will take the time and put forth the effort to create it. We, just have not yet learned the truth of these words. Remember the words on "Focused Concentration" given on (2003 2/21). He spoke:

Remember, too, that no matter how much you create for yourself, it doesn't diminish what others may have; it is all spirit. You are not hording or taking away from those who have less or from those who have more. Those who have more or less than you have the same ability as do you to create anything and all that they desire; hence, as the scripture says: "...Ye have not because ye ask not." (James 4:2)

2003 5/30 - "*The messages and miracles earlier in your life were given that you would know with certainty who is speaking to you later on.*"

The miracles let me understand, and continually remind me of the invisible realm and its unlimited power. Often I am reminded of the voice that told me to wash out the spilled gasoline on the bulk plant loading platform just before the fire flashed (Page 108 of *The Last Enemy*) or of the dematerializing trip through the gasoline semi-tanker when I turned in front of it (Page 111 of *The Last Enemy*), or warning of a child on the bicycle (Page 65 of *The Last Enemy*), or the terrifying experience in the high Canadian Rockies when I had to turn my forty-foot motor home around on a narrow road on the side of a high mountain, when I thought, "We're going over!" (Page 131 of *The Last Enemy*) I realize now just how much I need this assurance. I reinforce my resolve, belief and faith constantly with the remembrance of these utterances and miracles from the spirit world.

WARNING OF A CHILD ON A BICYCLE
(Story from page 65 of
The Last Enemy - Teachings From Beyond the Veil)

I took a job with Sears in Augusta, Georgia, selling tools in their hardware department. Jonnie Ann and I lived in a two-room, upstairs efficiency apartment in Aiken, South Carolina, not far away. We had to park our car behind the apartment building. To exit the parking area, I had to drive down a narrow, blind alley between two buildings to reach the street.

One morning about 6:00 a.m., as I was driving down this blind alley, an urgent voice from somewhere shouted, *"Stop! There is a bicycle!"* I screeched to a stop at the edge of the sidewalk just as a bicycle passed in front of my hood.

"Stop! There's a Bicycle!"

Someone had just saved a teenage boy's life and saved me from the heartache of what could have happened. But, where did the voice come from? There was no one around, just me, shut up in my car. I was dumbfounded, and I was delighted. Apparently, an angel, God, or someone else, had just shouted at me, and saved this kid's life. Who would ever believe this?

"WASH THE GASOLINE OUT NOW!"
(Story from page 108 of *The Last Enemy,*)

After planning to go to Alaska with the Atlanta Body (part of an interdenominational church), I felt I needed to quit my job with A.O. Smith so I could stop traveling and prepare to move to Alaska. I left A.O. Smith and joined my local A.O. Smith distributor in Atlanta as I began to get ready for the move to Alaska.

First, I had to find, purchase, and prepare a vehicle to transport my family and all our belongings to Alaska. It would have to endure the fifty degrees below zero arctic temperatures throughout the long winters. Secondly, Jonnie Ann and I had to advertise and sell our home and most of our belongings. Then we would have to buy wilderness gear suitable for the homestead we were planning to occupy. Meanwhile, I began working with the local A.O. Smith distributor selling petroleum equipment, and servicing problems that would come up on the A.O. Smith valves and meters.

One evening after Jonnie Ann and I had gone to bed and were nearly asleep, a huge explosion shook our house. Both of us jumped out of bed thinking something must have just blown up in the neighborhood. As we opened the doors to go outside, another explosion rocked our house, and we saw the sky light up over toward a petroleum bulk plant about five miles away. I knew it was a customer of mine where I had been installing and calibrating some new A.O. Smith tank-truck loading equipment. Other explosions erupted, both large and small. I jumped in the car and raced to the site, but fire fighting equipment was all over the place, and the streets were closed off for a mile around. I could get nowhere near the place. I went home and stayed up all night watching the flames and hearing more explosions as the bulk plant was leveled. One of my friends was killed in the initial fire.

We eventually found out exactly what had happened. The bulk plant was located on a hill overlooking a small subdivision. During the night, the plant was receiving gasoline from a pipeline that ran through the area. The plant manager miscalculated the amount of product one of the largest tanks could receive; consequently, the tank, a floating roof tank, overfilled, tilting the floating roof so that gasoline ran over the top and down the side, filling the dike around the tank. The gas fumes being heavier than air, eventually flowed over the dike and downhill to the nearby subdivision. The fumes entered the crawl space of the first six houses and eventually found the pilot light of one house's furnace. The crawl space, being full of gasoline fumes, exploded and blew the house away killing all the occupants. Then fire erupted under other houses, and they began to burn. The tank farm manager heard the initial explosion in the subdivision, and ran out to see what was happening. He ran down into the storage tank diked area and suddenly realized what had happened. He was standing ankle deep in gasoline. He knew a tank had run over, and the fumes had rolled down the hill into the subdivision. Then, in a panic, he realized the flames were surely headed up the hill to the tank farm and straight for him. He raced for the edge of the dike to try to escape the flame that was surely going to come over the dike into the gasoline-filled, dike area. He never reached safety. The flames caught him about ten feet from the dike edge. That is where they found his charred body.

It was three days before all the flames were extinguished and salvage crews could enter the area. It took some time for the wrecking crews to cut up and clear out the burned and twisted tanks, buildings, and loading platforms. Then the rebuilding began. My company furnished the pipe, pumps, valves, meters, and loading equipment for the rebuilding operation.

Within eight weeks, two storage tanks were ready for service, and eight lanes of the truck loading station were ready for calibration. The oil company management wanted me to personally check out, calibrate, and prepare the loading stations for customers. The oil company was losing thousands of dollars a day as long as the loading platforms were down.

The way the loading system works is that a semi-tanker truck drives up to a loading station. The driver opens the top covers of his tanker then guides a drop-tube arm and spout from the loading platform into the semi-tanker's tank compartment. Then he goes over to the meter set-stop counter and pre-sets the amount of product needed in that compartment. This set-stop counter counts down from his setting amount and shuts off at zero gallons. At least, that is what is supposed to happen.

A.O. Smith had just introduced a new model set-stop counter, and it had problems. Sometimes it did not turn off at zero. This, of course, would run gasoline over the compartment in the tanker, and gasoline would run down the side of the tanker onto the loading area cement floor to a drain which led to a 'slop tank,' or holding tank on the other side of the bulk plant. Normally, there is no immediate danger, since truck drivers many times dialed in the wrong number and ran the compartments over. They would jump for the emergency shut-off switch before more than ten to twenty gallons overflowed.

However, while I was trying to calibrate these new prototype set-stop counters, they were constantly failing to shut off and overflowing. I was filing plastic gears and shafts and mechanical latches to correct manufacturing defects to try to make these new set-stop counters work.

After two days, I had corrected the problems on six of eight of the loading stations and was working on the seventh. This particular set-stop counter was constantly failing to shut off and were overflowing; consequently, I was standing in two to three inches of gasoline all day working in the loading area.

In the afternoon, as I was trying to adjust station seven, an urgent thought penetrated my mind. It was like someone shouting loudly in my ear, *"Stop! Wash the gasoline out, now!"* There was nobody around. There was no one in sight. I knew immediately it was the voice of a spirit from within.

I stopped what I was doing and shut off the gasoline valves and pumps. I grabbed a high-pressure water hose and started washing out all the gasoline in the loading area. I washed it off the tanker, off the loading equipment, off the concrete, and even off my rubber boots. I washed it all down into the large drain located under the tanker, which carries it to the slop tank located on the other side of the tank farm from where I was working.

When I finished, I turned off the water and returned to the side of the tanker to think about what I had just heard, and to what I had just responded. As I stood there looking at the tanker, considering what this was all about, fire erupted up through the overflow drain under the tanker, blowing off the drain cover and licking at the bottom of the tanker. It went out immediately after burning the fumes in the pipe. I just stood there stunned. My mouth uttered, "Praise your precious name, Lord." Then, I began to tremble all over as I realized the gravity of what had just happened.

It seems welders rebuilding the tank farm had just moved to do some welding work on a pipe directly over another drain on this same slop tank pipeline, but on the other side of the tank farm. Red-hot welding beads fell into the gasoline-fume-filled drain and ignited the gasoline fumes in the pipe. The fire traveled in the pipe across the tank farm and up through my drain. If I had not heeded the warning and followed the command, I would have been burned to a crisp right there along with the tanker truck and new loading rack.

I quit for the day and reported the incident, informing the contractor and the oil company that I would do no further work on the loading stations as long as there was welding going on anywhere at the facility. The welders found other work to do until I finished on the loading stations. Needless to say, I spent much time that night in PRAISE.

"Wash Out the Gasoline Now!"

DEMATERIALIZING TRIP THROUGH A GASOLINE SEMI-TANKER

(Story from page 111 of *The Last Enemy - Teachings From Beyond the Veil*)

An A.O. Smith petroleum meter failed on a truck-loading platform a couple of hundred miles away in Alabama. My company asked me to take a replacement meter over to the Alabama location the next day, Saturday, and install it. The company would send John Holman, our service manager, with me. It would take all day to drive to the site, install the meter, test it, and drive back. It was extra money for both of us, so we were eager to do the job.

The next morning, John and I loaded the meter in a white company pickup and took off. We drove out I-20 from Atlanta and within four hours were near the petroleum terminal, which was located about five miles off the expressway. We turned off the expressway onto a two-lane state highway and headed toward the tank farm.

John and I were talking as we topped a hill and looked over a river valley below. The two-lane road led straight down a hill about two miles, across a small, two-lane river bridge, and then up the next hill about two miles to the crest. We could see for miles. About a thousand feet past the bridge, I could see a side road turning off to the left, and about a quarter mile down that road I could see the bulk plant and loading platform. It looked like we had arrived.

I drove down the hill, across the bridge, and prepared to make my left turn onto the side road. I looked and saw nothing was coming either way, so I started turning left. Suddenly, a blast from a semi's foghorn petrified me! I slammed on the brakes and looked to the right. There it was! A semi-tanker was bearing down on us—right on top of us. His radiator was within six feet of my right fender and barreling towards us at full speed.

I saw John throw up his arms and try to brace himself as I just gritted my teeth, clenched the steering wheel, froze, and waited for the impact. Our pickup was dead still in the road in front of the speeding semi-tanker, in his lane. There was no way for him to avoid crashing into us.

My life did not flash before my eyes. I just cringed, gripped the steering wheel, and waited for the impact. It seemed like eternity. Finally, I remember well that my first thought was, "If I had not stopped, I would have had time to get out of his way!" Then I thought, "Why am I still alive? I can't believe this delay. Why has he not hit us? " I slowly opened my eyes. The semi was not there! I thought, "Where is it? Was I just seeing things? Was there really a semi there? Am I crazy?" I knew John saw it, too, because I had seen him throw his arms up, and brace for the impact.

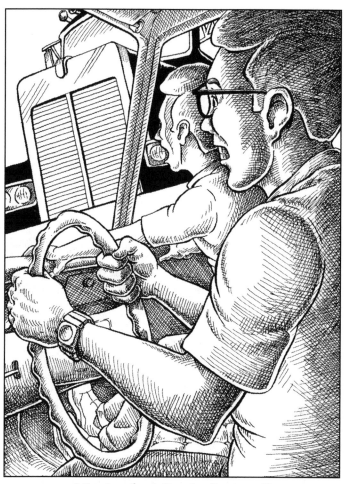

A Semi-tanker is Bearing Down on Us

Then I looked down the road to my left. There it was! The semi-tanker was nearly to the bridge, white smoke billowing from his trailer tires, and all his brakes still locked.

"Where is He? He Missed Us!"

Jack Bentley

"He Didn't Miss Us!"

Black skid marks from his locked wheels continued all the way back up *under* our pickup. "What's this? Has God just intervened in my life? Did that semi just go through this pickup and us?"

I looked over at John; he was seeing exactly what I was seeing. There was no explanation for what we were seeing now. John was even more terrified by what he was now seeing. Neither of us could speak for a moment. We were still stopped on the highway right on the skid marks. John finally spoke. "Jack, I will never again speak to you about this as long as I live. I wouldn't touch this with a ten foot pole." Then he just sat there, intently staring straight ahead. I worked with John for another eight months, and he never mentioned the incident again, as if this miracle had never happened. We installed the meter in Alabama, and drove back to Atlanta.

Strangely, as the years have passed, I have often wondered, "If the driver of the semi-tanker knew he had not crashed into us, why were his brakes still locked a quarter of a mile down the road? It looked to me like the semi driver thought he had crashed into us and was desperately trying to get the heavy rig stopped. Was this one of those situations where the crash did happen, and we were seeing the crashed semi trying to control his damaged tractor until he could get it stopped?" I wish I had stayed there a while to see if there was a white pickup in the ditch near the bridge where it was thrown by the crash. Was there a totally demolished white pickup truck with two very dead bodies inside in the ditch near the river? If so, were John and I propelled into a parallel reality that day? I know this incident happened, but I don't know if our Father intervened, by de-materializing our truck and us, or did we just switch realities? This scene is as vivid in my mind today as it was in 1973. Since then, I have found others who have experienced similar incidences, and I surely appreciate their sharing those experiences with me.

As I think further of the implications of this incident, I realize that neither John nor I was injured, nor were our bodies altered in any way by the experience. Moreover, the pickup in which we were riding with all our tools and the replacement meter were not altered or changed in any way. Everything appeared exactly as it was before the incident.

Through modern day science, we have come to understand that what we see as physical substance in this 3-D realm is mostly space, yet we perceive it to be physical matter. For example, If a hydrogen atom were enlarged so as to have one hundred yards between its one nucleus and its single electron, and the nucleus were then located at the center of an NFL stadium, the nucleus would be a pin-head size, not even a viewable material object at the fifty yard line, and the grain-of-sand sized electron charge would be orbiting around the last row of seats in the upper stands, traveling at nearly the speed of light. You see, it is 99.99999% space and the balance is just positive and negative charges. It is not physical matter at all. We just perceive it as such. What incredible intelligence created it all and is continually energizing it? That incredible power can cancel the physical attributes and operation of it at any given instant, as it did there in Alabama.

No wonder that in the Bible story, the lions could not harm Daniel when he was thrown into the lion's den. Our Father either changed the lion's appetite or Daniel's nature.

"I Must Turn This Truck Around or We Will All Die Here."
(Story from page 131 of *The Last Enemy)*

We were about three days into the Yukon Territory heading home to Georgia from Alaska. There was a fork in the road that I did not remember. There were no signs indicating which way to go, but in the snowstorm, it seemed I should turn left. I did, and we proceeded climbing up a mountain, but before long, I realized the road was winding tightly around the mountains, and was narrower and steeper than I had remembered. I must have taken the wrong turn at the fork. I decided to turn around at the first turn-off and go back to the intersection where I had made the left turn, but there was no place for us to turn around! There were no intersections either, so I kept going. Surely, somewhere ahead, there would be a place to turn around. We were traveling up a mountainside between two mountains on this road for miles, with sheer cliffs above us on one side and a deep canyon on the other. The road was getting steeper and narrower every mile we proceeded. It was at least 2,000 feet to the bottom of the canyon. Eventually, we came to an intersection, but it was a turn-off onto a narrow, one-lane bridge that spanned the deep canyon between the two mountains. The bridge had no side rails, and the entrance to the bridge was too narrow for our forty-foot-long truck to make a turn. We had to keep going, and find a place to turn this forty-foot truck around. We proceeded up the side of the mountain for another thousand feet before the road just ran out There was nothing but sheer cliffs ahead of us! Using just the mirrors, I backed the truck down the mountain for a thousand feet, in the snowstorm, to the narrow bridge. It took a while, but after some scary moments, we finally made it back to the bridge.

I got out and looked at the bridge. The entry intersection was too narrow for me to swing the truck into it. If I tried to back onto the entry of the bridge, the right canyon-side wheel would run off the edge of the road, and the truck would tip over into the canyon and tumble 2,000 feet to the bottom.

It was below zero and snowing steadily. This was the front of an approaching blizzard, which would likely close this mountain side-road for the winter. I knew I could never back the truck all the way down to the main road, the Alcan Highway. If we stayed here, we would freeze to death in a few days when the food and propane ran out. Again, I got out and looked at the intersection and the bridge.

There was only one way for us to survive. I had to turn the truck around, some way, on that bridge. After a time of thought and prayer, I reasoned that if I pulled ahead a hundred feet or so, and then backed up toward the intersection as fast as the truck could go in reverse, I possibly could, at that speed, turn the rear end of the truck onto the bridge without it turning over into the canyon. I reasoned that the centrifugal force of our top-heavy load trying to tip over to the left as I was turning right at high speed might keep us from tipping over to the right into the canyon, as I swung onto the bridge. This quick-turning maneuver could keep the truck from tilting into the canyon as the right rear wheel dropped off between the edge of the mountain road and bridge in the intersection. It was the only chance we had to survive!

I asked Jonnie Ann to take Tina, our six-year-old daughter, and stand on the road while I tried to turn around. Her answer: "If you go off the mountain, what would I do then? Tina and I would just stand here and freeze to death. I would rather we both go over the side with you. It would be a quicker end, and we would all three be together."

We agreed to stay together in the truck. I prayed, "Lord, it is all up to You now!"

Looking for a Mountain-side Turn-a-round

I pulled ahead about a hundred feet, stopped, cleaned the mirrors, and began backing up.

Backing up with Mirrors Only

Pushing the Peddle to the Metal—in Reverse

I pushed the accelerator to the floor. As I turned onto the bridge, I felt the truck first lean sharply over to the left as if it wanted to turn over. Then I felt the right wheel go off the road's edge. The truck then tipped severely to the right, and it felt as if we would keep going over into the canyon

Backing onto the Bridge—"We're Going Over!"

It seemed we tipped much too far to ever recover, and we were going over. Then I felt the right rear wheel climb up onto the bridge, and the truck straightened itself up. I slammed on the brakes. We stopped in the middle of the narrow one-lane bridge, dead center.

Jack Bentley

"We Made it!" "How?"

I realized we had, somehow, made it, *half way*! Since that time, I have come to realize we had tipped much too far to recover naturally. There was someone there who forced the truck back upright on the bridge. The truck had tipped so far over that I was looking down at Jonnie Ann and Tina in their seat on the right side of the cab.

I knew after being successful in reverse that I could now back up far enough on the bridge to have room to build even more speed going forward and then turn again onto the narrow mountain road. I backed nearly across the bridge. I pushed the truck in low, then second gear, and third as we gained more speed to turn back down the mountain. This time, the left rear wheel ran off the bridge as I made the turn, but this time I had enough speed that the truck tilted into the canyon very little. In fact, I nearly turned the truck over on the other side, against the mountain, as I made the turn. Now we were on our way back down the mountain. We found the intersection where I made the wrong turn and turned south on the Alcan Highway. We drove all night.

Presently in my meditations and life experiences, the messages are becoming much more bizarre and other worldly, so I can see why I needed the mental, emotional and spiritual reinforcement of these former miracles.

Some who read and have read these words will think I am a lunatic and feel I need to be put away. Don't fret friend; sometimes, I feel the same way.

2003 5/30 - *"During local and remote healing diagnostics, feel the patient's aura. It will help determine where to place your hands on the patient."*

You might want to try this technique until you become proficient with its use. Sometimes, as you pass your hands closely over another person's body, you will feel a greater buzzing, tickling, or heat in a particular area. Put your light-energy right there. Other times, you might feel a hole or blank spot somewhere on the body. Put your light-energy there. You will come to recognize these trouble spots. Sometimes, you will even get a <u>knowing</u> of what the problem is and where it is located inside the body. Treat it with touch-healing love-light-energy. We must learn to use this technique. It always works!

It even works in remote healing when the patient is located hundreds or thousands of miles away. Just bring the person to you in your imagination, lay him or her down in front of you and pass your hands closely over his or her body. You will feel where the healing energy is needed. Remember, time and space (distance) are illusions. You can circumvent time and/or space and bring a person's essence to you anywhere.

This can be done remotely from hundreds of miles away. Just imagine placing the patients on a cot in front of you and then treat them as instructed above just as if they were present before you. You will feel the hot spots and blank spots on their bodies just as if they were lying on a cot before you.

2003 6/11 - *"You are a part of Me, but not a separate part of Me.*
You are all of Me with All My love and power, living in the flesh. The
only limits you have are those you chose. You are omnipotent; you can
cancel the limitations any time. You already know this!"

The limitations we chose are amnesia and time-delay as revealed in my first
book *The Last Enemy,* 11/24/98,

> *"Your thoughts are omnipotent, creating those situations exactly as you*
> *imagine them. You ordered time-delay on your creative thoughts, and*
> *amnesia on your memory, before you were born into this dimension."*

There can be no such thing as a part of God. He is All-in-All. To have Him
in your consciousness is to have all of Him dwelling in your awareness. You
think with His consciousness presently, just as I do. We are all one with
Him living in flesh with blinders on our awareness of being Him and also
blind to being each other. One cannot be partially God! **You are one**
with God Almighty. If you are one with the Almighty, then you are
Almighty. Possibly, you just don't choose to believe it, yet!

Only you and I can remove our blinders and accept our omnipotence
and union with the Source of All-that-is. This is what we refer to as
awakening.

How long, Oh Lord, will I keep falling back in inaction? It seems to me
that I always limit myself. I know you will, someday, bring experiences
that will totally stabilize my mind about who I really am, and the absolute
oneness of our relationship. I have learned to look forward with great
anticipation and yet to shudder at what you are going to use to bring me
to that relationship, but I do get excited about the outcome.

2003 6/12 - *"As you go about your day's activities, spend more*
time in light-energy ingestion and meditation. Immerse yourself in
the light; it is Me."

I have begun to do this by starting with deep breathing relaxation and then
imagining forming a sphere of light in the celestial realms and bringing it
down through my crown chakra into my heart. I increase the intensity and

size of this sphere of Love, Joy, Peace, Grace, Truth, Healing and Union until it encases my entire body. I continue deep breathing of celestial light into this sphere while bringing in the complete color spectrum of light-energy from every known and even any unrealized Chakra on my body. I breathe in deeply this light-energy for a time while praising our Father. After a time of this exercise, I stop the deep breathing and just dwell in the sphere of light, quieting the earthly thoughts that try to invade. Many times, this is when I see or hear His next message. AIfter this, I again increase the light-energy sphere until it engulfs the Earth, the solar system, and all the universes. Then I empower the quest of every entity in the sphere. I bring them love, peace, joy, grace, truth, healing and union with All That Is. Then I release them all to their quest, but I continue my immersion in this light sphere for some time as I relax.

2003 6/12 - *"You must travel into those parallel realities you have created; heal and give release to your secondary selves. You are primary and have the power to free them."*

I then asked, "How? How do I get to these parallel realities and to these secondary selves?"

He answered, *"You get there the same way you put them there—through* **emotional imagination."**

He is referring back to the utterance given in this book on (2002 11/13). *"Global-thought-forms are living spirits created by us, the sons of God. Yes, we are omnipotent, ever able to create eternal spirits like ourselves, just as the Father created us. Negative spirits or negative global-thought-forms, must be CONVERTED (re-polarized) to become positive. There is only* <u>love</u> *(Positive), or* <u>fear</u> *(Negative). Knowing this, you can lovingly deal with every negative spirit. Love (passionate compassion) is the only force that can affect that change."*

This is interesting. We create our secondary selves in parallel realities during highly charged emotional and highly focused moments.

Now, how do we go to those parallel realities where these secondary selves reside? We have to, in our imagination, match that emotion or focused intensity involved when we created those secondary selves in order to switch to that parallel reality. Don't fear, we will always be able to return to our original reality when we let the emotion and focus subside.

Some of these secondary selves exist in our present reality as conditions (spirits) we have created or allowed in. They are, or might be, affecting us and plaguing us physically and/or mentally. Just love them. Love them! For your own sake, love them and deal with them as the faithful servants they are that are performing exactly what you ask of them. Now ask them to do something different. You cannot destroy them since they are eternal spirits created by you, but you can lovingly re-polarize them. Ask them to help you.

When we say "I don't want to be a cripple," (a negative statement) or "I don't want to have cancer," (a negative statement) your body hears, "I want to be a cripple," and, "I want to have cancer." You must always state your position in the positive, saying "I am in perfect health." Remember, you are creating now! It may take a while for the fullness of the healing in the body to become apparent because you made the laws of time delay and your amnesia for this incarnation. Remember Isaiah 40:31, *"But they that wait on the Lord shall renew their strength; they shall mount up with wings as eagles; they shall run, and not be weary; and they shall walk, and not faint."*

I notice that, as I go about my business, and even sometime during my time of meditation, I will have some little pains in my jaw. The thought comes, "This may be pain indicating another heart attack." I have to pause and remind the thought form coming through, "My Father said I will not die in this incarnation, so I reject this pain." It stops immediately. Then I instruct it to help me realize I am well.

Some of us have persistent maladies that continue coming back to torture or aggravate us, like possibly a back problem that began when we first hurt our back years ago. At the time of the injury, we **painfully** and **emotionally** thought, "Damn, I may have just done permanent damage to my back!" Out of this painful, emotional experience of fear that you may have done permanent damage to your back, you created a spirit to permanently affect your back with pain and its memory of that damage for the rest of your life. You are omnipotent! What you emphatically declare is created to be an eternal spirit (living entity) diligently performing the duty you declared to be its mission—permanently reminding you of damage to your back! Aren't these spirits wonderful? They will not shirk from their duty that we as omnipotent creators assigned them when, in a creative emotionally charged moment, spoke them and their mission into existence. What this newly created thought-form (spirit) heard was, "I have permanent damage to my back." These spirits MUST fulfill their assignments until you **emotionally focus on that back problem** and change your orders to them. No human being on Earth is more faithful than these wondrous spirit entities.

In our bodies, these spirit entities might appear as plaque in our arteries, calcium in our joints, cancer in our lungs or any other malady know to man. Sometime, they appear genetically and were created in a former (parallel) life-time, but you can be sure that what they are doing today is out of deep love, respect, and loyalty to your desires. Loving them is the only response you can possibly have as you ask them to aid you in changing the negative order you gave them earlier. They want to please you. **They live to please you!** Don't ask them to kill the cancer cells—ask that they become healthy cells once again. Ask the plaque in your arteries to be dissolved back into the blood stream to help accomplish healing elsewhere in your body. These cells love your essence. They want to help you. They live to please you.

These eternal spirits are absolutely faithful to their mission. You must understand, spirits once created cannot be destroyed just as your spirit cannot be destroyed. They can only be re-polarized, or re-assigned to another mission. They are in total obedience to you, their creator. You can trust them to continue to do their assigned task until you, their creator, assign them another, different task. You should love and cherish them for their faithfulness, and reassign them to a loving ministry to yourself and others. We should praise these spirits for their faithfulness and love for us. We should praise our Father in them as in ourselves. Is this not the same thing our Father is accomplishing in us—teaching us to live continually in love that we might function as omnipotent son's of God in these universes?

2003 6/12 - *"You will always do what I ask you to do. That is your nature."*

I replied humbly, "Thank You, Father! I don't see this faithfulness in myself, but I certainly will accept your word that this is true. That is exactly what I want my life to be—lovingly obedient to Your will. Father, I'm always chanting, 'Teach me Thy ways, oh Father, and cause me to walk in them!'" I think, in my case maybe the scripture applies here "The spirit is willing, but the flesh is weak."

2003 6/12 - "*Make sure you teach relaxation meditation techniques.*"

We are all the cells of God's body—the universes. We each are the God's of our little universe—our bodies. Our bodies know our voice and are absolutely faithful to our commands.

If the creator "God" of your body (you) tells it to relax, it must relax. You are the one-with-God person who envisioned and formed your body. Change it if you wish. Tell it to relax. It will obey you. Remember to be involved emotionally—make it happen.

What is a good relaxation meditation technique?

First, try to find a place that is relatively quiet, and if possible, have some greenery (even artificial green plants) in view. Green enhances relaxation. However, you can learn to relax in total darkness and even in total chaos, but for beginners, it's best to set the stage for the most success.

Second, start by sitting—not lying down, because you might go to sleep if you lie down. Rest your hands and arms on the arms of a chair or your legs if you are sitting on the floor. Have your feet flat on the floor if you are in a chair, or folded yoga style (if you can) if you are sitting on the floor. Balance your head erect as you do most of your waking hours. Just don't get in a position that is so comfortable that you will easily fall asleep—unless falling asleep is the purpose of this relaxation. Normally one is trying to relax for meditation and does not wish to fall asleep. Now, take a few (ten to twelve) deep breaths. Be sure to inhale deeply in to your abdomen and then force all the air out with each exhale. Close your eyes and concentrate on your scalp—tell it to relax and feel the tightness disappear as you do this.

Third, begin to relax the muscles of your body in the following manner: Tell the forehead and eyes to relax as you squeeze your eyes shut, and then relax them, Feel your forehead and eyes relax and feel the tension that causes the horizontal wrinkles to relax. Next, relax the ears—just tell them to relax and try to sense the (physical feeling) changes in the ears. Relax the mouth and jaws—just let your mouth fall open if it wants, and let it relax. Also, tell your neck and lower skull to relax.

Start at the base of your skull, telling and feeling each vertebra to relax. Note: If you are sitting on the floor move your legs straight out in front, and let your body lean forward. As you relax each vertebra, you will feel a small jolt when the tension releases in each vertebra. Then your body will begin to lean forward more and more with each release. When the entire line of vertebra is relaxed, you will probably find your face resting on or near the floor between your legs. The first time I did this, it was so relaxing and consuming, I didn't want to straighten up.

Next, after a time of enjoying your back relaxation results, sit upright again and go down your arms relaxing upper and lower arms, wrists, hands, fingers and thumbs. It feels great!

Then, begin to relax the hips, upper legs, knees, lower legs, ankles, feet and toes. Feel each part relax. Now, go to your head again and tell the brain to relax. You may get drowsy. Tell the glands in your head to relax—try to feel them relax.

Now, let's go inside the body. Move to your chest and tell your thyroid to relax—it is just behind your upper breast bone. Tell your heart, lungs and arteries to relax. If you have some green plants or objects in the room, open your eyes and stare at the green color.

Before you discontinue the exercise, do some more deep breathing, and with your inhale, say, "re", and as you exhale, say, "lax". Feel your body relaxing. Your heart will slow down, and the more you do this the more your blood pressure will fall (to a point).

I did this heart relaxation just before a nurse was to take my blood pressure and when she took it she shrieked, "Oh my God, it is 60 over 40!" I had to calm her down and tell her what I had just done. I told her to take it again and it would be normal, and I would behave. She did and it was 110/75. Her boss, my doctor, asked me not to scare the nurses like that again. Anyway, it is always fun.

Now, move on down the organs of the body relaxing each one all the way to the genitals. Just begin with the glands of the head and work your way down the body through all the glands and organs. They will all appreciate this gentle power.

By the way, if you read my first book, you know there are light-energy transducers (chakras) attached and corresponding to each organ and gland in the body from which each organ gets its life force. (And you thought the life energy comes from the food you eat.) I'm sorry to say, most of the food we eat, most of the time, interferes with life force in the body.

If you want an extra boost while you are relaxing these organs and glands, just concentrate on breathing in light-energy to each of them as they relax. Just imagine light coming in from the front and back and each side chakra of that organ directly into the organ. If you have read about the corresponding chakra light colors, imagine that color; if not, just imagine white light coming in—it contains all the colors.

This might sound like a time-consuming task each day just to relax the body, but it becomes routine and can be done very quickly after a time, and your body loves it and deserves it.

2003 6/16 - *"If you are having a problem accepting your own omnipotence, consider the following: Can the almighty God in you be partially omnipotent? It is like thinking a woman can be partially pregnant. Accept and rejoice in your power as God. You really are omnipotent. You really are one with Me."*

Don't make Jesus a liar by trying to say you are not one with God. Speaking to the Father about us, Jesus prayed in St. John 17:21-22, *"That they all may be one; as thou, Father, art in me, and I in thee, that they also may be one in us: that the world may believe that thou hast sent me. And the glory which thou gavest me I have given them; that they may be one, even as we are one."*

2003 6/16 - *"A person's primary reality looks and feels exactly like his or her secondary selves in parallel realities. Some who read these words will instantly understand this and transfer to their primary reality. They will then continue to fulfill their eternal quest in this life span. They may not even realize they have transferred from one reality to another."*

Said another way, they will become conscious of having a primary reality. For better understanding of the reference to "Primary Reality," I would refer you back to the words given to me on 2000 11/15 and 2000 11/20 as recorded in my first book: *The Last Enemy.*

(2000 11/15):

> *"Every entity has a primary reality where all other entities are supportive to him." In your primary reality you have absolute control of that reality. You form everything, every situation, every relationship and every experience. In your secondary realities, you have a supportive role to the entity whom is primary. The experiences and wisdom gained in these secondary realities as a supportive entity are then reflected into your primary reality and help your own quest."*

This message should speak volumes to us about the tendencies people have that don't seem to fit their present life situation, such as homosexual tendencies.

The Last Enemy (2000 11/20):

> *"If you are having problems with each person having their own primary reality, look at the sky at night for the probabilities and the proof. There are trillions of physical realities shinning out the confirmation of this truth. They are there to help you understand this truth."*

What he is implying is that each one could be a dwelling place for someone else's primary reality. There are multiple trillions of these worlds.

2003 6/16 - *"Never forget what I told you earlier about guarding your words."*

(The Last Enemy) 2001 1/15 - *"You must now and forever guard your words. They are omnipotently creative in your primary reality. What you declare about others, they are obliged to support. You speak into form their character and life-style. Speak only positively, and empower their quest. Remember, everyone is just supporting and fulfilling your expectations in this, your primary reality."*

We all think with and through the consciousness of the Source of All-That-Is. We are each assigned a primary reality among our many other secondary realities. In our primary reality, everyone else is involved, everyone is playing a secondary role, a supportive role, helping the one who is primary to find and know himself or herself. The one who is primary is also carrying out his own prearranged, preordained commands as he carries on with his present incarnation.

If the primary one says a particular person is a no-good, lying bum, he or she, the secondary person referred to, is obliged to fulfill that proclamation and become a no-good, lying bum. This lying bum must continue to act so until the primary one changes his character proclamation with, "He (or she) is a good, truthful person of integrity."

The most despicable person you know is here just to help you know yourself and help you proceed to ascension and union with your Creator.

"I told you in that message that what you declare about others they are obliged to support here in your primary reality. Their deepest quest, however, is the same as yours—union with Me. knowing this, you must help them by empowering their quest of seeking union with Me. Focus! See their Union. This truth will immediately reflect into their primary reality."

You should try to remove any negative mission you placed on others by declaring they were such and such. If you declared someone was a worthless drunk and thief, worthy of nothing but Sing-Sing prison, you should make an emotional counter statement about that one declaring that he is a new son of God worthy of all the blessings of out Father, no matter what his present actions.

This does not mean that we should try to direct his spiritual journey. We need to make sure we keep our meddling hands off his life. Love him, empower his quest, and leave him alone!

2003 6/18 – *"We are in this together. I am your consciousness. All thoughts originate with Me. Remember the Mercy Mission incident in Hawaii? Remember when you were demoted on the spot, and sent into an office to write an apology letter to the General? It was I who told you to direct the letter through General Kudar's office. <u>I knew what he would do with it.</u> You did not even know how to direct a letter to him. Others need to know how I work to bring them through their troubles."*

He is always on the scene. His consciousness is there because you are there. Your consciousness and His consciousness are one. You think with the mind of the Source of All-That-Is! Allow this to happen. Invite our Father's consciousness to the forefront in your thinking. Praise Him and allow Him to direct your life and thinking. He will.

This was in reference to an incident in the US Air Force in 1957 and written about in my first book *THE LAST ENEMY* and copied below, The Scripture declares, "And we know that all things work together for good, to them who love God, to them who are the called according to His purpose. (Romans 8:28)

The Mercy Mission – 1957
(Page 22, *The Last Enemy*)

Eventually, I was put in charge of Transit Maintenance, which included all maintenance and refueling of all transit aircraft that passed through Hickam Field from 12:00 midnight to 8:00 a.m. I inherited a fine crew of military and civilian maintenance people. Our job was to repair any problems with the aircraft and get them back in the air as soon as possible. Most of the time, this was quick and easy. Normally, there were very few problems with the aircraft that came through Hawaii, and all we needed to do was clean, refuel, and pre-flight them. If there were major repairs, the aircraft would have to stay on the ground in Hawaii until our people and the daytime crews could get the parts and make the repairs.

A large jet bomber landed, and the pilot, a General Robinson, who was ferrying it back to the states, handed the day crew a list of problems. These problems included the navigational radios being out of service. The day crew did not have the right parts to repair the radios and navigational equipment and ordered them from a mainland supply depot. The parts were supposed to arrive the next day.

As usual, when I came on duty at 11:30 p.m., I met with the civilian maintenance foreman and reviewed the daily maintenance logs to see what work was in progress. I noted from the maintenance log the status of work on all the aircraft under repair and the estimated completion times.

Then the other shoe dropped! All was well until about 2:00 a.m., when the base received a "Mayday!" distress call from a C-97 air force transport plane inbound from the mainland and loaded with military dependents. This reciprocating, four-engine aircraft had just thrown an outboard propeller, which took out the inboard engine next to it.

The aircraft was now being powered by two engines on one wing, and losing altitude. The only way the pilot was able to keep it flying straight was by pushing the opposite rudder-pedal as hard as he could. This was so exhausting that he and the co-pilot had to rotate pushing the rudder-pedal, as each would eventually lose all strength in his legs. The rest of the crew had to jettison everything on board, including everyone's shoes and personal belongings, to reduce weight and try to keep the aircraft in the air.

Part of my job was to make sure, at all times, that three rescue aircraft were fueled and ready to fly. Each shift leader made sure these rescue aircraft were ready. Each shift performed preflight inspections and engine run-ups on these aircraft. I was supposed to always keep maintenance people and fuel trucks on standby, just in case one of these rescue aircraft had a problem, and this particular night, two of the three had problems. As the first rescue aircraft was on its takeoff roll, an engine failed. It taxied back to the hanger. I had to find another aircraft to take its place. A local general had a four-engine C-54 transport aircraft assigned to him, and it was presently in a hanger nearby. I took it, but it needed to be refueled and given all the pre-flight checks first. I called for fuel. It was a gasoline engine aircraft, so I had to use one of the two available fuel trucks to refuel this aircraft. The other fuel truck contained jet fuel. My crew was on it immediately.

When Murphy's Law kicks in, it sometimes kicks you right in the teeth. About ten minutes into the mission, the second rescue ship lost an engine. Now, there was only one rescue aircraft headed for the struggling C-97, which at this time was just over the point of no return—a midway point in the Pacific Ocean of the 2000 mile, over-water flight path—in the flight from the U.S. mainland to Hawaii.

The Navy had, at that time, a naval vessel assigned to the area at the point of no return. Their mission was to help any aircraft in distress. They would spread a blanket of foam on the surface of the ocean in case an aircraft had to ditch in the ocean. If an aircraft could just get to that area, they would have a chance to ditch and be rescued. This crippled C-97 was presently circling this ship and steadily descending. The navy ship was already spraying foam on the ocean surface. Then, at about fifty feet above the surface of the ocean, the pilot noticed the aircraft leveled off and its altitude stabilized. He had found an area of additional lift just above the water. He decided to circle awhile and see if this vapor cushion he had discovered would allow him to sustain this altitude. It worked, and he decided to try to make it another 1,000 miles at an altitude of fifty feet, to Hilo, Hawaii, on the Big Island. At about 200 miles per hour, he was looking at a hair-raising ordeal of five more hours.

I, on the other hand, had to find a third aircraft to use in this rescue effort. The only other transport aircraft I could find on the base, ready to go, was the one assigned to General Kudar, the Pacific Air Force Commander at the time, but it, too, needed refueling. The second fuel truck was full of jet-fuel, so I had to have it dumped and filled with gasoline before I could refuel this third aircraft. I got it all working, hoping this rescue plane would stay airborne.

I looked up when a master sergeant appeared at my desk. He was the crew chief of the jet bomber that a General Robinson had flown into Hickam the evening before. He said, "General Robinson will be here in an hour to ferry the bomber back to the mainland." I explained that the aircraft was not yet refueled because it was grounded for lack of navigational radios and other problems. It could not go anywhere, and besides, presently, I had the fuel tankers refueling a mercy mission. I explained that there was no way I could refuel the bomber right now, even if it were ready to fly because both of my refuel trucks were presently full of aviation gas. He said, "You want me to tell General Robinson that you are not going to get his aircraft refueled before he gets here?"

I said, "Yes, that is all you can tell him at this time." I thought about how that might sound to the general and decided to call my superior, our maintenance officer, Captain Smith. He agreed with my actions and said he would contact Major Green, the base operations officer. Both Captain Smith and Major Green showed up within thirty minutes. Both agreed that I had done the right thing and that I didn't dare take the refuellers off a rescue mission aircraft. We continued the refueling operation and listened for further reports on the fate of the crippled C-97.

The office door slammed against the wall. I looked up from behind the counter and saw stars everywhere. General Robinson was marching straight toward me. Two stars were flashing on each shirt collar, two stars on each jacket shoulder, and two on his cap. His face was red as sunburn as he blared at us, "Who in the hell said I can't get my plane refueled?"

We were all standing at attention now. I looked around at Captain Smith and Major Green. They were both petrified. No one spoke. Sheepishly, I said, "I did, Sir."

General Robinson looked past me at Major Green as if I were invisible and demanded of my superiors, "Get fuel trucks on my aircraft now!"

Major Green reached around me, picked up the phone to the fuel farm, and instructed them to get the fuel truck off the rescue ship, dump the aviation gas, fill up the truck with jet fuel, and refuel the general's jet bomber immediately.

Of course, the general was not done with me. He demanded an explanation from Major Green as to why a staff sergeant was in charge of Transit Maintenance, when a commissioned officer is supposed to be in that position. Before anyone could answer, he demanded that I be reduced in rank to airman basic—a private in the Air Force and reassigned to a position befitting an airman basic. He then instructed Major Green to see to it that, before I was allowed to leave the flight line that day, I write him, the general, and my personal apology.

Major Green instructed me to go into the next office, remove my staff-sergeant stripes, sit down, and write an apology to General Robinson. I must then proceed to my residence and wait until I was called with a new position. I could not believe the gutless reaction of these officers to this egomaniac general. They knew I had done the right thing and that I had followed Air Force Standard Operating Procedures.

I went into an adjoining office, closed the door, and sat down at a desk. I was scared. As an airman basic, I would face a nearly impossible task of supporting my family and paying my college expenses. I began to pray and ask the Lord to help me.

I had an idea! Maybe it would work. (At the time, I didn't realize the Lord had just spoken to me. The Lord would clear up this "idea," years later.) I would write the apology letter to General Robinson and route it through the office of General Kudar, the Pacific Air Force Commander. I removed my sergeant stripes, wrote the apology, and in doing so, copied all the entries from the logbook exactly as everything happened that morning, explaining why I did what I did, and the consequences. I sent the apology to General Robinson and directed it through the Pacific Air Force Commander's office.

I waited at the flight line until I heard that the C-97 had safely landed at Hilo. It was interesting to note that the pilot of the crippled C-97, upon arriving at Hilo, wondered what all the commotion was about on the ground. Beside all the rescue equipment, a huge crowd had gathered to watch and share in the jubilation after the landing.

I was demoted to airman basic and assigned to a flight line office position procuring parts for the aircraft on the line. I worked hard and soon again had the full confidence of our maintenance officer, Captain Smith; however, we never talked about the General Robinson incident. I know part of the reason was that he was ashamed of the cowardliness he displayed the night of the mercy mission.

I did not take the usual coffee breaks with the troops, but used these times to study the Bible. Occasionally an airman or a civilian crewman would come up and ask questions about the Bible. I would use this opportunity to lead him to an experience with Christ. It was working wonderfully. I had a number of young men profess their faith in Christ and begin to study with me. This activity eventually began to irk Captain Smith.

One morning, Captain Smith summoned me to his office, and demanded that I leave my Bible at home. I complied, left my desk edition at home, and just carried my pocket New Testament. It was perfect for soul-winning work anyway. Captain Smith became aware that the soul winning was still going on and summoned me back to his office. He said, "Airman Bentley, I thought I told you to leave your Bible at home?"

I replied that I had left the desk Bible at home, but that I always carry my New Testament with me. I said, "Sir, with all due respect, I don't believe you have the authority to demand I not carry a New Testament on me, nor do I believe you have the right to demand I not share my faith with others who show interest." He then threatened me with a summary court martial if I had my New Testament on me again.

I called the base chaplain's office and made an appointment for lunchtime. At noon, I laid out the problem and what had happened over the past few weeks. This chaplain, who would become a close friend, then called the base air inspector's office and reported the incident. The air inspector called Captain Smith, and reprimanded him soundly for his actions.

When I returned to the flight line, I found I was now a "follow-me" truck driver and mechanics taxi driver. This was strange, but it gave me an even greater opportunity to work with young airmen about their spiritual standing with Christ, since they were captive prospects in the truck. Many more young airmen found Jesus Christ as their personal savior. Some of the new converts would team up with me in the truck, and we led many others to Christ. This was one of the greatest opportunities for soul winning I had ever found. I taught many young men to lead others to the Lord using only a few verses in the book of Romans in the New Testament; it is called The Roman Road method. I knew Captain Smith was aware of what was going on because it was the talk of the flight line. I think he was perplexed about what he could do about it.

Then, a confidential envelope came to me from General Kudar, the Pacific Air Force Commander. Inside was my apology letter to General Robinson with a note sprawled across the bottom. It read, "Sergeant, you did exactly the right thing! Put your stripes back on. I'll take care of General Robinson. Also, I am directing you be reassigned to a base back on the mainland. You need to be in a different environment."

The next day, Captain Smith and Major Green called me in to the operations office. They did not know about my confidential letter from General Kudar. "Well, we won! We got your stripes back, and General Robinson has been reduced in rank. But, we have to ship you back to the mainland because of the incident." They had the audacity to imply that they had fought on my behalf and prevailed. What frauds! Soon, I got my orders to proceed to my home in Milledgeville, Georgia, and await orders for my next reassignment.

2003 6/19 - *"Primary selves and Secondary selves in Parallel realities, are all in the NOW.*

Secondary selves in parallel realities can exist in current or totally different time periods, with different parents and possibly a different gender and/or race. Every secondary self is still connected to you.

Actually, all the other entities in existence are you. You see, you are Me, so they are, in fact, all your secondary selves in your present or parallel realities. You are all one; all one now."

Since there is no such thing, actually, as linear time and space, all creation and its activity are occurring in the present—the NOW. Our Father's consciousness is the "I Am" of each of us; I can see how we are all one, NOW.

2003 6/20 - A shampoo bottle fell in the shower at exactly 4:30 a.m., awakening me for meditation. I had forgotten to set the clock.

When we establish an appointed time for fellowship with the Spirit Realm, they keep the appointment, so shouldn't we? How He puts up with us is a mystery to me. This incident should teach us how our spirit guides always lovingly and tenderly keep us on track. They miss the meditation fellowship and opportunity to teach us when we don't keep our appointments.

2003 6/24 - I have begun catching sight of human-like figures of various colors appearing near me and then disappearing as I look toward them.

This has been going on for years, but here-to-fore, they were just dark shadows. Now I see them, but just for an instant in color. I don't yet know what they are doing or wanting. I will have to wait and see. They may be my guides and helpers, or some other ascended beings working on my behalf. At times, I even get a quick glimpse their facial features. Some, I seem to recognize, others are strangers to me.

2003 7/9 - *"Black holes in the heavens are galaxy-sized chakras, converting light-energy back into pure consciousness. Everything in the physical plane is a manifestation of light. Light-energy, when its purpose is completed, is drawn back into and through these black-hole Chakras and converted back to pure consciousness from whence it came."*

David Filkin, in his book, *Steven Hawkins Universe,* (Pages 102-103) tells us that Hawkins seemed to agree with Roger Penrose, a mathematician at Oxford University that black holes draw all matter into them and congeal it into super-dense matter that he calls the "singularity." Steven, it gets better than that—IT IS CONVERTED EVEN HIGHER—BACK TO PURE CONSCIOUSNESS! The dense physical matter is no more. This is good to know since we are heading for a galactic alignment on December 21, 2012, and we may be basking in a stream of consciousness from our galactic center black hole.

Jack Bentley

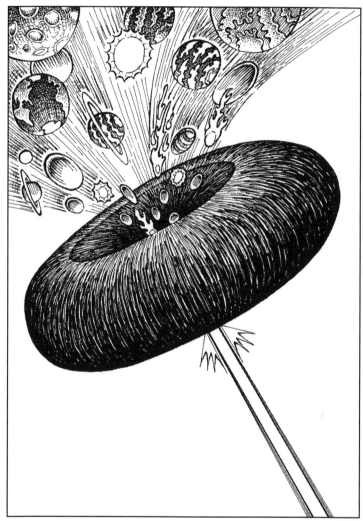

Galaxy's Black Hole

2003 7/10 - *"Be careful in your request and desire for manifesting Divine Love in your life before you are spiritually capable of handling its power. Divine Love can be devastating to the unrealized mind.* <u>*Passionate Compassion*</u> *for all entities and all creation can overwhelm one's mind if that one is less than fully realized. Love grows deeper and more powerful until all creation becomes absolutely irresistible."*

This will be more fully explained in the future 2004 5/6, and other messages. Even at this time, I realize that, in my live so far, I can imagine the desperate anxiety I would feel as I observed the hopeless situations of others if I loved as my Father does.

2003 8/1 - *"I told you before (2002 ll/13), **'Global-Thought-Forms are living spirits.' They cannot be destroyed. You must change, convert, re-polarize them _in yourself,_ or they will continue negatively affecting you. This is why, no matter how hard you fight a negative habit or thought, it keeps coming back. It will continue coming back until you deal with it! Deal with these spirits with gentle love, _seeing them as they will be and not as they now appear._ Love them into union with you and Me."***

All kinds of thought-forms invade my mind especially when I am trying to fast. There are the Global-Thought-Forms: "You have to eat or the body will begin to feed on itself until it destroys itself." "You can stop this fast and try again later when there is nothing to interfere." "You really should stop tonight and eat with the guests that have been invited for dinner." "You have plenty of time to fast; you are still young and in perfect health." These are some of the constant barrage of thoughts that invade my days while I am on a sustained fast.

Yes, since being given the techniques for fasting in 1997, I'm still having trouble completing a sustained fast for my "Youth Recovery Process." It is a tremendous spiritual battle. The longest total fast I have been able to sustain so far, was 28 days, but most of the time I start eating again after 4 to 10 days. However, I intend to keep at it until I do sustain a fast for months and until I know I can live on light-energy alone.

Now I have the technique for overcoming these negative thought-forms. Love them into harmony with my desires.

NOTE: I have prepared a special collection of messages on fasting in an Addendum to this book. See **Addendum "A."**

2003 8/3 - *"The slaughterhouses produce terror-and-confusing in the animals they are killing. These terror-and-confusing Emotional-Thought-Forms are embedded in the animal's cells. These Thought-Forms of terror and confusing are then transferred to those who ingest this animal flesh. Cooking the meat does not remove these terror-and-confusing Thought-Forms."*

It appears that the tortuous life and violent death experience of slaughtered animals are imprinted or embedded in the indestructible (DNA) cellular essence emotions of these entities. As such, these "terror-and-confusing" emotional thought-forms are transferred to the subconscious mind, or (DNA) cellular consciousness of those who ingest the flesh of these animals.

Is it any wonder then, that we are so fearful, violent and confused? <u>Could we reduce the fear and violent tendencies in ourselves and throughout the world by changing our diet, by just not eating any animal products</u>? Could we eventually eliminate the violent potential in ourselves by ceasing from eating animal flesh or any animal products, fasting regularly, and ingesting light-energy? It does seem to make sense, doesn't it?

Could this possibly be the root cause of much of the confusion we see around us in education, politics, and religion, in the business world and even in international relations? It seems most of those connected with these institutions don't know what is right and wrong anymore. We sit and scratch our heads wondering what our politicians and educators are thinking.

The problem in our society is that we don't see the violence and terror inflected on the animals we are eating; if we did, we probably wouldn't eat them. We are too far removed from the farms and from personally tending of the animals to see and understand who they are, what they are going through, and how they feel.

Also, we need to think about how meat eating is affecting us physically. The antibiotics and growth hormones are causing a world-wide obesity PLAGUE. Most obese people believe they allowed themselves to become overweight and therefore blame themselves and despise themselves because they let this happen to them. They have no clue that the growth hormones force-fed to the cows, pigs, chickens and turkeys are still active in the slaughtered, dressed and cooked flesh they are served at their own dinner table and at their favorite restaurant.

Just like the force-fed cattle, we who eat their flesh are ingesting the same chemicals and medications from their flesh. These antibiotics and growth hormones are not destroyed by cooking just as the "terror-and-confusing" thought-forms of the slaughtered animals are not destroyed by cooking. The growth hormones are making us hungry continually (That's what they are supposed to do in the farm animals so they will grow faster and bigger and fatter for the slaughter.) The antibiotics are causing us to become immune to antibiotic drugs and susceptible to the very diseases they are formulated to prevent.

We can look forward to a human race (all colors and creeds) in the near future (even now) that is so overweight, introverted, suspicious, scared, confused, paranoid and vengeful, full of hate for themselves and everyone else, that they are capable of any violent terrorist act we can imagine. Look at the news on TV and your local news paper. It is here NOW, and the cause is at your local meat counter. Wake up and investigate the chaos around you!

I would hardly recommend you read David Wolf's book, *The Sunfood Diet Success System*. It really makes sense.

2003 8/6 – This morning I asked, "Father, teach me to praise you more completely."

A strong thought immediately rushed into my mind: ***"Obedience to My words is a type of praise—that is, <u>complete obedience</u>. You see, you are praising Me more deeply everyday. <u>Intent</u> is praise, because all is just consciousness. Even before you walk-out or act-out the words you have received, you have already <u>intended</u> to do so. You have already been in praise. You believe my words; that is praise.***

Now you know what the Scripture means when it says, 'Abraham believed God, and it was counted unto him for righteousness' (Romans 4:3). Believe My words and walk in My ways."

I needed that! When He says *"Complete Obedience"* He means, following His revelations and instructions that you have received during your times of meditations, NOT what your religious institutions and (frequently edited) scriptural writings tell you to do. To begin with, trust Him to speak to you and tell you what to do and how to live. He will take you along at your own best pace and will never overwhelm you. You have never had anyone love you as much as He does, and you can trust Him to guide you day by day. Don't get anxious, just keep meditating, praising and waiting before Him; it will happen. Just believing He loves you and will communicate with you is the beginning of praise. He will respond. When He does begin speaking to you, record the words and be obedient to them. You will grow spiritually by leaps and bounds.

2003 8/6 - *"There is a Chakra that corresponds to every organ and gland in the body. In your light ingestion work, actuate each Chakra and bring in its light frequency and color."*

This means memorize and imagine the various colors of each chakra's light-energy and sensitivity. Bring in each Chakra's color if you know what it is. If not, tell the Chakra to bring in the color it needs. Then, just allow light-energy to flow into it.

Just for your information, the basic Chakra locations and colors are shown below.

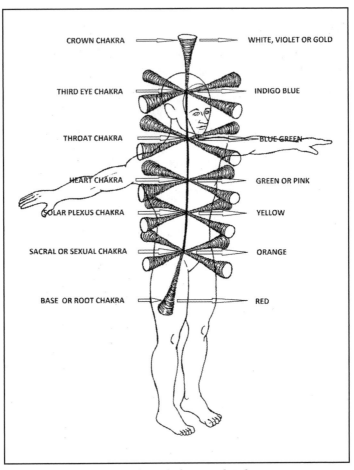

Our Body's Chakras and Colors

Think on your preference or delight when your eyes are exposed to some color they seem to want to feed on. They seem to hunger for certain colors—feed them those special colors. Could it be that your body, through the operation of your eye's color preference, is telling you it needs those color energies? Concentrate on those colors and bring them into your body, asking your body to use these particular colors as it needs. Your body knows?

Concerning the thought that your body be telling you something: read David R. Hawkins M.D., Ph.D., *Truth v/s Falsehood, How to tell the difference*. Also, another of Dr. Hawkins books, *Power v/s Force*, is tremendous. After reading his book(s), I think you will be convinced that your body knows best.

It is interesting that the Hopi Indians have known about the body chakra locations and their colors long before we "civilized" Europeans arrived on this continent.

2003 8/21 – Today, I experienced an apparent heart attack while working on a ditch at my mountain house.

I thought the intense pain in my jaws and chest was just acid indigestion as I was digging a ditch and moving cobble stone, but since it returned every time I started digging again with my mattock and shovel, and was so painful, I finally got the message. I asked Jonnie Ann to drive me to the Longmont Hospital Emergency Room to check it out. On the way to the hospital, I became convinced that it was probably a heart attack and was the incident the precious Father was using to force me to "PROVE THE WORDS" on fasting. I had been instructed to do this fasting five years ago, but had let circumstances delay an extended fast ever since then. Now, I realize It is time for me to get on with a total fast until I RENEW MY STRENGTH AND YOUTH, until I know beyond a doubt that I can live on light-energy, ALONE.

At the hospital they found three arteries were partially restricted. They performed angioplasty and implanted three titanium stents. I was in the hospital overnight and shopping at a local mall and celebrating my good fortune at a restaurant the next evening.

2003 9/10 - *"Prove the words for others and for your self. Hosts of angels are awaiting your success."*

OK, here it is; He is admonishing me to prove fasting and light-energy ingestion. Prove that a bite will satisfy my hunger. Prove I will have more strength, clearer thinking, and detoxification from fasting and light-energy ingestion. First thing is to begin a sustained fast.

2003 9/17 - *"Water is dormant energy. Drink good amounts while fasting. Water is broken down in the body's cells to use as oxygen and hydrogen to energize the body."*

I intend to follow this utterance to see what the underlying message is that it is teaching, or suggesting. There is more.

2003 9/17 - *"After your successful, sustained, healing, fast, your other parallel and secondary selves will then have this light-energy ingestion victory experience embedded in their deeper consciousness. They will know that they, too, can have this victory."*

Interesting! Since one consciousness resides in us all, and our secondary selves also share our personal consciousness, one victory will be realized by all and increase the enlightenment of all. It will never be as difficult for other secondary selves to believe, intend and accomplish a sustained, youth-recovery fast when it is achieved by any one of us.

2003 9/30 - *"It is all about proving the words, Jack!"*

WE NEVER IMPROVE UNTIL WE PROVE! So, we must go through all the trials, tests and situations until we prove, believe and are able to walk in the truth we are being taught:

2003 10/8 - *"While fasting, <u>spend traditional mealtimes ingesting light-energy. Make this habitual.</u> You must train yourself to spend more time in light-energy ingestion."*

Our spiritual growth is probably proportional to our time in focused meditation. I know that not much happens spiritually in my life outside of meditation. My quiet, sacred place is my power base.

2003 10/8 - In meditation this morning, as I was praising my Father, I declared, "I love praising You, Father. I think I want to be one of the elders before the Throne praising You."

A voice answered, **"*You are one of the elders praising Me!*"**

I was referring to where the Bible tells of a scene where a multitude of elders are gathered around the throne praising our Father. (Revelation 4: 4, 10-11)

"*4. And round about the throne were four and twenty seats: and upon the seats I saw four and twenty elders sitting, clothed in white raiment; and they had on their heads crowns of gold. And out of the throne proceeded lightnings and thunderings and voices: and there were seven lamps of fire burning before the throne, which are the seven spirits of God.*"

"*10. The four and twenty elders fall down before him that sat on the throne, and worship him that liveth for ever and ever, and cast their crowns before the throne, saying, 11. 'Thou are worthy, O Lord, to receive glory and honour and power: for thou hast created all things, and for thy pleasure they are and were created.'*"

2003 10/10 - "*Love is Real. Fear is an illusion along with all its manifestations of hate, envy, violence, and untruth. Love is of the highest dimensions; fear is of the lowest dimensions. Love produces ascension; fear imprisons in the lower dimensions. Love brings us closest to the Source; fear increases our distance from Him.*"

If we analyze our thoughts, we will find that each emotionally charged thought has its origin in either love or fear; therefore, with every emotionally charged thought, we are creating a situation in this or in parallel realities in secondary selves that is either positive or negative—either a beneficial situation for us or something negative that we will have to overcome later.

Really, what have we to fear? We are all one with the Father. We are all omnipotent beings. We are in a dream world, dreaming. This present reality is all illusions of our own making. The worst that can possibly happen to us is that we wake up in a higher dimension! And, that's also the best that can happen. The trick is for us to realize that we can change the script for this dream now and thereby change our circumstances and our futures.

The cycle of reincarnations continues until we can rest and dwell in love, where fear will have no place in our mind. Love is closest to the Source; fear is most far away from the Source.

2003 10/29 - *"You are now creating your way home. Remember, you and I are one, and so <u>your words and My words are one</u>. Some of the truths you are receiving were hitherto unknown on Earth, even to the ancient spiritual masters. Believe the words, and walk in them."*

I replied, "Lord, who am I that you should entrust your precious truths to me? You have said previously that I am the third who would tear through the veil and overcome death. Sometimes I wonder if I even desire to overcome death as I see what is going on in this world and as I see those I love growing old, sick and dying. You need to show me why I should want to continue living in this incarnation."

2003 11/13 - *"Ask yourself, 'Is this thought I am having coming from love or fear?' If it is from fear, it is not just a passing thought. It is an operative, eternal spirit that will remain negative, and growing, in your life until you deal with it—until you convert it. These fearful, negative spirits were created by you or others and allowed by you during your spiritually immature, weaker moments. Now, they have to be re-polarized so they might be positive, loving spirits; that is, they might be changed to love, peace, joy, grace, truth and wisdom."*

I think this utterance especially pertains to our thoughts during meditation. It seems we are plagued by superfluous, annoying thoughts that are interrupting our prayers, meditations, and healing sessions. Here, He is telling us to watch the thoughts and deal with them one-by-one as they appear. Some may be invading our minds, desperately hoping we will re-polarize them—hoping we will change them to positive, loving helpers. Help them so they may in turn help you to a deeper experience during your meditations. I think this activity of re-polarizing negative spirits is an eternal activity for us.

2003 12/8 - *"When the experience is finished and you have proven the words, you will KNOW!"*

Knowing, then, is a state of being—an ascended state of being. Every experience is given to teach us an eternal truth. We will continue to go through some of the same experiences over and over again until the knowing comes. Relax; don't resist the situations. ALLOW them to happen. There are no accidents. And there is plenty of time.

2003 12/27 – *"She is worth the wait!"*

I am anxious to find out what I am waiting for, and who "SHE" is. I trust "she" is my wife, Jonnie Ann, or our precious Mother Earth.

2003 12/30 – *"Before you were embodied, you had INTENT. You needed a way to prove that intent, but could not. The physical body was given to you that you might be able to prove spiritual intent by physical obedience. Proving intent by physical obedience is for your edification, not Mine. I know you! You will eventually accomplish everything I have asked of you. You have plenty of time. Rest in Me."*

I said, "Resting in You is sometimes hard, Father. I forget that there is much going on behind the scenes in the spiritual realm that requires time. I am sure it is I who am causing the delay by my constant interference and seeking answers right now. I have a hard time letting go and just waiting on You."

This seems to be an extension of the truth given to me in my first book *The Last Enemy,* on 1999 7/22, when He spoke of the two types of life experiences.

He said: *"There are two ways to experience life: linear sequential, or simultaneous experience."*

You might ask, "What does this 'proving intent' mean? Intent to do what? What were the intentions that I could not prove in the spirit realm?" Evidently, I did not know what I might be capable of without the knowledge of who I am and what is my relationship with my Father. Suppose I were left to my own way and rebelled against our Father? I wanted some method of proving my love and allegiance to our Father and to myself, to know that my basic character or being is safe, reliable, and dependable, and that it is eternally loyal, to my Father.

I realized that my soul or spirit must be isolated away from the King and Kingdom and away from any knowledge of my relationship with it and my Father. I must devise a plan to disguise who I am to my own mind—to go away from the King and Kingdom—to ostracize myself to a place where I am able to find and develop my real self.

Before I decided to come into physicality, I lived in a state of simultaneous non-time where anything I imagined appeared before me instantly, but I was not even aware that I created it. Being an extension of the mind of the Source of All-that-is, I had omnipotent creative ability. I just accepted that this was the way things work.

Eventually, I came to realize I could not possibly communicate on an appreciable level with our Father, because I am just one facet of his being and personality. I needed an education! I realized I must find a way to grow up into Him to become completely cognizant of His communication and activities, especially as pertains to His love, joy, peace, grace, truth, creativeness, omnipotence, omniscience and omnipresence.

It seems much goes on before we come from the spiritual realm into physical reality. First, our particular part of the essence of our Father is separated and becomes individualized.

We still love Him with all our being and want desperately to please Him, but we are at a loss because of our innocence and ignorance. We love being in His presence and feeling His love and energy, but we eventually realize that we must find a way to gain the knowledge and experience to communicate more directly and on a level more relative, more conversant with His energy and understanding. He has prepared a place to do just that. Very soon thereafter, we realized our innocence and our incredible ignorance.

We decided to give up this glorious spiritual realm existence and explore what we really are by giving ourselves amnesia and living in a physical realm where our creative power is not apparent. We would still be able to and could constantly create everything and anything we imagined, but we would not be aware of our creative ability because the created things would not appear immediately. We would have to draw them to ourselves by learning a disciplined practice of emotional focus. Eventually, we would learn to again create in the now and would also begin to regain our memory of who we really are.

We decide to experience separation from our Father for a time to gain this experience and knowledge, but, alas, both He and we can hardly bare the thought of that separation, especially since it involves the time delay of our creative abilities and amnesia of who we are. We must forget we ever knew Him! We must forget who we are!

2003 12/30 – *"First, there is revelation. Revelation produces understanding. Understanding produces intent. Intent brings obedience. Obedience brings KNOWING. Knowing is Union!"*

There is the process in a nutshell. The spirit world speaks to us, or gives us a vision or a miracle to help us understand a truth. Understanding that truth causes us to want—intend—to experience that truth. The experience/obedience of that truth gives us KNOWING.

2003 12/31 – *"All is consciousness. All consciousness is spirit. Intent is obedience! Therefore, you no longer have need of a physical body to prove spiritual intent by physical obedience. From here on, you may intend your way to ascension."*

I see now why our Father wanted me to finish the first book and then begin this one. Some might try to skip obedience. There is a spiritual progression, as I have shown in my first book, which must take place to develop us through intent, then through obedience, on to knowing and ascension.

Finally, the hour comes when we will realize that we are obedient by our intent. Then we will realize that if we intend something, it is done.

Once we realize the process above, we are far enough along to leave the body and progress into the higher spiritual realms. Glory!

2004 3/30 – *"There are many realities operating in your present three dimensional experience. You see some of them all around you, but you are invisible to others of them. Each reality is bound tightly its accepted global-thought-forms. Also, many of the higher levels of realities (dimensions) are invisible to you."*

This probably has to do with vibratory rate. Reality in our three-dimensional experience is produced by the vibratory rate of an individual and his or her acceptance of a group of global-thought-forms. Some realities are so far apart spiritually (in depth of consciousness) that those people dwelling on the lower consciousness vibratory realities are not even aware of those in the higher levels, thereby making those in the higher level realities absolutely invisible to the lower levels. The higher vibratory consciousnesses may observe the lower, but are not seen, nor affected by them.

You may experience situations where you will realize you are not being seen nor perceived by others, nor even perceived by other physical objects. (Yes, objects: stones, plant life etc., have perception of other life forms.)

2004 3/31 – *"Your individualized mind, or ego, as some might refer to it, is still My mind. You are learning to bring it back into harmony and union with you and Me. But, presently, the ego's process in your life is similar to that of a teenage child's rebelling against his or her parents. This is a natural stage you all go through on your journey home. It, too, does not know who it really is."*

Here, He is telling us that as we try to cope with our divine identify, we are all like rebellious children trying to face adolescence. He says we all go through it; we all have to grow through it into harmony with All-That-Is and realize our union with the Father.

2004 4/27 – *"Your ego is part of your deeper consciousness. It is trying to avoid living in the NOW because the NOW appears to be THE VOID from whence it came, that awesomely lonely place where it and you existed when you asked, 'Am I?' It wants to think of the future and past only. This seems safe to it."*

Therefore, we must realize that our ego has a veiled memory just as we do, of the VOID prior to its incarnation in, as and with us. It tries to stay away from the fearful veiled memories of that existence by trying to dwell in the future with its planning, worrying, and fantasizing, or in the immediate past with its regrets, and grief.

Our individualized ego has amnesia concerning its former state of existence in the void just as we do, but the memory of that state and its doubts of existence are still in its deep background consciousness, haunting the ego with the age-old question and doubts such as, "AM I?" Just like us, the ego's only escape is to flee into the busy future with its fantasizing and planning, or possibly the memory of the incarnations past. It must avoid the present, the NOW. It seems the present is ominous and threatening, but it knows not why. It is just scared! It is afraid to face life and anything else that threatens its everyday existence.

"I Am" is a declaration of one living in the NOW, the ever present, which actually is all there is. The past and the future are all just experiences in the Now. The awakened one does not dwell in the "I will be" or the "I have been," but in the "I Am" state of being.

Help the ego find its way out of its fearful state. Love it into the now and let it help you climb to the next dimension. It really wants to be your best friend and most loving companion.

2004 5/6 – *"Divine love is experienced as the overwhelming awareness of the deepest feelings of another entity. It is experienced as the <u>awareness of being one with that entity</u>. At that time, you are experiencing union with that other entity. You are feeling what they feel. You truly love that one as yourself. This experience can be* *unsettling and overpowering emotionally, and should not be sought after, but simply allowed when it occurs."*

This helps explain the *punishment and reward* we must all experience when reaching the next higher spiritual realm. There, we become aware of, or actually experience, the emotions and feelings in the now of those we have harmed and likewise the joy of those we have helped.

Every individual will eventually awaken to the fullness of divine love and have to face and re-live the experiences of every individual or entity he or she has ever wronged—feeling the very exact pain, agony, loss, grief, and terror he or she has caused in others; actually going through each experience just as the victim did.

When our veiled mind is uncovered, and our amnesia healed, and we become "one" with every entity, what else could possibly happen, but the awareness, or memory of the emotional damage, of those we have harmed, or the emotional gratitude of those we have lovingly helped?

Since we are then in the timeless now of eternity, it matters not how long it takes to experience every second, every instant of the life of each individual we have wronged. This is the hell and Judgment we must face before we can understand and forgive ourselves for the wrongs we perpetrated on others, but really on our own self. Then we shall go forth triumphantly.

2004 5/27 - *"I never instructed you to exercise; only to fast, and ingest light-energy for perfect health."*

I responded, "Lord, you never told me not to either, but evidently the script we wrote for my life does not depend on physical exercise." Evidently, it probably does not depend on eating, drinking or even breathing if we really knew the truth. I have always loved manual labor and physical exercise—especially on my mountain bike. However, my Father, in the past, has advised me to fast and ingest light-energy for perfect health, not mentioning the need of exercise.

2004 6/20 - *"My nature is a totally integrated, male/female, father/ mother nature, with the Mother's gentle love dominating my essence. As you grow in grace, love, and truth, you too will exhibit softer female attributes. Your love will be more patient, allowing, and detached, but totally compassionate."*

Since His explanation of the operation of divine love as that of being able and willing to experience the feelings of other entities, I can understand that the female, or Mother-Nature, must dominate; otherwise, the male, or aggressive nature, might not be able to endure.

2004 8/3 – This morning during my meditations, **I saw what I believe was the spiritual essence of our Father expressed in light-energy.**

I was praising Him when, suddenly, I saw an awesome scene. In my dark study, with my eyes open and/or closed, I saw a cluster (ring) of bright golden/reddish lights appear around a circular center network of flashing violet lightning strings. The violet lightening strings looked like a nearly solid web of violet light in the space at the center of the golden/reddish light ring. The violet lightning strings seemed to be originating at a center point and flashing out in all directions to the golden/reddish ring. The golden/ reddish light ring and the inner violet web resembled a round eye—the iris and pupil. Then, all around the golden light ring in the black background were many tiny white lights brightly flickering on and off and darting about. It was breathtaking to watch.

I believe I was seeing here displayed in light-energy, the essence of our Father's consciousness. It was incredible!

2004 8/4 – This morning during my meditations, I saw the same scene as yesterday morning. This time, however, the intensity became even brighter, and the scene began to change. The golden/reddish light ring began changing colors. The golden/reddish ring changed to bright yellow, but the violet web-work in the center remained. Then, between the yellow light ring and the violet web network, a bright red ring formed. The bright flickering lights outside the yellow light ring were even bigger and brighter this morning. As I watched, the black background beyond the flickering lights, turned from black to foggy grey, and in the background beyond the fog, I became aware of something whirling like helicopter blades, spinning slowly just out of sight. These whirling images were turning both clockwise and counter-clockwise. This scene lasted through my entire meditation.

I then began to feel intense pain in various parts of my body, especially in my head. Other parts of my body that became quite uncomfortable were my shoulders, my middle back, and the area around my right kidney. I asked why I was experiencing so much pain, and the answer came, *"Your body is in healing trauma. Your body is experiencing the gouging out of calcifications in the joints and around the vertebra of your back, which was quite painful; the removal of plaque from your arteries, leaving exposed, damaged, artery walls which are emitting pain. The removal of these accumulated toxic substances must precede the healing process. Just endure it. You are being healed."*

2004 9/28 - *"Your arteries are being cleansed."*

This is very interesting. After a routine stress test on 4/27/05, I had an isotope imaging session that showed one artery that was partially clogged a year ago, and, at the time I was told I might need angioplasty and stint treatment, but it was now clear. How about that?

I wonder if it will stay clear since it was my thinking process that caused the clogging in the first place. Have I learned the lesson the clogged arteries were supposed to teach? If not, I will have to go through this again and again until I do get it. Knowing my Father's past methods with me, the answer is probably yes, I will.

2004 10/2 - *"My words are health and life to you; stay in them!"*

Sometimes, I allow my schedule to limit my time meditating and reviewing His words to me. That is a mistake. Lord, your words are health and life to me. I have proved that too many times. I must keep my meditation appointments and review constantly His words to me.

2004 10/26 - *"Embrace the thought forms that are warring against you!"*

All thought forms are living entities, and all living entities are thought forms, even the inanimate are living entities.

I must embrace negative thought-forms and re-polarize them as I was instructed earlier. I must see the negative thought-forms for what they are—spirits created by me as I emotionally considered the likelihood of some illness, disaster or negative situation.

These thought-forms are my obedient servants. They love me and live to serve me. **I am the one who gave them their life's existence and assignments,** and they are faithfully following my directions. I must love them back into a positive being. Then, I must re-assign their tasks and purposes. I do this by affirming positive statements concerning their new life assignments until they become positive thought-forms.

2004 11/6 – *"You are moving from the experience of intent to the reality of knowing. This means knowing 'I am well' makes you well. Knowing 'I am younger and stronger' makes you younger and stronger. Knowing that you can live on light-energy alone MAKES YOU IMMORTAL."*

I move into this experience by knowing first that "I am," that I am one with the Father; that I am the Father; that I have His power to create whatever experience or condition in the physical or spiritual realm I desire. All that is necessary for me to do is to simply use **high emotional focus** on the situation or experience I desire, and then accept it and embrace it into existence.

2004 11/10 - *"Think on FORCE-OF-WILL. This force-of-will is absolute determination to create the situation desired."*

Often, I consider the force of will that was necessary to blast this universe into being from pure consciousness. How much mental/spiritual force, and how long did it take to develop that technique? How much focus does it require to sustain this creation?

2004 11/11 - *"Think on Creative-Force-of-Will."*

He keeps coming back to me with this. Of course He does; it is the most important lesson we must learn as awakening gods. This was previously taught on 2003 2/21.

> *"Remember the creation of the Sun? That light beam was focused consciousness. Consider this and learn to focus your consciousness on what you desire."*

This vision about the sun being created was revealed in my first book and inspired the cover scene of my standing in a doorway watching a beam of light focusing on a spot in the universe eventually forming the sun.

I'm praying about this Creative Force of Will and the focus that accompanies it. I want to know exactly what He means by Force-of-Will. I'm sure it is a technique of focusing emotions during a time I'm trying to change a situation or possibly heal someone. He will make this known to me.

2004 11/11 - *"Everyone lives in his or her own rigid thought-form reality. Each creates and fashions his own reality to conform to his own beliefs as to how things are and how it all operates.*

Therefore, the criminal thinks everyone else is just like himself—a liar and thief, and must be dealt with as such.

A person of integrity, on the other hand, believes most are like him, honest and reliable, therefore, in his innocence, the person of integrity is gullible. Without laws to protect him, he will be victimized and ruled over by the criminal.

This goes much deeper. Some opposing realities are even invisible to others."

Note: Many of our own thought-form-realities are spirits we have created along the way when we were in an emotionally charged situation in our life. Sometimes we continue to reinforce these spirit entities by creating new and more related entities from the same highly emotional attitudes until we become quite rigid in that particular area of our life. In past religious experiences, they were called "demon spirits," and we thought they originated from outside ourselves—not so—they are our own creations! Now, we have to deal with them.

He speaks of us who are of integrity are gullible. Now that's interesting! The criminal understands our nature. No wonder the politicians who have gained rule over us can dupe us so easily. They realize we are innocent and gullible, so they have learned to tell us what we want to hear over and over again, and we will soak it up no matter how many times they change their story. We want to believe everyone, even to our own detriment.

There are really no laws to protect us from lying politicians. Think about it: <u>Do we ever hold a politician accountable to perform as he promised in his campaign</u>? No, we don't! They call what they promised "campaign rhetoric" (Real meaning: Excusable Lies) and turn from these promises as if the very suggestion of performing as promised is a repugnant joke. After they are elected, they will follow their own greedy agenda until they are eventually voted out of office. This system is wrong, but it was designed that way as an experiment as George Washington noted. We should realize, <u>the world of politics is mostly populated by criminals</u>.

The politicians along with their media collaborators, self serving religious institutions, greedy medical and pharmaceutical professions and the progressive propaganda touting educational systems rule over us and cruelly deceive us until we are completely enslaved by their devices, and helpless to resist.

The scripture says in Psalms 12:8, "*The wicked walk on every side, when the vilest men are exalted.*"

2004 11/23 - "*The area beyond the universes is not empty space; it is <u>non-existence.</u> I designate it the VOID because it does not yet exist; nevertheless, My consciousness is there because My imagination is* *there; therefore, the non-existence of the void is full of My omnipotent All-That-Is and also All-That-Is-Not.*

Consciousness is all that exists and all that does not exist. <u>Actually, there is no void and there are no created things; there is only consciousness— imagination; I AM.</u>"

Wow! That is a mind twister. I am being told to consider non-existence as if it exists? Is He saying "Nothing exists?" Or, is He saying, "Consciousness is all that actually exists?"

He is saying this: all that exists in the physical realm are figments of our/His imagination or thinking process. It is not real (eternal mass), but temporary illusions appearing as mass thought constructs or thought-forms. The only thing that is eternal is spirit or omnipotent consciousness.

2004 11/23 – *"The reason a straight line eventually curves back on itself in the vastness of this universe is that it cannot extend into non-existence; it and everything else, every physical object, must stay confined to this created physical dimensional reality."*

In all our science, physics, and mathematics courses, did any professor ever have a clue why this was the case? They could not even tell me how they knew a straight line curves back on its self. Some spiritual seer in ages past must have made the statement about a line curving back on itself in outer space or they received this revelation and it stuck; however, you and I now know it is so.

You and I have no such constraints. We are able to move into non-existence and out of it at will. We are actually creating new universes right now in the void.

2004 12/09 - *"Use that creative consciousness that is within you to heal yourself and help others. That consciousness that is you is Me. We are one and the same person. <u>Share</u> that consciousness with Mother Earth and the Celestial Realm, for that consciousness is omnipotent.*

Sharing is the place where you will find the FORCE-OF-WILL to accomplish the seemingly impossible."

SHARING LIGHT-ENERGY WITH MOTHER EARTH AND THE CELESTIAL REALM (From *The Last Enemy*, 1997 11/5)

The illustrations below show a technique of meditation of sharing light-energy nourishment between Mother Earth and the celestial realms.

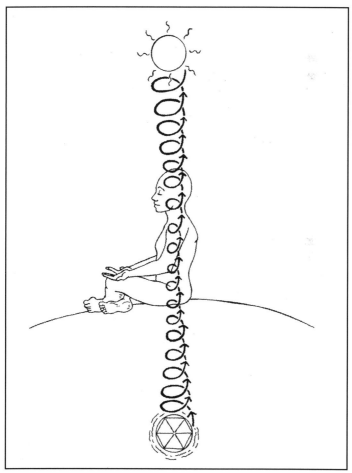

Sharing Mother Earth's Light-Energy with the Celestial

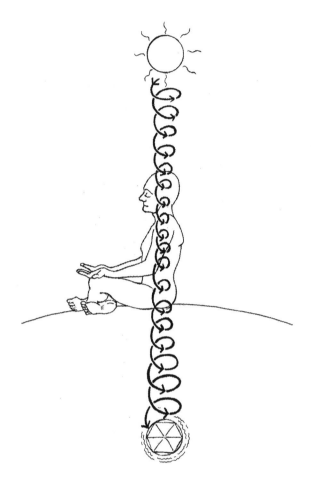

Sharing Celestial Light-Energy with Mother Earth

When I do this meditation, I sit on the floor or the ground. I concentrate, while breathing in deeply, imagining bringing up red light-energy from the core of Mother Earth into my base chakra, holding it a few seconds and then exhaling completely through the next chakra, the genital chakra. During the next deep breath, I imagine bringing the red light-energy up through the base chakra, mixing it with the orange light-energy of the genital chakra, holding it a few seconds, and then exhaling out through the solar plexus chakra. I do this mixing of light energies all the way up to the third eye chakra, from which I exhale through the crown chakra. This seems to awaken the whole chakra system. Then I breathe in deeply from the depths of Mother Earth straight up through each chakra; then I breathe out through the crown chakra into the celestial realms.

Immediately afterwards, I breathe in pure, white, celestial, healing light-energy through my crown chakra down the spine, to the base chakra. I then exhale it into the center, vibrating crystal core of Mother Earth. I call this sharing light-energy with Mother Earth.

My consciousness is omnipotent! I can change anything in my reality at will, for it is all just my imagination. I am able to change or re-create anything that displeases me. So why do I allow something in my reality that I don't want or like? I must seek to understand and use this "Force-of-Will" that I possess. I know it is available for me to use.

2004 12/10 - *"827436."*

I really have no idea what this number means at this time. I received a number years ago and tried it as a possible winning Lotto number, but it didn't work, so I doubt such an earthly, selfish, exercise would be what He has in mind here.

2005 1/17 – *"You are allowing your consciousness to be occupied by annoying thoughts from news print, radio and television news and trivia. Return to praise, light-energy work, and meditation when you are alone and while you are driving."*

I needed that! I do get too concerned with the political situations in this country and others around the world. Bully boys will be bullies and they grow up to be bully men (big *little* boy bullies). They will always be the belligerent, aggressive, little bullies that they have always been. Tragically, these nasty little bully boy minds rule the world.

Remember Psalms 12:8. *"The wicked walk on every side, when the vilest men are exalted."* We exalted them! We elected them to their exalted positions. Our indifference, little concern and non-attention to the character and deeds of those running for office has led to our present situation. Yes, we did it!

Look at the national leaders in the world today. They are always envious of what others have, always lying when the truth is a better story, always threatening and intimidating weaker nations, always finding something to start a war about, always willing to commit your and my sons and daughters to war to face death while they and theirs are ensconced in their palatial mansions in their capital cities. They are constantly finding new innovative schemes to enrich themselves and cover their backsides.

We watch in disgust and wonder how they ever got into office. Why did we ever vote for them?

Have we not yet learned that our political system is irredeemably corrupt? Nothing will change no matter what party is in control without direct divine intervention or an unavoidable national revolution. Then, who will rule over us?

Just turn the television news cast off. Ignore it all and proceed with your quest for union with the Father. This is our only hope. If you lived in the fifties and sixties, you read and watched the news daily and were scared to death of a Russian nuclear war that seemed imminent. Yet, it did not happen, so we worried for nothing. What will happen, will happen whether you worry about it or not. Just learn to turn it off and live in peace.

<u>Remember, everything is exactly as it should be.</u> It is best to turn off the news programs and throw the news papers in the trash.

There is nothing new under the sun. The Scripture says in Ecclesiastes 1:9-11, *"The thing that hath been, it is that which shall be; and that which is done is that which shall be done: and <u>there is no new thing under the sun</u>. Is there any thing whereof it may be said, See, this is new? <u>It hath been already of old time</u>, which was before us. There is no remembrance of former things; neither shall there be any remembrance of things that are to come with those that shall come after."*

Sounds like he is saying we won't learn by reading history, doesn't it? The fact is that we are not interested in history, just like a teenager is not interested in listening to his parents when they council them that they have been there and done that, and it got them in trouble or got them hurt. We seem to want to experience failure for ourselves. .

2005 1/24 – During my meditations this morning, I had an exceptional praise and light sharing experience while increasing my sphere of light to all entities. It was electrifying and very powerful.

Afterward, Jonnie Ann asked me what I was doing because during my meditation time, she saw a "snap shot" of me running with a huge smile/laugh on my face. I was wearing all blue denim clothes and also large-lens glasses.

Evidently, I am going to be doing a lot more jogging/running in the future. At this time, I have a work-out schedule that includes indoor cycling nearly every day.

2005 2/2 – *"The answer to all life's questions has always been, 'Christ in you, the hope of glory'* (Colossians 1:27). *Heal yourself and others with that power that resides in you, not from outside you. You are the Source of All-That-Is."*

Remember "Christ" means anointing, so we must rely on that deeper spiritual anointing of our Father. That is our own deeper self, the Source of All-That-Is.

The purpose of all my writings and ministry has always been, and will always be, teaching others to seek the anointing within, seeking our Father in our own heart—finding our deeper self (our Father) and listening to His still, small, voice within. This is the one and only truth every human being must somehow, some day, learn: "We must find that omnipotent one within our own deeper self." All else is just religious folly and will never satisfy our deepest longing nor lead us out of this continuous life/death, life/death reincarnation cycle.

2005 2/2 – *"Give! Give first and always! Give of that healing, loving, omnipotent life-force from within your own heart."*

I responded, "Somehow, this sounds like your eternal mission and life focus, Father. I want to be just like you—make me so. You are the ultimate giver."

2005 2/3 – *"Your healing is from within you. Your knowledge is from within you. Your union is from within you. You are the Source of All That Is. Send healing light to the Universe! Heal the universes. You have the power!"*

That Force-of-Will that He is asking me to use for healing comes from the focused energy of my center of light—my heart chakra. I must learn to FOCUS EMOTIONALLY from my heart.

2005 3/3 – *"What a privilege we have to share God's consciousness— to think with His mind."*

I agreed, "Father, let me not misuse this precious gift. Let Your integrity and righteousness guide my thoughts and actions. All my life I have been aware of Your changing the situations around me to keep me from danger and stumbling. I praise you, Father!"

When we eventually awake and realize we are actually thinking with the eternal God's consciousness, we will be frozen with the awe of the responsibility, the stewardship, and the glory He is sharing with us. We will be both ashamed and dismayed by how we have used this consciousness— the wicked thoughts and the wicked deeds we have perpetrated using this power on the one hand. But, on the other hand, we will be gratified by the grace and truth we have given to others. We will realize that everything we do every instant is, and has always been, open and naked before Him. We will stand without excuse, except that we are sons of the Most High and objects of His love and are safe in union with Him forever.

2005 3/3 – *"Let's talk about the veil. There is a veil across or a sphere above the strata of consciousness between your thinking and the deeper contemplation of the Source of All-That-Is. This veil is what you are learning to penetrate to receive truth and wisdom. There is but one consciousness—that all-knowing consciousness that created the illusion of physical substance and time, and it knows their secrets. This consciousness penetrates time to its ultimate limits, both forward and backward, continuously. It sees from the beginning to the end of* *time, simultaneously. **It knows! It knows all! It sees all! It remembers all! It is all—now!**"*

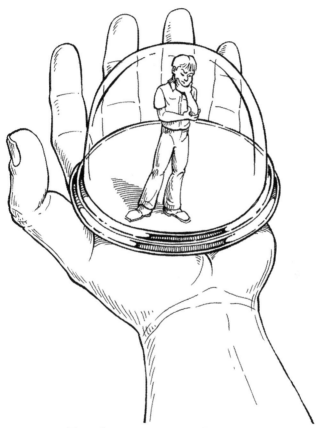

The Sphere Over Our Understanding

This veil or sphere is what prevents our understanding of how this world came into being, **from nothing**. It disallows our being able to understand the eternal nature and existence of the Almighty; moreover, it disallows us seeing our limitations, and the veil prevents us from learning the secrets that would allow us to penetrate its mysteries.

There has always existed a way for a devotee to gain entry to this understanding and all-knowing. Jesus said, *"It is harder for a camel to go through the eye of a needle than for a rich man to enter into the kingdom of heaven."* (Matthew 19:24) He did not say it is impossible—but extremely difficult. We must want this enlightenment more than anything else in the world. Now our glorious father is teaching us to penetrate this veil and regain our full nature as sons of God. Glory!

Do you think you are having a hard time reaching and searching for enlightenment? Consider how deeply and earnestly David, Solomon, Isaiah and the other prophets must have searched.

2005 3/16 – *"Everything and every entity is already in union with Me. <u>Much of creation knows it is in union with Me</u>. Keep that in mind as you share light-energy."*

Wow! Much of nature (the animate and the inanimate) knows it is in union with the all-knowing Source. If we learn to communicate with the animals and the inanimate, we may find a new source of wisdom—wisdom from the Source of All-That-is.

After reading this, should we hug a tree, or ask a thorny rose to help us understand our Father's mysteries and the workings of His omnipotence? Could I, alone in the forest, the mountains, or the desert wilderness, ask the sand or the rocks for help, wisdom or comfort? Would I be so foolish as to hold a stone or a crystal in my hand and earnestly believe my Father would speak to me through it?

Certainly, I should be so foolish! The scripture says the foolishness of God is wiser than men (1 Corinthians 1:25). Let's think about the enormous impact these words could have in our lives.

2005 3/29 – *"I am all that exists! Everything is Me. Just Me! The only way anything or any entity can exist is by being Me. You are Me! We are one—you cannot exist otherwise. You are My consciousness, otherwise you would not be!"*

Can this truth be stated any simpler? I and the Father are one being. All that He is, I am. I was from the beginning, and I formed all that is, and it is all sustained by me. Everything we see is our Father, be it the table or chair, the sun or a grain of sand, another person, or a fly; it is all our Father and it is ours to enjoy, not to fear. It is all His consciousness corresponding to our sight, touch, smell and taste. Actually, it is all me!

2005 3/29 – *"You exist by the force of your own will, because you are Me, and I WILL you to be. You and I wrote the script and set the stage for this life. It is all you and Me. We are one."*

I replied, "Yes, I understand. I was originally an essential part of Your consciousness that You and I individualized. We then planned this life (and many others) and the circumstances of this life that would give me the best chance for the lessons I needed at this time in my spiritual development. We then prepared for Me this life experience by giving me amnesia and placing me in a time-delay physical realm so I would not know who I really am, and what enormous creative powers I have."

2005 3/29 – *"You are entering that realm where you feel the words more and before you understand them."*

I replied, "Yes Father, and before I can express them." The truth of the words comes first, then the ability to articulate them. Sometime, the messages I feel are deeper than I can express. I have to wait for the messenger to interpret them to my level of thinking, understanding and expression.

2005 4/14 – *"You are going to experience the scripture that says, 'For this corruption must put on incorruption, <u>and this mortal must put on immortality</u>. So when this corruptible shall have put on incorruption, and this mortal shall, have put on immortality; then shall be brought to pass the saying that is written, Death is swallowed up in victory. O death, where is thy sting? O grave, where is thy victory?'* (1 Corinthians 15:53-56) *It is necessary that you know that this will be a supernatural moment."*

I shudder at the thought of what this all means. Is He saying that I am going to be at death's door soon—so near dying that I will know my surviving the experience is death being swallowed up in victory? I believe that is exactly what He is saying. I have to rest in His words that I will not die this time from whatever is facing me.

2005 4/20 – Today I had blood work done to determine my progress since my heart triple stent implant in August of 2003. This blood work and a treadmill stress test were ordered a week later to see how well I was doing.

2005 4/22 – Today, I rented a garden tiller and spent some five hours tilling a plot of land for our vegetable garden. Even though I fought with this machine for five hours pulling and jerking it around, I had no physical discomfort or problems at all.

2005 4/27 – I had a treadmill stress test today to complete my physical progress examination, and it went very well indeed. I was able to run three minutes longer than a year ago and faster with no discomfort or problems.

2005 4/30 – While shoveling snow off our deck at the mountain house today, I realized I was having pain similar to my heart attack twenty months ago in my back, chest, shoulder and jaws. This was especially strange to me since I had just successfully completed my stress test three days ago, but there was no mistaking the signs; it was another heart attack.

I decided that if this could kill me, contrary to God's word, I would let it try. I drove home from our mountain house and was kept awake all night by intense pain in my chest and jaws. Sunday, and Sunday night were restless bouts with the same pains. The pain got so intense that, at times, I thought the death angel or someone from the other side would be coming to get me. Nothing happened. I just suffered and lost sleep.

2005 5/2 – I met with my cardiologist today and after reviewing my blood work and stress test results, I was given a clean bill of health. He said he didn't need to see me for six months.

I then told him of the pain in my jaws, chest, shoulder and arms, and about a fever and runny nose I have been fighting for a week. We both eventually agreed, after reviewing the tests, that my fever, runny nose and pains were probably the result of a viral infection (flu) that was going around. It caused aching muscles, weakness and pain in various parts of your body much like a heart attack. I went home.

2005 5/5 – After three more sleepless nights with intense pain in my chest, shoulders, arms and jaws, I decided I didn't want to live with the pain any longer since it looked like I was just going to live through it, and with it, no matter what. I checked into the Emergency Room at the Longmont Hospital. They admitted me immediately as a heart attack patient. Within two hours, I was in the operating room having another three stints implanted. Three days later on Sunday, May 8, I returned to the operating room to have two more stints implanted. Now, I had eight titanium stents in my heart's arteries.

2005 5/9 - Today, one day after the last stent implants, I was released from the hospital.

I felt very well. I was a little weak from lying in a bed for four days, but otherwise, I felt great.

2005 5/10 – In my meditation this morning, I asked, "Why did this heart attack have to happen? You said I would not die this time, so why did I nearly die?"

The answer came immediately, *"If you are to teach about engaging The Last Enemy (DEATH), you must know what it is like to face him; hence, your present situation."*

During the five day struggle with death, I came to realize Death is not an enemy at all, but a trusted friend who is carrying out our plans and following the scripts we have written for this life. Maybe, that is why he is called an angel—the Angel of Death.

2005 5/12 – Jud Manning, a deceased former president of our company, CPS Distributors, Inc., came to me this morning in my meditations and asked me to go with him to swim the "river." I realized he was referring to the river of death, and so I refused to go with him at this time.

2005 5/14 – Jud Manning returned this morning during my meditations and asked both Jonnie Ann and me to go with him to the river. We both refused to go swimming in the river at this time.

At this particular time, Jonnie Ann was very ill, too, but we both refused to swim in the "river." Jonnie Ann and I both seemed, to others, to be at the point of death, but because of my Father's words, I refused to depart, and Jonnie Ann wouldn't go without me.

2005 6/7 – *"There is always plenty of time. You created linear time— you can extend it or diminish it as you wish."*

Now, here is an interesting message. Do we do this extending or diminishing unintentionally at times already? If time is an illusion existing as the result of our conscious manipulations, then we probably do unknowingly, increase or diminish its incremental durations. We can all remember times when time flies or when it seems to drag. Are we changing the intervals between seconds at those times? Now, it seems to me it is quite probable we are doing exactly that—manipulating time. We really are awakening Gods!

2005 7/17 – *"There is more to 'I Am' than you have realized. Jesus said, 'Tell them I AM hath sent me,' Indicating that 'I AM' is a reference to God the Father. However, 'I AM' also describes a state of being; that is, 'I AM' is an unfinished phrase. It solicits further description of*

that action—I AM doing some thing—I AM healing—I AM creating.
I AM doing all the activities an omnipotent being performs as I AM
All-That-Is."

Everything that exists is "I AM" doing the work of sustaining the illusion
of physical existence in this present three-dimensional reality. Now, since,
my Father and I are one, then it is I whom is doing the sustaining work in
this physical illusion. "I AM THAT I AM!"

2005 7/17 – *"When you are meditating during light-energy touch-*
healing, use My words, 'I AM' with the description of your action, such
as 'I AM sending healing, love-light-energy.' Invoke My presence with
your action—I AM there."

2005 7/18 – *"Before you sit for meditation, review My last messages*
to you. This will help you understand the next utterance."

I believe He is implying that no subject or revelation is finished in a single
message. There are always more and deeper disclosures of truth. It never
seems to end. This is why I have been instructed to review the past recent
messages before I sit for meditation each day. Review of past messages is
necessary because our spiritual progress is assembled truth upon truth,
"precept upon precept," until we are able to understand the next deeper
concept.

Some wonder why they seem so far behind in their spiritual journey and
become dismayed and discouraged. You cannot build a building from the
top down. You have to begin with the foundation, then the walls, and
finally the roof. Our spiritual growth is much the same. Some truths we
receive today are but conceptual braces to hold up the spiritual structure
until we can build the walls.

Understand this: When the deeper truth comes, it may even seem to
contradict earlier, but necessary, building blocks of truth. Eventually, we
will see why the (seemingly) contradictory earlier words and experiences
were necessary.

I believe this constant reviewing of past messages from the spirit world is what King David was talking about in, Psalms 119:11, when he wrote, *"Thy word have I hid in mine heart..."* He continually reviewed the words the Father had spoken to him. Then he recorded them in what we know as the Psalms.

2005 7/18 – *"Think on the emotion of an auditorium full of people in a successful religious healing service. Yes, some people are healed during these services. The extreme emotion of the excited congregation is what made the healing service a success, and that is the kind of emotion you and your patient must produce for a successful touch-healing session. Think on the times when you have seen success in healing others—there was tremendous emotion involved. Later, that emotional intensity will come naturally to you when you are light-energy touch-healing."*

He is saying my patient and I must produce as much emotion as an entire congregation? Yes, but the emotional quality, not the quantity, and we can—we must learn how. Just knowing that light-energy touch healing always produces some change should invoke the emotion to finish the work. I will eventually get there. There is always some healing energy produced when you lay hands on someone for healing, but we must be very careful; "healing" might not be in their plan for this time in this incarnation. Let them ask for the healing, or wait on your spirit guides to tell you when you are to lay hands on them.

2005 7/27 – *"Stay in My words. This is the place you will find the strength and determination to carry on to victory."*

I asked, "What victory, Father?"

He answered, *"The victory of awakening to the full omnipotence of your being."*

He certainly is not talking about staying in religious writings passed down through the centuries that have been translated, interpreted, and doctrinally edited until they are nearly useless to a true seeker. He is talking about reviewing constantly the messages He is giving you and me personally; however, I do use some ancient Biblical Scripture and other references because I can *feel* their truth, because so many accept them, and because truth is truth, no matter where it is recorded.

The Apostle Paul in Colossians 1:26-27, writes, *"Even the mystery which hath been hid from ages and from generations, but now is made manifest to his saints: to whom God would make known what is the riches of the glory of this mystery among the Gentiles; which is* **Christ in you, the hope of glory***:"* Christ means anointing, and Paul is saying the Anointing in you will give you the glory. The Anointing—the Source of All-That-Is, your own deeper self; the, I AM, within you is what Paul is talking about. That is the place the words, messages, and miracles will come to enlighten and awaken you to the fullness of your own omnipotence. In The Epistle of James 1:5, it is written, *"If any of you lack wisdom, let him ask of God, that giveth to all men liberally, and upbraideth not; and it shall be given him."* If you are earnestly seeking wisdom from the Father, He will enlighten you.

2005 7/27 – *"The incredible in your life is just beginning. I am opening new worlds to you."*

I cried, "Father, the words You have already given me are incredible. If You stopped talking to me today, it would be more than I could have expected in ten lifetimes."

2005 7/27 – *"Think of the promise of Strength, Health and Youth— Make S.H.Y. (shy) your mantra."*

Remember the Bible verses in Isaiah 40:29-31, *"He giveth power to the faint; and to them that have no might, he increaseth strength. Even the youths shall faint and be weary, and the young men shall utterly fall: But they that wait upon the Lord shall renew their strength: they shall mount up with wings as eagles; they shall run, and not be weary; and they shall walk, and not faint."*

Isaiah is talking about **us old folks** here, my brothers and sisters—read it again. Life is not nearly over at eighty; we can live well into the 200's and a lot more if we choose to do so. Let's claim our heritage and our omnipotence. The writer Isaiah saw the truth about overcoming the ageing process, even though he himself eventually died, I guess (?)

Isaiah is writing here about the "faint" and "them that have no might" as contrasted against (in the next verse) "the youth." He tells us he has been shown that when the situation becomes so grim and terrifying that the young men faint, grow weary and utterly fall, then the old men shall mount up with eagle's wings (eagles have always been symbolic of God in the Bible). In other words, he is saying, "We shall mount up as gods with eagle's wings, and persevere as gods.

The course is not over just because you think your body is aging and wearing out. Let's disregard appearances and claim our victory. Really, it becomes obvious.

2005 8/3 – *"How do I, as the omnipotent Father, as pure consciousness, understand and improve myself? I take each thought, MY MENTAL IMAGES, and incarnate them so that they may find their way through the maze of positive and negative experiences until they realize (KNOW) that the PATH OF LOVE is the only way to peace, joy, fulfillment, and union. This is why I told you long ago that, 'You are an eternal thinking process.' This is why it is written that man was created in the IMAGE of God."*

(1999 5/3, *The Last Enemy*) - *"You are a thought-in-progress, a thought that never ends, an eternal, omnipotent thinking process."*

Sounds as though He is describing God Almighty, doesn't it? Actually, He is! Welcome home!

We too should understand the path of love that we are undertaking. Love sees no evil in others, but understands everyone else is just like us, living out what they must to find union with their Father.

Here, our Father is expanding on, or clarifying His words on the creation of mankind. Each is an image (imagination) of the Father. Each person is a separate individual expression of our Father's consciousness that He has individualized temporarily to find its own life experience. Then, we will all come together again as **"separate but united"** and equal entities, gloriously co-existing in love and understanding, excitingly creating and enjoying eternal life and glorious situations for all. My expression "separate but united" means we will still be individuals, but completely united, and in perfect harmony with the Father. This may seem double talk, but it will eventually make sense.

2005 8/3 – *"All you are dealing with is eternal mental IMAGES in-and-as yourself and in-and-as others. Human beings, animal beings, spirit beings, and the inanimate entities are all mental IMAGES— THINKING PROCESSES, making their way to re-union with the creator and sustainer of all-that-is. You must deal with them all on a spirit or consciousness level to help them in their quest."*

You should ask, how? First, we must realize that each of us and each of our mental images, exist in an illusionary world in illusionary bodies, whether human bodies, animal bodies or in inanimate bodies—all physical bodies which are not real. The real person, animal or rock, is an invisible consciousness that may or may not have amnesia concerning their eternal existence and relationship with the Source. Some inanimate entities are completely aware of who and what they are. You think you know what they are, but now you know you can communicate with them on a deeper level. Have you ever tried to do so? Have you ever tried to communicate with a dog or cat, a rock or tree, or even another person on a much deeper consciousness level?

Have you ever stared into another person's eyes to observe their inner self? Sometimes it is a beautiful face—sometimes it is hideous. You can know right away whether to embrace or be apprehensive of that one.

Have you ever stared into your pet's eyes to see the deeper longing in their lives? Have you held a rock in your hand and meditated on it until it communicated with you?

When you were in deep grief or distress, did you feel the soothing relief as a tree took your pain away? Did you remember to thank it for its love-light-energy? We can help those entities the same way by sending them love energy just like the tree does us.

Do you feel thankful toward Mother Earth for her steadfastness to always help us? We explode hydrogen bombs on her skin and try to drain her blood to use for fuel as we frolic in our SUV's. We pollute her air and water every day and in every way imaginable. I cringe when I think that we use her precious water to flush our toilets.

If you are truly thankful and appreciative toward Mother Earth (Gaia), then send her your love energy and thank her every day for the wonderful environment she selflessly provides for us for our incarnation experience.

2005 8/4 – *"Let's talk about emotion. All miraculous action demands great emotional stress, and this emotion can be positive or negative in nature. That means, great fear or hate is just as effective as a creative emotion as is great love or joy because you are omnipotent. Your emotional decrees MUST produce the results you emotionally command because your consciousness is the source and creative power of All-That-Is. Think on this!*

Remember the emotional 'fear' you experienced during the Mojave Desert car stall when the rain cloud appeared? Remember Jonnie Ann's healing in the Fort Collins hospital? Recall the joy (emotional elation) you experienced when you said you didn't have the faith to pray anymore. I told you to 'be obedient, I will be faithful,' and she was healed. The first incident was emotional fear, the second was emotional joy—both produced miracles."

He says, your emotional decrees (or statements and thoughts) MUST produce the results you emotionally commanded because your consciousness is omnipotent, the Source and creative power of All-That-Is.

You say, "Well, where are all those results we have created during these emotional experiences?" Some, you have already gone through—some you are living with presently, and some are awaiting being drawn into your now from a parallel reality. Hopefully, you are only dwelling on and drawing to you the positive imagination creations, and not the negative thought-forms. What ever you emotionally dwell on, you will eventually experience. Be careful, my brother or sister, you are omnipotent and you are creating all the time.

(The First Incident)
Stranded in the Mojave Desert - 1958

Finally, my tour of duty on The Rock was over, and I was heading back to the mainland. There was a problem: While in Hawaii, I purchased from and had Sears install, a rebuilt engine in my 1951 Plymouth. The new engine began knocking just after the two year warranty was up while I was still in Hawaii. I asked Sears to help me, but they would not. My credit account with Sears was at its limit, and they would not repair it under the warranty because it was expired by two months. I decided to repair it myself, but when I disassembled the engine, I discovered Sear's overhaul facility had installed a different size bearing on each of the six rod throws. To overhaul it, I would have to remove and regrind the crankshaft to all the same size throws or buy six separate sets of rod bearings and use one bearing out of each set. I could afford neither. I had just enough money to make the trip across the country from San Francisco to Milledgeville, Georgia.

I had a month off, so if I could get this car back to Milledgeville, Pap would help me get it fixed or buy a different car. I could find a temporary job during that time off, to pay for the repairs. I had to try to make the trip across the country from the West Coast to the East Coast in this loud, rod-knocking 1951 Plymouth.

The Air Force sent us back to the mainland by commercial ocean-liner, and we docked in San Francisco. My car was also on board, so the next day I went back to the docks and picked it up. The engine seemed to be knocking worse than ever. I thought maybe I should see what a Plymouth mechanic would say. Maybe it was just some common wrist-pin noise in one of the pistons.

The mechanic was not sympathetic at all. After he listened to the engine with his stethoscope, his remark was, "I would not try to drive this thing across the Mojave Desert with a new one pushing me. It has one or two rod bearings about to come loose."

What could I do? I had no money to rebuild the engine for the 3,000 mile trip to the East Coast, but I had to make the trip. After consideration, I thought, "I will pray about it. Hopefully, if I hold my speed below 50 miles per hour, the engine might stay together." We loaded up the Plymouth, and set out for the Mojave Desert.

Things were going well the first few hours. We were the slowest car on the road, but the knock did not seem to be getting any worse. Then, we crested a hill and the landscape changed from plush green grass and orange trees, to desolate brown desert. Wow, was it hot! I pulled into a service station to fill up with gas. Also, I needed to buy some water and ice to take along, since we had two young kids and a long, hot trip ahead. The folks there showed me a way to have cool water along the way, without ice. They had canvas water bags that tie to the front bumper. The bags hang down in the wind as you drive along. As the canvas bags sweat, the moisture cools the water inside by evaporation. What an excellent idea! We could have ice-cold water to drink all day. I bought two, filled them with water, tied them to the front bumper, and off we went.

It was well over 110 degrees on the desert that day, and my Plymouth was just not up to that kind of heat. Within about 150 miles into the desert, the engine began to overheat. It seems I was driving too slowly for the wind across the radiator to cool the engine. Then, we had our first fuel system vapor lock. The engine stopped, and we had to wait for it to cool. I eventually got an idea to pour cold water on the fuel pump and the fuel lines. This helped, but about every twenty minutes, the engine would vapor lock and quit again. We were now out in the middle of the desert and not getting along very well. I saw a long hill up ahead and knew this would heat up the engine, causing it to quit again. I got up a little extra speed and started up the long grade. As we got about halfway up, I thought, "We are going to make it!" Then, the engine quit again, and I coasted to the shoulder. The kids were hot and crying, and we needed to refill our water jug from the canvas bags while we were stopped. I got out and lifted the hood. Then, I reached for the canvas water bags to cool the engine. They were both empty! I had hung the bags too low on the bumper. They had dragged on the pavement, and the dragging wore holes in both bags. What had I done? If no one stops to help, I will have killed my family! This was in 1958, and there were few cars on the highway that day. I thought, "It might be hours before another car comes by. Then, would they even stop?"

I leaned over the engine under the hood, and wept, "Lord, I have run out of options. In a little while my family will die from this heat." I cried, "Lord, please help me!" All of a sudden, I felt better, but I could not understand why. Nothing had changed. We were still out of water. The car was still dead in the road, and the temperature on the desert was still over 110 degrees. Somehow, my begging the Lord for help seemed to encourage me. Now, all I could do was try to start the engine. I got in, pushed the starter button, and the engine started instantly. I thought, "It has not had time to cool off! It should not have started!" I quietly thanked the Lord for His intervention and pulled out into the road. The engine did not overheat again until we got on top of the hill about a mile away. I thought, "Well, at least we got over that hill, so I will coast as far as I can, and then I'll pray again, and He will start it again. I turned the ignition off as I topped the hill to try to cool the engine while coasting down the other side of the hill.

As we coasted down the long incline, I noticed a small cloud begin forming in the sky over us; it grew very quickly. Soon, we were coasting in the cloud's shade. I thought, "That should help cool the engine. Thank you, Father."

Then, in the middle of the Mojave Desert, in the middle of the day, it began to rain! The rain cooled the air. I put the car in gear and let out the clutch; it cranked, and began running, cool. I began to praise the Lord. The rain from this little cloud continued to fall on us and stayed with us all day until we crossed the desert

A Miracle in the Mojave Desert

I realized we were safe for the rest of the trip. We stopped in New Orleans and visited friends; then we drove on to Georgia without another mishap; however, I traded the Plymouth as soon as we arrived back in Milledgeville, Georgia. There, I began working with Pap to renovate his rental houses.

(The Second Incident)

"SHE PROBABLY WON'T MAKE IT THROUGH THE NIGHT."

Jonnie Ann began having a new health problem. Out of the blue, she came down with a debilitating case of diarrhea. "No problem," I thought as I sat down with her to lay hands on her and pray. We prayed together, but it didn't change a thing. Finally, after treating her for a week with no change, I dejectedly went for some medicine. After another week, I saw the medicine had done nothing for her. I took her to a neighborhood clinic, and they prescribed a stronger medicine that contained paregoric. She took this mixture for two weeks and continued to get worse. I was still laying hands on her every day, asking our Father to heal her. Nothing seemed to help.

She was now developing arthritis in her joints and, within two more weeks, she could not walk. She lost her appetite and was unable to eat anything. She had now been ill for six weeks and was growing very weak. She could not even sit up by herself.

I took her to a doctor in Fort Collins, who brought in a specialist in intestinal disorders. He put her in the Poudre Valley hospital that very day. By that evening (Monday), he put her in intensive care. I was working in Denver, but I came in every morning and afternoon to sit with her. Jonnie Ann's doctor was not very optimistic about what was happening. He was unable to find the source of the problem. He did find some *Giarrdia* bacteria in her colon, but he felt like there was not enough to cause this problem and they could treat Giarrdia. She was not responding to any medicine or treatment. She could not eat without losing the food, so she was now being fed intravenously.

On Tuesday, she was worse, and much weaker. I held her hands, and we prayed together for her healing for hours. On Wednesday, she was worse but I continued to lay hands on her and pray for her healing. This had worked so often on so many ailments. Why not now? Had I failed the Lord some way? Was I doing something wrong? I was completely disheartened. Nothing the doctor was doing, and nothing I was doing, was helping. All I could do was wait and see if she could snap out of it on her own.

Thursday afternoon, when I arrived at the hospital, the doctor met me in the hallway. "Mr. Bentley," he said, "come with me to my office. I have to talk to you." I went in his office and sat down. He closed the door. He spoke softly, "I hate to have to tell you this, but your wife is now in a coma. She has not responded to any medication, and now her vital signs are degenerating. Her liver and kidneys have failed. Her blood pressure has become dangerously low, and her temperature is dropping. Mr. Bentley, I am so sorry, but I don't believe she will make it through the night." He patted me on the shoulder and left. I began to sob.

After a while, I regained control of my emotions and left his office. I entered Jonnie Ann's room and sat down at her bedside. She was so still and was hardly breathing at all. Her color had faded to a pale yellow.

I was finally beaten. I felt totally powerless and spiritually dead. I had nowhere else to go, and no one to ask for help. So often before, the Lord had intervened and helped me. Why was this so different? I began to sob again as I prayed. This time I knew it was too late for help, so I just asked, "Why, Lord? She loves it so much here in the Rockies. Why does she have to leave so quickly?"

A voice I knew so well softly spoke, *"Remember the scripture, 'Lay your hands on the sick and they shall recover?'"*

I replied, "I have for six weeks, Lord, and nothing works. I'm totally beaten down, and I don't know what I believe anymore. I just don't have the faith to pray for her again."

The voice, louder now, and more stern, spoke again, *"You be obedient; I will be faithful!"* The hair stood up on the back of my neck.

Chills coursed through my body, and I began to shake with excitement. I shouted, "Yes Lord, I can do that, now!"

I put one hand in Jonnie Ann's hand and the other on her abdomen. I committed her to the Lord and began to thank and praise Him for her healing. My hands began to tingle! They became hot as I sat there waiting for what would happen next.

Hours passed as the heat and tingling continued. Suddenly, the tingling stopped and a pulsing began. I instinctively knew the treatment was finished. Then I experienced an incredible inner assurance of, *"It is done!"* I realized she was healed completely. I knew now what the old preachers, back in the south, meant by "praying through." I was so excited that I grabbed Jonnie Ann and shook her. She woke up! Yes, out of a coma, she awakened. I cried, "Jonnie Ann, the Lord just healed you!"

She was dead tired and only managed to say, "OK." She went back to sleep. Later, she would not remember waking up and speaking to me.

I went home, called my sister Sally, and told her what had happened; then I crashed for the night. I didn't awaken until nearly 10:00 a.m. the next morning. I drove to the hospital and was met in the hallway by Jonnie Ann's doctor. Excitedly, he exclaimed, "Your wife is finally responding to the medicine! I said, "I'll bet she is!"
He hesitated, and then continued, "She is going to be fine. She awakened at 6:00am this morning demanding real food, and they gave her some breakfast. Now she is demanding more food, and she is keeping it down. Her blood pressure is normal, and her liver and kidneys have recovered. She can probably go home this afternoon. Go in and see her. I'll be in there shortly. I need to talk to both of you."

Jonnie Ann was sitting up in bed eating her second breakfast. Her color was back to normal, and she, of course, wanted to go home. She didn't know she had been in a coma, nor how ill she had become. She didn't remember anything that had happened the night before. She didn't remember talking to me when I awakened her. That was all right; she was well.

The doctor came in and advised us that Jonnie Ann had Crohn's Disease, a chronic inflammation of the colon. He said it was a life long disease and would demand diligent care to keep it under control. He said, above all, that she must avoid all milk products such as cheese, ice cream, coffee cream, milk of any kind, and she must take a heavy steroid (prednisone) every day for the rest of her life. If she failed to adhere to his advice, she would be right back in the hospital and, next time, she might not be so lucky. After the doctor left, I told Jonnie Ann about her miraculous healing. She wanted to believe me but she was afraid. She was not awake during her healing experience. She felt she had to take the advice and the steroids as the doctor ordered. I did not try to argue with her. It had to be her choice. We actually checked out of the intensive care unit and the hospital the same hour that morning. We went home and Jonnie Ann began taking the steroids. She also stopped eating or drinking any type of milk products.

Within three weeks, Jonnie Ann's hair began falling out from taking the steroids. When I got home one afternoon, she was sitting at the table with her comb in hand crying about her hair loss. She said she would rather have died than be bald. I said, "Jonnie Ann, remember my telling you what happened the night before you left the hospital?"

"Yes," she said, "but I have been afraid to believe it."

I replied, "Honey, you were completely healed. You don't need this medicine and you don't need to avoid milk products."

She studied my face for a moment; then she exclaimed, "All right," let's go get a pizza." She threw the prednisone in the trash and we headed out for a Godfather's pizza. Then we followed up the pizza with a banana split. We have eaten pizzas and ice cream and drank milk shakes ever since. That was in 1985, twenty years ago, at this writing.

2005 9/22 – *"In this body, I Am. In dying, I Am. Between worlds, I Am. In ascension, I Am. Forever, eternally, I Am."*

Father is here speaking as me in this body. He says He is the one living in my body incarnations. He is the one who dies, and lives between incarnations, and He is the one in me, as me, who ascends and is eternally the, I AM.

2005 10/13 – *"You need to be more aware that everything you touch is Me. Everything you see is Me. Touch Me. See Me. I am you and everything else in existence. As I told you before, 'If it exists, it is alive.' It is alive and I am its life and consciousness."*

I exclaimed, "Amen! You continually remind me of this truth. I hope I will soon allow it to be fixed in my spirit."

We need to pause and just look around us and consider this truth. Fix your gaze on any person, animal, insect or inanimate object, touch it and consider "This is my Father's manifesting Himself as this rock." Ask Him in the rock, "What message do you have for me, Father?" See what happens. Give it time…

2005 11/13 – *"Believe My words Jack. They are life and health to you and all the people of Earth. It is all truth; receive it."*

I replied, "I do believe your words, Father, and they have been life and health to me. You seem to indicate that many people worldwide will receive life and health from the words in my books. Thank you, Father, for your encouragement."

2005 11/13 – *"Water is the balm of healing for the body and for the worlds. Its secrets will heal the Earth and its people."*

I have been told by the spirit realm for years that there are secrets about water that will heal the worlds. This is not only speaking about human body healing, but the healing of world wide problems, such as a source of fuel for the planet and for all planets throughout the universes.

From the hieroglyphs of the ancient tombs of Egypt, Babylon and beyond, Zachariah Sitchin, in his book, *The Lost Book of Enki*, and many other of his writings, has translated hundreds of clay and lapis lazuli tablets that tell of ancient astronauts who claimed their spacecrafts were powered by water as a fuel, and also used water to power their weapons, *The Lost Book of Enki* (page 69-70) One ancient astronaut told of blasting his way through the asteroid belt on his way to find Earth. He told of his space ship even having to land on the planet we call Mars many thousands of years ago to refuel from water there. There was water available on that planet at that time. These ancient writings even tell why we see no water on Mars today.

Soon, someone will learn the secret of economically fracturing the water molecule to produce free hydrogen and oxygen and thereby produce a fuel burning process with over one to ten efficiently. What a perfect fuel! It contains the flammable agent hydrogen and also oxygen which aids in burning, and these fuel agents are in just the right mixture in water.

There is some discussion about a process being over 100% efficient, or being able to produce more energy out than is required to drive it. I agree with them, but I just don't know how to describe this other-realm process that gives you more energy than you invest in it. This process would require a small number of watts of electricity to operate and produce hundreds of watts output when its thermal output is converted to watts.

2005 11/13 – *"Drink only Holy Water—water that you have infused with love, joy, peace, grace, truth, wisdom, healing and thanksgiving. Give your attention to water, then listen, watch and wait."*

I think this truth was picked up by the Catholic Church hundreds of years ago. Holy Water is still used in their services today. Somehow, they learned that Water is alive and **conscious** and when blessed, carries that power to whatever purpose it is intended.

The profit Nostradamus used water in his meditations to predict the future. The seer used a bowl of water during his meditations and stared into the water. It would eventually form pictorial scenes of future events. Many of his prophecies were extremely accurate. We realized this, of course, after the events he predicted actually occurred.

2005 11/30 – *"Remember long ago I told you to 'Consider the Water'? That was one of My most important admonitions to you. Again, Consider Water!"*

As an ongoing project for more than thirty years, I have been trying to <u>efficiently</u> fracture the water molecule to produce hydrogen and oxygen to use as the perfect fuel. Many have fractured the water molecule, but not efficiently—not over better than one to one. Our Father would like to teach us that the science we trust so much now is not the full knowledge of science or technology that is available to us. As a friend asserted thirty years ago as he was helping me on this water-energy project, "Jack, are you saying that there is a energy window in the universe that allows energy to flow that we heretofore have known nothing about?"

I answered, "Exactly, and that is our Father's other-science energy that is now available to us. We will eventually find it, and learn how to use it."

Our Father knew that when He placed us on this planet, we would eventually come to burn fossil fuels until we reached the "Peak Oil" point. This is a point when our oil wells and refineries can no longer supply the run-a-way demand for oil. He knew that shortly thereafter, the oil wells will eventually be drained, and world wide chaos will follow. Without oil, we could not heat our homes, nor drive our cars, nor cultivate the vegetables for us and feed for the cattle we think we must eat, nor produce electricity for industry, hospitals or our homes.

Knowing this, He prepared this planet for its eventual over-population and the extreme fuel shortages it brings. So, our Father designed this planet, with oceans of fuel all around us. Three quarters of our planet surface is water. This is adequate to provide the energy with adequate planning to build the huge dwelling complexes for countless future populations, and still leave ample land mass for cultivation.

Note: The effluent of burning water is steam. We would no longer pollute our land and air and destroy our atmosphere. But, I'm sure our gracious government would find a way to tax even this process.

2005 12/14 – *"Foolishness grips the mind of man. Even the most spiritual must guard against its folly. Dwelling long on its folly creates negative intention, and unabated negative intention produces corruption."*

We are rewriting our life's script constantly. A well-intended life can be changed very quickly by dwelling on negative situations and erotic pleasures because our thoughts or imaginations are omnipotently creative. Each thought creates the situation we envision immediately in a close, parallel dimension. Then, as we emotionally dwell on its folly, we draw this situation into our present time and into our present experience; on the other hand, if we realize our mindless folly and consciously reject its nonsense, we will cancel the created scene and avoid its consequences.

Much of what we are seeing today on a national scale is the consequences of some of our politicians dwelling constantly on their own frivolous follies instead of promoting and protecting the welfare of the people. Our own political leaders are drawing a destructive economic situation upon us all, and we can see it beginning to unfold all around us today.

The Scripture declares: *"The wicked walk on every side, when the vilest men are exalted."* (Psalms 12:8)

Our indifference to what goes on in Washington, D.C. is what has brought us to this hour. Remember the patriot talking about vigilance. We have totally disregarded his admonition. Don't despair; it is all in our script.

Also on this subject, the Scripture declares: *"The righteousness of the perfect shall direct his way: <u>but the wicked shall fall by his own wickedness.</u>"*

2006 1/12 – *"Think of water as the liquid consciousness of the Father."*

We have a special relationship with water, or we should have. The prophet Nostradamus knew its power.

2006 1/28 – *"Only as long as you are in this realm are you allowed to affect this realm. Presently, you may influence this realm with your energy. Share, meditate, and pray. That is the urgency. When you leave this realm, there are protocols greatly restricting inter-realm activities and communication. Remember the Scripture; 'There is a great gulf fixed.'"*

There must be a restriction, or else we would come back and interfere with the lives of our loved ones and even interfere with our national leadership. This would be to the detriment of both our loved ones and our national destiny. <u>We are, as individuals, and as nations, exactly where we are supposed to be.</u>

A new friend of mine, and a proof-reader of this book, Geoff Cutler, pointed out to me that our Father did not say the protocols restricted all influence, and that is a great point. We have all experienced or known of deceased men and women reappearing to help or teach others still here in the physical realm; however, the contacts are "greatly" restricted.

If our deceased loved ones could come back and interfere in our lives, this physical experience we signed up for would be useless as a spiritual growth situation. Those deceased loved ones, who love us and are still concerned for us, would constantly try to change our minds and defend us from the negative appearing situations we ourselves scripted for our own spiritual advancement.

Think about this: If our loved ones couldn't or wouldn't straighten us out while in their body, why would we think they could as spirits? The result would be that because of their interference, we would never progress character-wise or spiritually. Just as some parents won't allow their children to face life and its eventual disciplines for themselves, but continually interfere and protect the child from life, they would also be trying to protect their children from growth experiences, both mentally and spiritually, even from the grave.

2006 3/18 – *"Think on, Spontaneous Human Combustion in your experiments in breaking down water. Be careful."*

Spontaneous human combustion is a mysterious phenomenon of a person bursting into flames for no apparent reason. The flames burn intensely hot and are quite localized. They destroy most of the body but leave objects in close proximity to the person virtually unharmed.

I have read on the internet and have seen pictures of people who have become victims of Spontaneous Human Combustion. One was of Dr. John Bentley (no kin) of Pennsylvania who apparently died of spontaneous human combustion in 1966. The spot where the body lay is burned, but the rest of the room, was not even scorched. Only the bottom of one leg remained to identify this as a human body. This anomaly interests me because we know that over 75% of the body is water—under certain circumstances, the most flammable substance on Earth (?)

You, the reader, may be aware by now that I believe water can be made to burn—extra-EFFICIENTLY, that is, more than 100% efficient. Of course then, I would be trying some experiments to do just that. Some of you have reminded me that there is nothing over one-hundred percent, for that is the whole. To our present understanding that is true, but there is other realm science where all things are possible, and an efficiency of over one-hundred percent is common. In the beginning there was nothing—nothing was the one-hundred percent; but, we are here and the Universe is here, so there is more than nothing. This process is impossible to the present 3D educated scientific mind. This, of course, is not 3D science, it is other dimensional science.

Father is telling me I will find the answer, and when I do, to be careful not to breathe in the free hydrogen and oxygen mixture. If I do, the result could be spontaneous human combustion. Think about it, if my lungs were full of a fuel that burns at thousands of degrees Fahrenheit, my burned shoe-prints would be all that could be found on the floor.

I have purchased a diving mask and tank to use when trying to ignite water. Am I nuts? Probably, but it is fun!

2006 4/10 – *"Think on this physical life as Basic Training Camp. Soon you will graduate and be allowed to come home. Finish the course!"*

I completed the US Air Force basic training program at Lackland AFB in Texas, and I hated every minute of it. It's a wonder I didn't go AWOL. My brother-in-law was probably the reason I stayed there. However, basic training is the only part of my Air Force experience that was remotely military. The rest of my Air Force sojourn was more like a civil service job with the exception of the constant disciplinary action against me for alleged insubordination. I respectfully contend it was no such thing. Even in the military, a peon (foot soldier) has some rights and should be accorded some basic human respect.

Now, the spirit world is reminding me that our physical life is much like military Basic Training in that it is designed to be uncomfortable, hateful, debasing, disrespectful, intimidating and lonely. In our normal physical life a loving, understanding, all-powerful helper is always near, "closer than a brother," to smooth the terrain and keep us marching on. We will, as the Apostle Paul said, "finish the course;" therefore, there is laid up treasures in this and the next dimension when we graduate.

2006 4/20 – *"Physical life is all mind games Jack. You are basically just consciousness, really nothing more, so use mental-construct to accomplish what you feel is your present mission."*

In my first book, the Spirit told me we are continually rewriting the script for our lives. He admonished me to rewrite the script if I am not pleased with the present program. He said, ***"Know who you are."***

2006 6/6 – *"Now is the time. I am going to show you how healthy and strong you can be."*

I am gaining strength slowly, but I think He is saying I will be getting constant teachings on upgrading my health. I can see that my ability to perform manual labor has increased by leaps and bounds the last year. No matter what happens in the future, I know I can overcome and go forth victoriously.

2006 6/8 – *"Make water rejoice with your words, songs and praise. It will respond and yield its secrets to you."*

Water responds to words, songs and praise. There will be more on this later.

2006 6/19 – Snickers dies—I miss him so much!

I have had doggy pets all my life, but Snickers was different. We had a closeness that was way beyond the normal man/dog relationship. He was my dear, close friend who seemed to know my every mood and thought. He was so very special.

He became very ill in his fourteenth year with many organs failing at the same time. We decided we had to have him put down.

First, I took him to his favorite place in the mountains to spend the day. Even though I had to carry my little exhausted friend some of the way on our walk there, he really enjoyed it.

My Eternal Little Buddy Snickers

Then, when we returned to our home in Mead, I had the veterinarian meet us to put him to sleep. First, the vet gave him the relaxer shot so he would go to sleep and not know what was happening. When he got the shot, he immediately gave me a last kiss and passed out in my arms. Then, a moment or two later, the vet gave him the fatal shot. Suddenly, Snickers rose up from his sleep and screamed three times like a human child and then fell over dead. When he was screaming and dying in my arms, I cried out to him, "Snick, I can't stop it now!" I was devastated! I felt I had just violated every ethical, decent and moral principle in my life. I thought, "What have I done?" For months, when I would think of Snickers, I would burst out sobbing. "Everyone felt I was going mad. Everyone thought, "How could you possibly feel that way about a dog?" Snickers was and still is a precious part of me. I shall never lose my love for him. "Snick, I still love you so much, little buddy!"

.

2006 7/10 – *"Look around you for the secret for fracturing water. Look at the trees and grass. The answer is obvious."*

I cried, "Lord, I am afraid that it is so obvious that I am overlooking it. I see the trees, the grass, the sky and everything else in nature, but I'm too slow-minded to see it—help me!"

2006 7/18 – *"You have the formula!"*

Once again, I cried, "Lord if I have it, where I am hiding it. I know the world needs this technology, and I am trying to find the right formula. I now realize that, one day I will, in an instant, know the answer."

2006 7/19 – *"You need to ask for the question. Listen for the questions you should be asking. Remember when you first asked about what the word 'water' meant in the Scriptures where it said,* (I John 5:7-8) *'the spirit, the water and the blood'? The answer came in volumes. Now you should realize that I gave you the question and then later on, the answer. When you wait for the spirit world to give you the question, your mind is ready and open for the answer, and then the answer comes."*

2006 7/19 – *"When you ask for the question instead of for an answer, and expect it, your ego controlled mind is baffled and goes blank. It surmises, 'This is not logical!' Then it loses control, leaving your mind open to Me."*

Wow! What a technique! Here He is talking about, during meditation, when the mind noise seems to drown out any voice or thought trying to come through, we need only ask our Father to give us the next question we should be asking Him. This totally confuses the logical thinking ego. The ego hesitates and lets the mind go blank while it tries to figure out what is going on and how it can respond to an unknown, unasked question. You and your ego then both pause and wait for the question.

Yes, this technique works, always, and it leaves precious blank moments for praise and patient waiting while our hearts and minds tune in to the spirit world.

2006 7/26 – *"What is consciousness? <u>Consciousness is awareness.</u>"*

Remember when He let me hear His/my first thought, "Am I?" It was the beginning of awareness; self-awareness. Awareness is the beginning of all life and that is where the struggle begins—and ends. Think about that.

2006 7/26 – *"Jack, think about Snickers* (My deceased doggy best friend).*Your grief multiplied by millions was what I was feeling when you left Me for your mission in the physical realm. I knew you must go and mature spiritually, but it is so hard to allow all that you must endure to grow, and I miss our relationship so much. I love you all so much."*

I reacted, "Father, I don't have sense enough to even imagine your kind of love. I just wish I could love on such a level. The contrast I feel between yours and my love is so immense as to shame me to no end. I cried for weeks after Snickers died, but to think of that experience multiplied by just two would have done me in.

When my daughter Jackie Lynn died years ago, I thought I would die from the exhaustion of sobbing, but I am realizing now this grief pales in comparison to yours on watching us depart Your presence. Praise You, precious Father!"

2006 7/30 – I want to honor you, Father; show me how.

He answered, *"Your life has always honored Me. You are a beloved son. I will always honor you!"*

I whimpered, Father, I don't deserve such love and devotion!

Again, He answered, *"Yes you do! I know you—you do!"*

2006 8/1 – *"Know your heart is healed and well. Know that your arteries are healthy and clear. Know you are becoming younger and stronger."*

I exclaimed, "I am trying to KNOW Lord, but so often I find myself looking in the mirror, or checking my blood pressure to see if it is really happening. Help me to believe your words Father, and force the changes."

I might as well accept the truth that I am healed. This truth will eventually work its way deep into my consciousness, or else I will have more lessons on knowing.

2006 8/9 – Father, I want to know you face to face!

*"I am spirit consciousness, Jack, and the consciousness of everything that exists. Know Me in a grain of sand. Seek Me in the animate and inanimate, in a leaf or mountain stream. You will find Me and **know** **it is Me.** Remember the scripture,* (Jeremiah 29:13) *'You shall seek for me, and you shall find me when you shall search for me with all your heart.'"*

I doubt if I have any inkling of what this phrase "With all your heart" really means. I am beginning to see You more and more in the animate, but so far, I haven't taken the time, or made the proper effort to find You in the inanimate. Help me, Lord. Remind me to seek You in everything that exists.

2006 8/25 – At the mountain house in Big Elk Meadows, while moving furniture and a television up and downstairs, I began to feel pain in my chest. I sat down. After a while, I told Jonnie Ann that I thought I was having another heart problem, and that we had better drive back down the mountains to the Longmont Hospital to have them check me out. We got in the car and headed for Longmont. We had gotten only a half mile to the Big Elk Meadows office when the pain worsened, and I decided we had better go back to the house and call the local paramedics—the pain was getting much worse.

When we drove up in the yard about three minutes later, the pain in my chest became nearly unbearable. I got out of the car to go in the house and immediately began vomiting there beside the driveway. I began to feel quite weak, so I sat down in the driveway. My strength then just faded, and I fell back on the gravel. Jonnie Ann was in the house calling 911. Within five minutes, I heard the sirens from our Big Elk Meadows Fire Department paramedics approaching. Then the paramedics were all over me. They were giving me oxygen, nitro glycerin, morphine, and relaying my blood pressure and EKG readings to the Boulder Hospital some thirty miles away. I could hear myself groaning, and I could not stop. I could not believe the pain. One paramedic said he could not get a heart beat.

I groaned, "It's still there." Finally they found it. I heard more sirens coming.

I was thinking, "How can this be happening? Father, you told me I would not die, but it appears I am about to die right here in my driveway. This has to be a major life-taking heart attack. I didn't know such pain was possible. I thought to myself, "Well, it probably will end soon...It surely hurts!"

Then I thought through all the pain, "Now this is getting interesting. Soon, I should be seeing who has been sent to meet me upon departing this body. Leaving the limitations of this body is going to be exciting. I soon shall see the next dimension and all the glory of that realm, Jesus, Isaiah, Gandhi, my parents and grandparents, my daughter Jackie Lynn, my cousin Bubba, and all my kin folks. Boy, this is going to be great."

I thought, "I had better say something to Jonnie Ann before I depart; something she can hold on to during her grief." So, I told Jonnie Ann I love her, and asked her to take care of our grandsons. Then, I waited for the visitor.

Time passed, but no one showed up. I was beginning to feel disappointed as I realized it probably was not going to happen just yet..

The paramedics picked me up and put me in an ambulance and were heading for the helipad at the firehouse. It had been only twenty minutes since Jonnie Ann called 911. The helicopter was landing. Soon I was strapped in, and we were lifting off for our thirty mile, fifteen minute trip over the mountains and down into Boulder Colorado.

I felt the chopper landing at the Boulder Hospital, but the pain was so great that I was unaware of most everything, except, from my position in the helicopter, I did see two people I knew, my niece Debbie Sweet and Lee Ann, a mountain neighbor's nurse daughter.

Then, I was aware that the pain had stopped, so I asked the person attending me, "What did they just give me for the pain? Remember what it was because it worked. The pain has stopped!"

A nurse said, "They implanted two stents. That's what they gave you." I had been asleep for about an hour's surgery, and for the next four days I remained in intensive care.

On Tuesday, August 29, I was released from the hospital. I went home, took a shower and sacked out in my soft sleep-number bed. As I lay there praying, someone said, *"You will have twenty visitors from the spirit world by lunch tomorrow."* I have to believe these spirits visited me, but I certainly don't remember the incident. I did, however, recover in record time.

On Wednesday the 30th of August, I began my walking therapy and some other exercises. After a good day of checking in with my company and bringing myself abreast of the latest goings on there, I showered, and we set out to Applebee's for dinner. I made the mistake of drinking diet coke, which allowed me no sleep all night.

I arose at three a.m. to mediate, and within an hour found myself intently watching a crystal entity in my dark study. It stayed at the center of my line of sight for over an hour. I asked his or her name, but only was able to praise it for coming to be with me. It finally moved to the left and after a while it disappeared. This entity was such a distinct crystal that I would recognize it again anytime. It had a triangle shape with the right side open and a bright white light emanating from inside. The bottom and left sides glittered and shimmered as it slowly moved. It was so beautiful. I told Father that I praised Him for sending this being, and I surrendered to whatever he needed to do to me or with me.

Friday, August 31st, as I was praying and meditating in bed in the early morning hours, I found myself sinking deeper and deeper into a red crevasse. Eventually, I realized this red crevasse was the damaged muscle tissue of my heart. I had just been reduced to a cell sized entity, and was frantically trying to help repair damage to the fibrous walls around me. The task was to construct new heart muscle fibers using billions of body cells that I was interacting with in this area. They were all red and perfectly spherical in shape with a number from 1 to 10 showing on the outside of each of them. It was quite uncomfortable here, very tight, and I was fighting to repair the area by directing the muscle fiber cells to align themselves in a certain way.

I was not progressing very well at all. It seemed I was losing the battle, when someone said, *"Relax and allow the body cells to do what they know to do."*

I drew back and said to them, "I allow you to repair the heart as you know to do." They began to drift into vertical, horizontal and diagonal alignment according to a predetermined plan. I marveled at what they were doing. Soon, I began to peacefully drift up out of the area and reassume my place as a body entity.

2006 9/5 – Again today, I visited the cellular entities in my body. This time I knew what was happening, so I just spent the time thanking and praising their work and faithfulness. I felt great love for these cellular entities and also felt great love from them.

2006 11/8 – *"You have been given words of truth and life, and you published them—read and heed them."*

When one has been receiving words directly from the spirit world, he should be reviewing them constantly. They are words of life and enlightenment to him. This is why King David said, *"Thy word have I hid in my heart that I might not sin against thee."* (Psalms 119:11) He wrote them down, memorized them and dwelt on them constantly.

It is so imperative that we seize the words of truth (words that we recognize are divine truth, because they resonate emotionally with us when we read or hear them anywhere, but especially when we hear or feel them personally). Stay in the truth that has been revealed to you, no matter from where it comes!

2006 11/28 – *"Being well is a state-of-mind, not the apparent state of your body. The body follows and manifests your state-of-mind. You are well!"*

We must overcome the global-thought-forms that bind us to <u>appearances</u>. You and I create what appears in our lives continually. We are what we think we are. If we think we are ill, we will be ill and stay ill until we change our mind and project wellness until we think we are well and whole. In my case, Father had to bring illnesses (heart attacks) to me again and again until I asked, "What's going on, Father?" I needed to rewrite the script for this life. I needed to understand that the heart attack situations were illusions I needed to lead me to the deeper truth of how to change the illusion of illness, to the illusion of wellness—both of which are illusions.

2006 11/28 – *"Water is waiting on you to be ready to receive its secrets. When you are ready, water will speak."*

Lord, I don't know how to be more ready! The world is nearing the point when more oil is not going to be available. It is running out! But, Father, your timing is always perfect. I rest in you.

2006 11/28 – *"You asked Me to teach you about Me that you might be able to teach others to know Me. I am the stillness of the mountain. I am the song of the mockingbird. I am the sweet smell of a puppy's breath, and the love in his eyes. I am every lovable thing in everything animate and inanimate in the universe. Consider Me."*

I exclaimed, "When I look over the breathtaking sights in the Rocky Mountains, I can see You Father. The mountain scenes are food for my hungry eyes."

Rocky Mountain Elk Herd

This makes me remember an incident while driving on Trail Ridge Road in the Rockies just west of my home in Colorado. I had just left the Alpine Lodge on Trail Ridge Road and was driving east back to Estes Park to return home. I spotted a herd of elk walking in a straight line formation making their way up the mountain to another group of elk at the top end of a long, wide, climbing, hardened, snowpack field which looked much like an icy glacier. The glacier spread down the mountain about 200-300 feet long. I pulled over for Jonnie Ann and me to see what they were doing.

To our amazement and astonishment, the elk were playing a game of follow-the-leader sliding down the snow pack. An elk at the top of the line would run onto the snow pack, sit down with his back and front legs out in front, guiding himself with his front feet and legs till he slid on his rump all the way to the bottom of the snow pack some 200-300 feet down the mountain. Then, he would jump up and dance up and down in utter joy and celebration of what he had just done. Then, he would return to the tail of the line and make his way back up the mountain to do it again. All the elk were ecstatically joyful and having as much fun as any group of children on a slide.

I wished I had brought a movie camera because I doubt I could ever catch such a game and such a human-like display of joy and emotion from a **wild animal** again. I have met one other person who watched that scene that day. He, too, didn't have a movie camera.

How could anyone who witnessed such joyous, intelligent activities, ever want to kill one of these beautiful, precious, creatures? I certainly could not ever do such an act again.

2006 12/8 – *"Your power to create is directly proportional to the enthusiastic emotion (Force-of-Will) you concentrate on it."*

Every person who wishes to continue on their spiritual journey should pay close attention to this message. He is saying we can have or do anything we desire if we will concentrate with the emotional force-of-will adequate to bring such a desire into our present reality. We, every one of us, have this creative power, and He expects us to learn to use it.

2006 12/9 – *"You are wealthy today because you gave up everything for Me. I know your intent to be at My disposal. I will use you and honor you. You are My beloved son."*

I cried, "Thank you, Father!" He, of course, was talking about my wife and me selling everything and moving to Alaska to follow him.

2006 12/13 – *"Men and women of conscience need a savior, because there is a voice speaking to them telling them what is right or wrong as they go about their daily lives; hence, when they do wrong, they have a feeling of guilt and remorse which troubles them spiritually. Religious institutions reinforce these troubling thoughts by labeling them sins and with their many laws and rules they bind these men and women to their institutions that promise forgiveness. They claim dominance over everyone's soul and everyone's relationship with God. Then, through their many laws and rules, men and women of conscience develop a <u>self-loathing</u> because they seem unable to live within these laws and rules. Then, only a Savior can deliver such a crippled mind/spirit to spiritual freedom and growth."*

Jesus Christ became a scapegoat for us for our grieving conscience. As we were told in my first book, "***Christ did not have to die…***" (*The Last Enemy*,

October 1994) Why? Because our Father never judges or accuses us of anything.

Every government, political, medical, educational, and religious institution is competing for control of your mind and <u>pocket book</u>, be it your priest, minister, doctor, congressman, mayor, boss, or even your spouse and family.

Break loose! You are a free-born son or daughter of the Most High with no limits on the expression of your life force. The scripture says, *"If God be for us, who can be against us?"* (Romans 8:31)

2007 1/11 – Duke, an English Springer Spaniel, came into our lives. Duke is teaching us how to "Live in the now." Also, Duke has proven to us that his presence in our lives was arranged in the spirit world with Snicker's help. Snickers even re-visited us and spoke to us about Duke.

My New Friend Duke

Before we adopted Duke, I was having a problem. After six months, I was still really missing Snickers. I talked to Jonnie Ann about it, and we decided to see if we could find a dog at the Humane Society that might help fill the void in my heart that Snickers had left.

We visited the Humane Society and lo and behold, there was a beautiful pure-bred English Springer Spaniel that no one had claimed. The reason no one had adopted him was that he was terribly sick with Kennel Cough, very weak and lethargic. When I saw him in his cage, he tried to be friendly and licked my fingers but did not get up. The attendants were feeding the dogs, and I watched as his plate with his medicine was put down to him, but he turned away and didn't eat it. The other dog in the cage gobbled it up.

We told the people in the office that we would like to adopt him, and we filled out the paperwork. They said we would have to visit him daily for a week and then we could take him home. But, the next day, they called us and said if we wanted him and would take him to a veterinarian, we could take him that day. We picked him up and took him to the veterinarian. The vet said we nearly waited to long to get help for him. We had to hand feed him tuna cat food to get his medicine down and I slept on the floor with him for a week while he coughed constantly and suffered through the illness.

When Duke recovered from his illness, we became aware of a big problem. Contrary to most of his breed of Springer Spaniel, Duke didn't seem to like people at all other than Jonnie Ann and me. He would bark, snarl and lunge at anyone who came to our house. We could not let anyone near him or even in the house without him going crazy. We hired a trainer from a company in Denver to come to our house and see what he could do for Duke. The trainer brought with him a shock collar and said it was very low voltage (when adjusted in the low range of twenty), and Duke seemed to respond very well to the collar. We checked the collar and acknowledged that in the low range the shock was quite gentle, so we thought this was all right, and the trainer assured us all Duke needed was something to get his attention.

Duke was "coming" and "sitting" on command, and we felt things were progressing nicely, until we noticed the drooling and jerking and Duke

Jack Bentley

pitifully trying to come to me for help when the trainer pushed the remote. We stopped the session and checked the remote. It was now set on eighty. This heartless, hateful trainer was hitting our dog with the voltage of a policeman's tazer. We fired him and removed the shock collar.

Now, we were exasperated and wondered what we must do. I finally told Jonnie Ann that I would return Duke to the Humane Society the next morning. We certainly could not have a mean dog around our grandchildren.

The next morning while I was meditating, I had a wonderful experience. There in my study, as I sat on my pillow on the floor during meditation, Snickers came to me and spoke as if he had spoken English all his life. He said, "Give him a chance, Daddy!" I knew immediately everything would be all right. I told Jonnie Ann, and we celebrated the day with our new family member.

Through the internet, my daughter found a dog trainer nearby who loved dogs and used only gentle positive commands and rewards for obedience training. We called her, and she and Duke made friends quickly. She worked with him for a time that day and finally told us that Duke was afraid someone that came to our house was going to take him away like they did before when he ended up in the Humane Society. She said we needed only to let him meet people outside the house and bring them inside with him so he would know he was not going to be taken away.

Overnight, Duke became the most loving dog we have met, with our grandsons rolling on him and wrestling with him all over the house. He is probably the most loving animal I have ever seen.

2007 2/22 – "Now you need to be in a meditation readiness continually. Forget about just an hour or so in the early morning, and seek my face and my truth continually. Dwell on this."

How far do we want to go with our journey to enlightenment and union with the Source of All-That-Is? Should we relegate just an hour in the morning or evening each day to meditation and praise, or should we have our heart and mind tuned in to His frequency (praise) continually, anxiously and excitingly awaiting His next message, vision or experience?

We have a long way to travel in a short time. We must press in to Him constantly!

2007 3/6 – *"Think on how your mind influences mechanical and inert objects. They each have a <u>unified</u> (unit) <u>consciousness</u> just the same as your body cells have unit-consciousness. Your physical body has individual body cell consciousness too.*

Think on how you may have influenced mechanical devices before in your life, and how in times of great trouble you may have influenced their body cells for your relief. You and I have the same omnipotent consciousness with the same powers."

This is interesting! Our own bodies are a collection of billions of separate, independent cells working together to keep the whole unit alive and healthy. That is their primary mission and responsibility. They have a common sense of union and body consciousness as they work and communicate to energize and heal the body. They go about their assigned tasks like tiny ants in an anthill, feeling personally responsible for the whole unit. They live and work and die and are replaced by new cells continually. Every new cell picks up its tasks and responsibilities where the last cell left off. Each cell is absolutely diligent to this body mission all its life. These body cells have individual and unit consciousness and are subservient to the ruler of their body universe—you! You are their god directing what tasks they are to perform. Whatever you emotionally think about and dwell on is their command. If you in fear think, "Oh God, I'm afraid I have cancer," They will faithfully and deliberately change their form to become a cancer cell. Be sure your fears will come upon you. The Scriptures say: *"For as he thinketh in his heart, so is he."* (Proverbs 23:7). Let this truth soak deeply into your mind and begin to reprogram your body's cells toward Youth, Strength and Perfect Health. Daily, let this affirmation be yours: **"My body is Strong! My body is Young! My body is in Perfect Health!"** Just remember the word SHY = Strength, Health and Youth. Think **SHY**.

Perhaps this unit-consciousness is the way alien space craft are said to be able to seemingly heal themselves. It may be a biomechanical/mind technique that was learned on some distant world ages ago. We are told in some alien/UFO periodicals, that alien space craft are able to take on a nearly biological life, repairing its selves when damaged. Now, I found that hard to believe until I found out that our own scientists are now working with some self-healing materials for future space craft design.

2007 4/1 – *"You need to be reminded of something I told you earlier. Many of your family and friends are going to die while observing you getting younger and healthier. Don't fret, they will follow later. As for spiritual truth, some will receive it, but most are so deceived by the world systems, they cannot understand. Let them proceed peacefully."*

Enough said—no comment.

2007 4/12 – *"Give me time, Jack!"*

My body spoke to me this morning. In my healing process, the first things I am observing presently are the sun spots fading on my hands, and the pain during physical exertion lessening. Also, I am hungrier.

2007 4/20 – *"You are beginning to be aware of the consciousness in the inanimate. Enjoy the show."*

Father, if I am becoming aware, I am unaware of it on a conscious level. Show me where, when and how I am doing this.

2007 5/4 – *"The discomfort in your joints is just a healing crisis."*

What is a healing crisis? A healing crisis is experienced when something you have done to help your body such as a fast or light-energy work causes your body to experience, in reverse order, the symptoms you experienced when you received the illness or injury. It feels exactly the same as the original injury or illness, except when it is over, that injury or illness is healed.

2007 6/14 – *"Your body is My temple."*

I asked, "Lord, Then, what is mine?"

A voice answered, *"I am yours! As I told you years ago; I am your inheritance."*

2007 8/2 – *"It is not what you do, Jack, it is what you think!"*

Yes Lord, I realize, it is only what I think! And, as I think with great emotional focus, things change.

2007 8/10 – *"You are what I want you to be. You can be nothing else. I know what you need to grow, and I know the place you need to be. We planned this present life experience together."*

It should be evident to us by these words that we are totally innocent of any wrong doing in this life. Here, again, He is inferring that we are exactly what He wants each of us to be in this incarnation. He and we planned these lives together to accomplish certain missions in our quest for perfect reunion with our Father. We planned it all with Him. We knew we were going to have amnesia concerning our relationship with our Father, about what personal experiences we must go through that would be both positive and/or negative, that we would be required to live in a sequential, time-delay dimension that is totally foreign to us, and among beings in similar situations who are on their own ascension mission. They too, do not know who they are or how they should act. We knew that each of us would eventually learn (though many incarnations) that the purpose of it all is for us to mature spiritually and mentally so as to be able to function with the fullness of our Father's omnipotence and have eternal harmony and communion with our Father. Again, we are exactly where we are supposed to be, so let's live with great joy and anticipation in the now. Be like that leaf drifting on the water in the mountain stream moving in any direction the water takes it. You see, we know the destination—union with perfect love, the Source of All-That-Is.

2007 8/16 – *"You have every age of social culture living on the Earth today, together! That is why there seems to be so much chaos and turmoil. They are all living in the now. These cultures range from primitive to the sublime."*

Yes, I can see this. I see the cave-man-mentality that thinks all women are theirs for the taking, who live in a kill-or-be-killed state of mind. They believe there is nothing but this present situation, so they are going to do whatever makes them happy and prosperous. These are those who are convinced everyone else is just as wicked as they are, totally selfish and hate filled, that it is best to take what they want and destroy anything and anyone who would or could deprive them of their desires.

Then, we have the peons who willingly work for the masters and never challenge the way things are, just the same as in the cast systems serfs of early Europe. They are peons in their own minds and will be peons all their lives. Even if freed, they will seek someone else to rule over them.

Then, ruling over them all, we have the aristocrats who think they have, by some kind of birth-right or high intellectual achievement, the right to rule over and dominate everyone else. These are the folks who love politics and being elected to the high offices that give them perpetual rule over the caveman peons.

Now, we have the 21th century democracies that believe all men and women should be free, equal and self-ruled. Most citizens are just one step above the caveman and peon mentality and are dangerously close to subscribing to caveman/peon lifestyles because very few of them are willing to get involved in the real moral social issues of their day.

It all gets a bit muddled in our present day when aristocrats, cavemen and peons have all gained control over us in this democratic society. They are all so busy pushing their own agendas that it leaves little room to live free, maneuver and enjoy life. The Scripture says; *"There is wickedness on every hand when the vilest of men are exalted."* But, remember, it is all as it should be!

2007 9/10 – *"Any time your hands begin to vibrate, send healing energy to whomever comes to mind. Someone is asking for help or healing."*

This now happens to me quite often, so I just pause and send love energy to whoever comes to mind. Sometime, days, weeks or months later that person will tell me of help they received about the time I was sending love-energy to them.

2007 9/18 – *"Give up your dreams for Me. When the time is right, I will tell you what to do."*

I do dream of what the world would be like when I unlock the secrets of burning water as a fuel. I know now that it is possible and that I will find the formula for the cracking (economically) of the water molecule.

Of course, I make plans of how to build, patent and distribute the power units; how to prevent greedy hands from stealing the patent rights, controlling the distribution, and swindling the people when they purchase the power units. But, He tells me I must let Him handle this as we move along. I agreed with Him, "Lord, I give up, do as you will with the process and with me."

2007 10/2 – I asked what the name of my chief guide or guardian is. The name *"Sabatino"* was given to me.

It looks like Jesus' words, "Ask and ye shall receive" are absolutely true. I asked, and I received his name. I have not yet seen Sabatino physically, but I know he is near.

2007 10/10 – *"There is no end to the creations of our Father. There is no end to the universes, and there is no word to describe this endlessness to His creations."*

This is interesting. Our Father's thoughts and creative works are so far beyond our ability to imagine, that we have no words to describe its extent, or its endlessness. Right now, He and we are creating universes and populating them with sentient beings, some like ourselves, some more primitive and some much more advanced intellectually. Think about it, there are no limits on omnipotence.

2007 10/11 – I saw Jonnie Ann in a red sleeveless vest, and she was busy with Christmas packages. She was as tiny as when we met.

I have come to realize that what I see in my visions during my meditations usually comes to pass. Jonnie Ann wants to lose some weight, but not as much as I saw here; nevertheless, she will weigh around a healthy one hundred pounds sometime in the future.

2007 11/5 – Today, I gave in to death. I surrendered to die if my Father wanted that at this time. I allowed the death experience. Then, I felt much better both mentally and physically.

I was having pain in my chest and jaws. I know the symptoms—another heart attack! This time I refused to fight it, or go for help. Instead, I said, "All right, if this is the day You have chosen to bring me home contrary to what I heard, Father, so be it; I'm ready" The pain receded and I went on about my business.

2007 11/15 – *"Allow love to radiate to the universes from your heart with each heart-beat. Your body is the temple of the Most High. He is love. Allow this temple to pulsate with love to all. When you radiate love, you are transmitting the highest essence of My being. Release these waves of love—release Me!"*

This is referring to my morning meditations and at other times throughout the day. He wants me to share this light-energy with others as I go about my days. I do and I will continue to do so, Father. I felt this already and am engaged in this practice.

2007 12/10 – I was warned some time ago to be careful of bonding with the consciousness of another being, but this morning during my meditation time, I felt I needed to try a brief bonding with someone I care very much for, knowing that I could back out of the bonding activity before I was too involved.

I wanted to see if I could bond mentally with another so as to help him or her in healing his or her body or other negative situations in his or her live.

First, I found a way to bond with a lady's consciousness whom I know, since I had been trying to do touch healing on her for months but it seemed to avail very little. She was suffering from lung cancer and had already lost one lung to surgery.

After bonding, I felt great depressing anxiety as I asked her what was going on in her life, and why was she letting this disease inflict her? Why was all the effort expended by me and others to no avail for her healing?

She cried, "I want to be free! I want to be free!" I felt her deep emotion, and I realized she was talking about wanting to die. This is why the touch healing is not bringing the results I thought and hoped it would.

I left it at that and broke the bond. I did not think I should pry into the matter of why she wanted to die, and I was very uncomfortable emotionally. I certainly did not want to feel this anxiety any longer or any deeper.

I don't know if she is aware of this incident since she has never mentioned it. Neither have I. I do know, however, that I don't need to worry, for she is exactly where she is supposed to be.

Next, I thought of a young man I know who has been in trouble since he was a teenager, and I could understand some of the reasons. He is now in his forties. I have known him since he was a child, living in a mostly dysfunctional family. His dad was a habitually absentee dad with a drinking and gambling problem. His mother worked to support the family of three children but lacked any meaningful disciplinary skills. He was on his own most of the time, even as a very young child. He grew up in a church atmosphere but found nothing there that would significantly affect his life. He married his high school sweetheart and fathered two children. Then, three or four years into the routine of family life, the trouble began. He started drinking and before long was partying most every night, wrecking his vehicles without having even liability insurance, having judgments levied against him and losing his driver's license; nevertheless, he continued to drink and drive without a license or insurance. Eventually, he started running with other women. Then he lost his family. He could not keep a job. He pawned his belongings and started conning folks, eventually begging money. He is now a confirmed alcoholic and drug addict, steals whatever he can find. He is probably destined for a long term in prison, or he will be killed.

I wondered if I could help him if I could see what was behind his problems. I then bonded my consciousness with this young man and asked him, "What is your problem?"

I heard, and felt him say, "I'm confused! I don't know what to do, or how to behave!" Knowing this young man and knowing that he is not open for help at this time, I decided to drop it. I have offered him my help, but he refused.

I realized both of these people are exactly where they are supposed to be.

I am reminded of my Father's words, 1999 10/23, *The Last Enemy,*

> *"Everyone's ultimate quest is the same: to reunite with the Source. Don't even try to guess what avenue or venture another is now on to achieve that goal."*

Again, on (2000 8/16) *The Last Enemy,*

> *"They are where they are supposed to be."*

This young man has chosen what he needs in this incarnation, and he knows that if he needs me, I can and will help. I have already offered to help him, but he refused. If he needs me he will find me and ask.

I also realized that I really don't want to bond with any others quite yet. The emotional despair I had to share with both of these people is not something I wish to repeat very soon.

2007 12/11 – *"You need to experiment with what you have been taught."*

He was talking to me about the water fracturing process that I am working on. I have been experimenting on fracturing water for the past twenty-five years, but so far, to no avail. Yet, I know our Father has given us water to sustain our lives on Earth in more ways than just drinking and flushing our toilets. I know water is the fuel of the future. I or someone else will discover how to burn water efficiently.

2007 12/18 – *"Before I created the first universe, My love and joy were there in the void because My consciousness was there. Love does it all."*

He is saying that love is the creative force throughout the universes. All creative energy is emotional love—passionate compassion—that must create more to love. He is love.

2007 12/20 – This morning I was talking to my Father about my life. I told Him I didn't see why I was still here. He is omnipotent and certainly does not need the likes of me. Why haven't I already been taken?

He answered, *"I do need you, Jack. You are part of the healing process all over the Earth. I choose to heal through you!"*

I am ready Father. Show me what to do next.

I realize that as I radiate love energy to the Mother Earth, the Celestial Realm, the universes, and every entity everywhere, they are healing.

2007 12/21 – *"The only* <u>REAL</u> *reality is eternal, omnipotent consciousness. All else is imagination."*

Father, I guess the reason you tell me this message over and over again is because it is so hard for us to deeply receive it. No matter how it is worded, this message always thrills me and gives me a spiritual lift as if I had never heard and considered it before. Help me to process this truth to the knowing!

2008 1/9 – *"Your well-being is inevitable. This is yours!"*

He was responding to my complaining about the condition of my heart and circulatory system. I reminded Him that he had told me earlier that I was healed. Then, I recited Isaiah 40:29-31 about waiting upon the Lord. *"They that wait upon the lord shall renew their strength; they shall mount up as eagles – They shall run and not be weary – They shall walk and not faint."*

He just reminded me: *"Don't look at the physical, it is an illusion. Look at the words I am giving you!"*

2008 1/16 – During healing meditation for others on our Healing-List this morning, I heard, *"I am in them too, Jack. Do you think you can do something for them that I cannot? Send My love to them. I will do what should be done. You will notice that your hands will radiate constantly now that you know what you are doing for others."*

I wondered if He was telling me to not send healing energy to anyone, any more. He will clear this up later. He is telling me to just send Love Light-Energy; it will accomplish the mission.

2008 1/20 – *"You are recovering from all your illnesses. You will live—you are well."*

I guess you, the reader, can tell, I'm still complaining. I am not yet in the active strength and health of youth. But, I know that situation is coming; so I sometime complain. I want everything to happen right now. I realize, however, that would cause no little commotion, and so I will go along with the program as He and I have written it.

2008 2/5 – *"Miraculous healings can kill human spiritual initiative."*

Illness and other negative situations are always sent to a person for instruction in living and growing spiritually. They are never sent to punish—only to help a person on his or her quest for union with the Father. Most don't know they chosen this incarnation as a continued quest for ascension and reunion with the Source of All-that-is. If some zealous, self proclaimed healer comes along and with his emotional energy combined with the patient's emotion expectation manages to see instant healing in the individual before that individual has received the full lesson written in to the experience script, what has the individual gained?

You say, "Some that are ill or in a tragic accident, don't even know God, How could such an affliction possibly instruct him or her about their relationship with God?" Everyone is here in the third-dimension to try to advance to a higher stage of enlightenment. They knew this very well before they arrived in 3-D and they had a plan in place to help accomplish more enlightenment during his or her present incarnation; therefore, be certain in your mind that this illness or accident was written into the script long before the incident happened. There are no coincidences in the universes.

You and I don't know the how or the why of the situation but we can be sure that the situation is generated from a prearranged plan by the individual and by our Father's DIVINE LOVE and leading. He knows what He is doing and what effect this situation must have on this individual as He draws each of us back to Him.

2008 2/7 – *"There are island universes in outer space so far removed from your universe that light from their suns will never reach your universe during its existence."*

My God! How great Thou art! What else is out there? There are trillions of star systems with planets capable of supporting human life, or human-like intelligent life. Life on some planets has evolved for millions of more years than ours on Earth.

So, contrary to the belief of many, man is not the highest evolved species in the universe. I personally hope not! I believe the reason some of the folks from the other galaxies, constellations and universes try to stay very clear of our primitive planet is that man, as a whole, has evolved very little spiritually and socially since cave man days.

It is well known by our government that beings from outer space have visited this planet, and, in fact, are residing here now with the permission (or without) of our world leaders and may be the rulers behind all governments on Earth.. Why our government leaders choose to conceal these facts is a mystery to me, unless they are under duress by the aliens, or stupidly believe it would panic the populace. The populace of this planet would probably be relieved to have someone other than our present inept world governments in charge.

We should remind our rulers that it didn't panic the Aztecs when aliens appeared in heavenly vessels flowing up over the edge of the Earth's waters in their magnificent sailing ships and landing on their shores. Yes, at first, they thought these visitors were gods, but these gold seeking, murderers soon proved they were not gods but maybe even more primitive than the Aztecs.

I believe that if a civilization survived long enough on other planets for them to learn warp speed and time travel, they would have overcome the blood lust, greed, and lust for power that exists throughout the citizens and governments on this planet. The would have eventually learned the folly of warfare and overcome their lust for power, control and property that rules mankind on this planet.

I believe they are here already, but don't desire to intermingle with such a primitive race as they have found here on Earth. They may, from time to time, find an individual they can reveal themselves to and communicate some truth and technology to, but very few.

Maybe we ought not to be so high-minded and so cruelly dominating over the other sentient beings on this planet. We must learn to respect life, no matter how, what form, or where it appears. Yes, we are very primitive!

Most likely any new technology they might share would very soon be utilized in development of new weapons of warfare and mass destruction.

I was trained in heavy radar maintenance in the US Air Force in the late 1950's and 1960's and was totally blown away by the new transistor technology that appeared seemingly instantly on the scene. I have often wondered where the transistor technology came from. Could it be ET, Inc.?

I think it is also interesting that this technology is susceptible to destruction by certain types of radiation such as a nuclear explosion or from electromagnetic sun flares **and the like**. Could all we on Earth possibly have been set up for some future takeover by using a transistor technology that could be destroyed instantly and worldwide?

2008 2/13 – During my meditations this morning, I re-lived the Alcan Highway mountain turn-a-round experience where I had to turn my motor home around on a one lane mountain road high up on the steep side of a snow covered mountain by backing onto a too-narrow, one-lane bridge. I remembered seeing Jonnie Ann's eyes as the motor home tilted over off the mountain bridge into the deep chasm below. Her eyes were locked on my face. This morning, I saw the people of our Healing List looking at me the same way.

Their eyes were saying, "I trust you. You will get us through this!"

2008 2/20 – During meditation this morning, I was thinking of something Father said to me earlier about sending His love to others for their healing.

I asked, "Father, how can I, a mere man, believe I can send the omnipotent power of Your love to others?"

He replied, *"Because I instructed you to do so and because you and I are one."*

Notice, He is not instructing me to send "healing" but just send His love.

2008 2/28 – *"When working with others, don't look at what they are manifesting presently, or what they have been manifesting in the past, Look at them as what they shall become some day—ASCENDED MASTERS. They really already are, you know. Remember what I told you, 'They are exactly where they are supposed to be in their spiritual evolution.'"* (2000 8/16)

We are all on the same path and in the same hateful boot camp. We are being instructed on how to handle the omnipotent position we will inherit as the sons of God. Some of us probably have been on this reincarnation wheel much longer than others, so we can be sure we have, in the past, manifested everything we are seeing in others, or perhaps, we will be manifesting it in the future.

2008 3/4 - *"Both illness and perfect health are illusions. Allow illusions of perfect health to emotionally dominate. <u>Everything in the physical is illusionary</u>."*

We are so accustomed to having life situations dominate us. When we are ill, we think of nothing but how quickly we can get to a hospital where our doctors can begin treating and helping us. Seldom, have any of us thought to seek our Father first when serious illness finds us. If we were certain it is just an illusion and we are exactly where we are supposed to be, we would probably consider our situations differently

2008 3/4 – *"You had to have an illusionary physical body experience to comprehend existence. Remember your first thought, 'Am I?'"*

"YOU MISSED SOMETHING!"

1997 8/10 - *The Last Enemy.*

In my meditations, I was still trying to understand the "Why" of the beginning. What is it all about, anyway? Why do we need this physical existence to be so long, so negative, so vicious, so savage, and so heartlessly evil, and why are we so unaware and oblivious to Your presence? When will this madness end?

Someone spoke, *"You missed something when we went back to the beginning. There was something before the loneliness. Let's go back there again."*

I was taken back to that time before the incident when I saw the first sun being created, back farther before the loneliness was felt. Now I was again in the void, waiting, but this time there was no doorway. Again, there was great relief and weightlessness. For a long time, I just tarried there. It felt strangely, but wonderfully, familiar. I was at peace, and I loved it. I was conscious, but not aware of my consciousness. A first thought, a concern, an anxiety, slipped into my mind. A question began to form in my mind: **"Am I?"** I began to wonder if I really existed. If so, how; why? What am I? I became confused. Then I became determined to find the answers. This, then, is the reason for it all. If I am, then I want to know what I am. I want to know all that I am, and what I am capable of doing. I want to know me! This leads us to today and the six billion soul expressions of me all trying to understand who and what I am by experiencing being me in every aspect of living.

Some of the ancients understood this original "Am I?" experience of the Father, so when the ascended master Jesus came along showing that He, too, knew the first thought of God by declaring, "Tell them, I Am, sent Me," He infuriated the religious establishment. The secret society of elders and priests knew exactly what Jesus was saying. He was saying to them. "I Am the Father, and I know that I Am." For this, they believed He blasphemed God, and they wanted to kill Him.

The First Thought, "Am I?"

In truth, He had gone much deeper in His spiritual quest into union with the Father than any of them. He had heard the first thought of the creator of the universe, just as I did. Jesus knew He was God!

The high priesthood knew of the "Am I?" theology, but they had not personally lived the spiritual experience. They did not understand that any person can experience God's life. We can experience His life in any creature, in any entity, and at any instant in linear time; in the present, the past, and the future.

"Jack, the physical body is provided to answer the question, 'Am I?'"

2008 3/10 – This morning I asked, "Father, how do I cancel the illusion of illness?"

He answered, *"You cancel it through the EMOTIONAL FORCE-OF-WILL! Concentrated, emotional, positive, statements (affirmations) will change the illusion.*

Notice: I said nothing about healing. An illness is the manifestation of a thought-form. You cannot heal an ingrained thought-form; you must change the thought-form. You all have the ability to do this. You now understand illness."

This is probably one of the most important statements He has uttered on illness and healing. Take it to heart and dwell on it often!

He used the words "affirmation statements" here. He has told me before that those **totally positive, emotional, focused, affirmations will change any illusion.** Since everything in this 3D physicality is illusionary, then anything, any illusion, or any situation can be changed instantly when I learn to use my omnipotent nature as the Source of All-That-Is.

Word your affirmation carefully—"keep it in the now."

2008 3/10 – *"This 'FORCE-OF-WILL', illusion-changing exercise is what the prophet was speaking about when he said in Isaiah 40:29-31, 'He giveth power to the faint; and to them that have no might he increaseth strength. Even the youths shall faint and be weary, and the young men shall utterly fall: But they that wait upon the Lord shall renew their strength; They shall mount up with wings as eagles; they shall run and not be weary; they shall walk and not faint.' The prophet was speaking of aged, decrepit people waiting and meditating emotionally on a new perfect body thought-form that will propel them into new strength, perfect health and mature youth."*

Look at Psalms 103:5. *"Who satisfieth thy mouth with good things; so that thy youth is renewed like the eagle's."* He is making it quite plain that there is a way to renew our youth, not just in mind, but bring our body to youth, strength and vitality again. Note: He will reveal the full extent of this truth later in this book.

2008 3/29 – *"Keep in mind; you are dealing with consciousness, not matter, in your experiments. All is illusion. All is just thought-forms."*

Sometimes, we forget that everything that is, at this moment, consists of thought energy from someone or some group of conscious beings. These beings have the ability to suggest that a certain condition becomes a continuous creation until they or we change it.

2008 4/23 -- This was my first morning with no bloating or water retention swelling since my last heart attack two years ago.

Normally, one who has had a serious heart attack realizes he or she has damaged or destroyed some muscle or muscles in his or her heart which he or she has been told, can never again function to aid the heart in its operation. They tell us that these heart muscle tissues have become just scar tissue.

In my case, my heart could no longer pump sufficient blood through the kidneys to remove all the excess water from my body. I would have to take water pills the rest of my life and endure the bloating every morning until the water pill took effect. Then the water pill would stimulate the kidneys to more strenuous action, but eventually overworking them in the process. Now, the bloating was receding and letting me know that healing of heart muscle tissues is proceeding. The day will come when I will take no medication at all, and my health, youth and strength will return.

2008 5/01 – *"Of all the creatures and entities on Earth, man is the only one who can choose NOT to do God's will. Our Father allowed us to have VOLITION that we might discover our destiny; therefore, you can now understand why He cannot let everyone quickly discover the truth of who they really are. They would destroy the universes. It* *requires many centuries of walking on Earth to come to understand that only love and allowance can survive and be of service to the universes."*

Why would He make us go through this hell again and again? He does not make us do anything. We asked—no, we demanded that we return here again and again, then lose our memory and live in an alien world where we don't even know who or what we are. We demanded the opportunity to come here again and again to find out what we are really capable of, and to stay here incarnation after incarnation until we learn that only love can survive eternally. To do this, we had to have the choice to eat our apple of selfishness, rebellion, and ruthlessness until we understand the truth and are capable of living in love and harmony with All-That-Is.

2008 5/01 – *"I have allowed the shortening of man's life-span on Earth in order to quell his desire and determination to devour the very nature that supports his life. <u>Man in his unenlightened state is extremely dangerous.</u> His negative emotions must be overcome by many lifetimes of experience that teaches him the path of love and peace."*

The first question here: Is He inferring that we used to live much longer? Certainly, He is. The Bible supports such an assumption since from Adam to Noah most lived over five hundred years, and many lived over one thousand years.

I certainly can see this! Few people are aware or even seem to care that we are facing tremendous long-term petroleum shortages, and few even know what one is talking about when he speaks of peak-oil (that point in the near future when the world's oil wells and refineries can no longer keep up with the worlds demand for petroleum). Within the next fifteen years, the Earth's known oil reservoirs will dry up.

Most are not aware of the calamities we will face with the estimated loss of five BILLION lives because of starvation from the lack of farm tractor fuel. Electrical production system fuel will very soon switch back to coal, but that will take a generation and will not happen in time to stave off the inevitable. We have not built or upgraded any new nuclear plants in a half century.

We are running out of fresh water. Our nation's aquifers are being depleted at an alarming rate.

We are polluting the air we breathe, and our government wants to tax and penalize us for our misuse of the atmosphere. Our government, whom is telling us that it is our champion of the GREEN exhortation, is the culprit who is said to be spraying chemicals in the air that we sometimes see as jet engine vapor trails, but some of these are what some refer to as chemtrails. What are these chemtrails and why are they spraying them in our atmosphere? Check the internet for the word chemtrails for more information.

We have a medical/pharmaceutical industry which is determined to provide and promote pills to treat every discomfort and/or medical <u>symptom</u> of disease we face without finding and correcting the cause of any.

Our political systems world-wide have become a conspiratorial group of self-serving despots unaware, uncaring and stupidly leading us to the edge of extinction. I predict that, because of our stupid and uncaring political leadership and our own indolence, sloth, lassitude, and indifference, our own United States of America will experience a complete moral, monetary and military collapse within the next ten years. We will either be facing an internal armed revolution, or else we will surrender to another nation, group of nations or an alien (extraterrestrial) race. America will be no more.

I'm afraid if some miracle does not happen soon, such as the water-as-fuel concept, most of the people of this planet will be dead or in dire straits within the next twenty years. Surely, man is the most dangerous species this planet has ever seen.

2008 5/1 – *"The water burning process is a new other-world science that, when proven, will convince many of the existence of other, higher realms of thinking. I could not allow this process to be known earlier;*

otherwise, total calamity would ensue. I am allowing the veil to be raised now. The Earth is ready."

With all the gloom that the present world situation is bringing to bear on us, this water burning process promises to be the panacea that will rescue us from our own thoughtlessness and destructive devices. Using water as a fuel will break the economic disaster we are soon to face and begin the long process of healing and restoring our planet to its original pristine beauty. We will switch from a petroleum, coal and nuclear fuelled society to a clean-water burning (water vapor effluent) society. It's about time.

2008 5/1 – Jonnie Ann had a dream this morning while I was meditating on the water burning project. She and an unknown woman put a new pot of water on the stove to boil. When it came to a boil, the water began to turn brown. She turned the stove off and was amazed that the pot now contained a four inch pile of gold slivers.

I think Jonnie Ann was seeing a confirmation from the spirit world that this water fracturing process that I am working on will become more precious than turning lead into gold. Think of what the value would be if you could turn a pot of water into a pot of gold!

I think this gives us conformation of the percent of efficiency we can expect from this water burning process; probably something over one to ten. (Yes, I know this is contrary to physics as we know it.) Energy will cost next nothing after the water-burning engine equipment is set up and operating.

2008 5/14 – *"If you must come back, why die? Finish the course this time."*

I think I am being pressed to get on with my light-energy ingestion regiment. I have been on many fasts of four to ten days, one for seventeen days and one of twenty-eight days. Yes, I do intend to go on, and stay on a water fast in the near future.

2008 5/21 – *"Jack, I'm here if here is here…"*

What? Obviously, He is saying physical reality is evidence of His being if we can see it. Sometimes, His words cause me to think much deeper than I am accustom in this present realm.

2008 5/22 – *"There is just spirit, Jack.* <u>*My consciousness is all there*</u> <u>*is. All that is manifested physically are illusions.*</u> *You will learn to manipulate the illusions when you completely accept this."*

Lord, I can hardly wait for the day when I can openly, willfully, and instantly manipulate the illusions around me. Teach me Father, how to accept and experience this truth!

2008 5/27 – *"The world is ready for the water burning process, but you are not!* <u>*Your constant planning ahead and fixation on the business*</u> <u>*and financial processes are not in line with allowance.*</u> *Let it happen! Planning for every future happenstance is the way the world handles worldly endeavors. This process is not of this world—it is other-realm spirit science. It works minute by minute with My directing the next move. Don't try to tie My hands. Remember the words in Mathew 6:34, 'Sufficient unto the day is the evil there of.'"*

I have been in business in this society far too long. In this business climate, business owners are forced to plan ahead, anticipate the pitfalls and protect their assets in today's world of commerce, or see their business hijacked or run over by their competitors. It seems sometimes like a real-life chess match with some unseen tournament champion opponents. You don't know when or what move they are going to make next, but you do know they are looking for an opportunity to check-mate you and your business in some way.

Just three years ago, the owners and directors (of which I am one) of our (then) public company, decided to take our company private, mostly because of the many new rules and regulations thrust upon us by the SEC. We hired a consulting firm to evaluate our company's stock, and then hired a second firm to give us a Fairness Opinion on the first firm's evaluation. Eventually, we satisfied the SEC and hired another consulting firm to make the notifications and work with the courts and stockholders to buy and transfer their stock. All was done in a straight forward, open, and honorable manner.

After most of the outstanding stock was purchased, and the company was again a private corporation we received a letter from a New York law firm notifying us of a class action lawsuit against us, alleging that the evaluation of the stock was unjustly low, that we were a bunch of crooks attempting to steal the stock from our investors. They asked the court that we be punished by the courts and forced to pay a much higher price for these investors' stock.

After researching the matter, we found out that this particular law firm watches the SEC web site and when a company like ours files their paper work with the SEC to go private, this law firm finds a stockholder, or creates one, who is willing to cooperate with them in a class action law suit against that company. They presently had thirteen such lawsuits in the courts. After eighteen months of haggling, tons of paperwork and hundreds of thousands of dollars in legal fees, we were fleeced for a million dollars. It was all legal with the New York law firm which brought the suit taking forty percent of the final settlement.

Eventually, in today's business climate, you learn to watch your backside and try to anticipate anything that could hinder, block or slow down or ruin your business.

Here, Father is saying He will take care of the business—just cool it. I replied, "O.K. Father, it is all your creation, you take it and tell us what to do. I like this program much better."

2008 6/10 – *"Keep it Simple!"*

He was talking about the water process experiment. He is saying to not get to technical with the science of it. Just do what I have been told, and the rest will be revealed to me.

2008 6/18 – *"Don't forget to cleanse your food by spirit radiation before you eat it."*

This is referring to a message from my last book, The Last Enemy, 2002 1/28:

"Cleanse and energize every food by hand radiation before you eat it."

Before you eat, place your hands over the food as shown in the illustration. Then bring in healing, cleansing light-energy down from your crown chakra, down your arms and hands into the food.

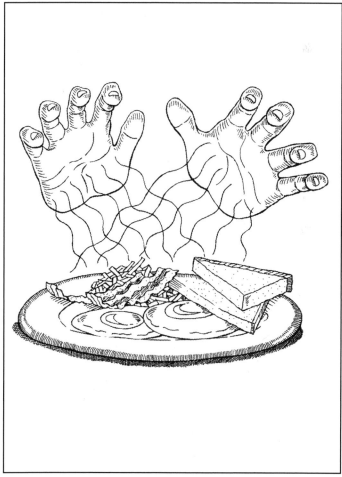

Cleansing Our Food Before We Eat

Lord, help me here. My mind is so unresponsive on this! It is so easy to forget to radiate our food before we eat it. We learned from our parents to say a blessing before each meal at the table but it goes deeper than that. We are eternal, divine beings with omnipotent power and the ability to change the very nature of a substance set before us. We must learn to hold our hands over the food or if it is small enough, grasp the food in our hand and bring light-energy radiation into it. This is the same method we use when bringing light-energy into our bodies. We live on light-energy. We must learn to obey and do what we have been taught to do concerning our food intake.

2008 6/27 – *"The world and its institutions are selling and promoting only hopelessness and fear. This is going on through science, education, government, politics, religion, commerce, the medical, and pharmaceutical industry, and the news media, <u>but mostly for monetary gain</u> and control over the people."*

I exclaimed, "Without you Father, all is hopeless." See how far we have come. All is for profit—materialism. All is negative but being sold to us as a positive way of life. Let's just briefly consider the institutions of science, education, government and politics, religion, commerce, medical and pharmaceutical industries and the news media.

First, **SCIENCE**: You can depend on the gods of scientific academia to blatantly reject any new scientific theory, invention or discovery until they are overwhelmed by the obviousness of the truth of the new scientific advancement and its use by the ordinary man on the street. Then scientific academia will embrace it and write brilliant papers about how many of them had been working on it all along. It has always been that way and always will be. Just ask Galileo and a host of others who have been thrown under the bus by these learned institutions.

I ask you now, how long has the scientific world known we are running out of oil? How many great scientific institutions have tried to alert the world of our situation in the near future when the worldwide crucial disaster will face us? Have they sent warnings to our government and the people of our country that we are fifteen to twenty years away from worldwide financial and social collapse because, of among other emergencies, NO ENERGY?

Have our universities and scientists investigated the thousands of clay tablets from ancient Egypt, Africa, Iraq, Iran, Peru and elsewhere, which tell us of extraterrestrials visiting our planet and giving us secrets of new sources of energy? Have they investigated these visitors' assertion that they burned WATER AS FUEL for their spaceships, and as power for their weapons? Sitchin, Zecharian, *The Lost Book of Enki.(pages 69-70)*

These clay tablets tell us of nuclear wars on this planet thousands of years ago and of human genetic engineering being performed on our ancestors. They tell us of their building the great pyramids and how they cut the great multi-ton granite stones by laser and set them in place with levitating vehicles, and for what purpose were such structures created.

But, when a gifted, life-long, archeologist deciphered and translated these clay and lapis lazuli tablets, what great universities are acknowledging Zecharia Sitchin's work and supporting and promoting the study of these incredible documents? Most of university scientific academia scoff at his and Erich Von Daniken's work and teach kindergarten level science in comparison.

Second, let's look at **EDUCATION**: There has to be a government/ educational conspiracy doctrine and edict that states, "We must dumb-down America, or we won't be able to control her when we put our plans in action!" Their underlings ask, "How can we do this?"

Their answer:

1. "Let's make sure we don't teach them to think for themselves."

2. "Let's get them addicted to television, computer games, sex and drugs."

3. "Let's make sure all the children and all our adult citizens are on fluorides so their brains will be pliable and non-resistant when we take control."

4. "As we do in the financial world, let's convince them of our awesome intelligence, undisputable knowledge and wisdom by our tremendous, palatial school buildings and universities but teach less and less until their minds are useless."

Third, let's turn to **GOVERNMENT** and **POLITICS**: Who believes anything that is spouted from Washington, D.C. or from our own state capitols? We know that each party has its own hidden agenda, and very seldom do we even get a hint of what it really is unless some one of these conspirators slips up and reveals some tidbit of what is going on.

Concerning the present recession/depression economic situation around the world and especially here in the USA, For years we have seen the maneuvering behind the scenes by members of our congress and executive branch and outside **world-order** groups that have planned and forced the financial institutions into situations that would eventually precipitate an economic collapse. Was this intentional? Of course it was! Did it result in the government and Federal Reserve gaining control over many private institutions? Yes, it did. Could this have been foreseen and prevented by those in government? Of course it could! Most of these people are criminals, not fools. Remember the Scripture: "The wicked walk on every side, when the vilest men are exalted." (Psalms 12:8)

Why is it that we go to war every few years with a foe that was formally a friend and poses little threat to us? Same people; same agenda.

Forth, think about **RELIGION**: Let us consider religion. We are told religion is supposed to give hope, faith, peace, love and salvation to all comers. We are told they have found the way to God and will eagerly help us to find our way to Him.

But, what the religious institutions are telling you is that you must be a part of their particular brand of religion or risk an eternity in torment in a devil's hell. They tell you that "God is Love" but He will happily to send you to burn in fire eternally if you do not accept **and support** their particular brand of religion. There are hundreds of denominations of the Christian religion, and hundreds of denominations of Islam all claiming they are the only way to God. The other major religions have their own numerous splinter groups as well.

Does this make sense to you? Why are you still a part of it if you understand this? Why are you not on your knees alone seeking our Father's leadership to show you where and how to find the way to Him that is real and right. I guarantee you it won't be through another man or his organizations. Our Father is quite able to bring you to Himself personally without anyone else's help. He is doing it all over the globe. People are waking up to who and what they are without any religion's help. Your only salvation is within you, and that is where you should be going and you will eventually find that way, though it may not be in this lifetime.

Fifth, let's deal with **COMMERCE AND BANKING**: How can leading financial institutions be so unscrupulous in their dealings? They are finally caught fraudulently and/or stupidly losing hundreds of billions of our investment dollars and still show no remorse but point their fingers at the stupid investors and government overseers they say should have known better.

Our federal government enacted new lending guidelines that proclaimed every American must have a home of his own, and then they enacted laws allowing people to buy a home with little or nothing down regardless of their income qualifications. The old adage: "If it cost you nothing, it is worth nothing." They walked away after the first few payments came due, some laughing and bragging about the free rent.

Sixth, we have to consider the **MEDICAL AND PHARMACEUTICAL INDUSTRIES**: The medical profession today treats symptoms and does little to cure the medical problems in their patients.

A doctor friend of mine let me read a letter from a hospital administrator urging the medical staff to prescribe more surgery so they could get their hospital bed occupancy rate up. Can you believe that?

I believe prescription drugs are killing more people every day because doctors and pharmacists don't know or don't research the dangers associated with the drugs or with their being ingested along with another drug or drugs that in combination could be deadly. Every day, there is another drug advertised to us for some inconvenience or disorder we might have or think we might have. Think about it, could the very scary advertisement actually give your mind the emotional FEAR that you might have this condition or ailment, and thereby bring it into being in your body? Think about it. Yes, it is happening every day, but you do not have to fall prey to it. Announce your perfect health to your body every day until it understands you are continually very well.

Now our bungling central government wants to control the doctors, pharmacists and the hospitals. Why? Control of all the people is the only reason. Bring your citizens to the place where they must depend on the government for every basic necessity of life and you have it all—enslavement!

Seven, we certainly can't skip **THE NEWS MEDIA**: The news media intentionally denies us the truth but instead, dwells on hopelessness, fear, murder, rape, drug and alcohol abuse, drunkenness, extortion, theft, robbery, burglary, natural disasters, hideous death scenes, larceny, war, enslavement and terror; seldom do we see the news media calling our attention to the good things that are happening around us every day.

We have learned that we can depend on the media to take a news story and so twist and distort the facts that you swear off the news media forever, knowing you cannot believe anything you read in the news papers or see and hear on television or radio? Yes, we finally come to the point that we realize the main-line news media is trying, and most of the time, succeeding to propagandize us into a mindless robot society, completely dependent on the media and our government to control our thinking and our lives.

Many of our people have disconnected their televisions and canceled their news papers. I still read the sports section and sometimes the want ads. I realize the comic section is the only truth in the paper, because it is labeled fiction.

Some people laugh at me for my conspiracy theories. What can we say about the present world situation? Is there a great conspiracy attempting to rule the planet?

Think about it. We teach competition to our children as soon as they can take part in any game or sport. The object is to win over others. Choose a team and go out there and win, and dominate the other teams. Is it any wonder that the concept of *us versus them* stays with people throughout their lives? Then, when we become adults, we join a group of other people in a business venture to compete for market share and profits. Do we care if our competition suffers loss or even destruction because of our activities? If our company were large enough, would we then enter the banking business and try to dominate that industry, even buying interest in other financial institutions and businesses and finally taking total control of them? Would we eventually try to gain control over all the other banks nationwide and eventually worldwide? Would we eventually try to gain control over all the people and governments of the planet? Folks, this is our nature if we are less than fully enlightened. Please understand that there are organizations out there that are intent on ruling the world, and will stop at nothing to attain their goals. They believe as Karl Marks did: "The end justifies the means." Don't be surprised at what you see in the near future.

2008 7/18 – *"Live it to see how far you have come!"*

I asked: What does that mean, Father?

A voice answered, ***"Live each new experience, observing how you react to the various circumstances that you face. Watch, you will be amazed. You really are awakening."***

We need to really examine our own lives today, and realize that we have traveled far down the road of enlightenment from where we were just a few years ago. Stop and take a long look at your life and rejoice! Let's really get involved in each day's activities and gain the full value of every experience.

2008 7/18 – *"Meditate every spare moment."*

A time of great awakening is approaching. We must set aside time to frequently communicate with our Source as much as possible.

We set aside time for everything else, why not spend more time with the one that created and sustains the universes? He is only a thought away from us at any instant, and He is always eager to communicate with us. In fact, He is communicating with us all the time, but most of us dismiss His words and thoughts as strange ramblings of our own mind or hilarious fantasy of our ego. Welcome back to Earth again and again and again!

2008 7/21 – *"I have shown you the secrets of water; use them."*

I answered, "Father, I am trying to put it all together. Please simplify the process in my mind. I keep getting more and more ideas about how to make the process work, and with them, more complications."

2008 7/22 – *"3200 feet!"*

I have no idea what this means. I have wondered: is this an altitude, or a distance to some place, or is it 1,600 peoples' feet marching to somewhere?

2008 7/30 – *"Your ego is an immortal spirit that is an eternal part of you. You will never be alone because you and your ego have agreed from the beginning that it would be dedicated and tied to you forever, and it, too, has amnesia. It, too, is a part of the Source of All-That-Is. The core of your ego's being is Love, just as your core is Love. You personally lay out your ego's overall mission by your continual mental activity concerning your wants, likes, dislikes, fears, fantasies, your intentions, and direction in life. Your ego wants to protect you and help you fulfill your quest in this incarnation. Your ego tries to help you think of those things you have demonstrated that you most like to think about.*

This is why you have so much trouble during your meditation times. Your ego is constantly and faithfully bringing up your dominant intentions and your dominant thought patterns."

Boy, have I thrown my ego and me a curve ball! It thinks all I want to think about is foolishness, folly, and fantasies, so that is what it is feeding back to me during my meditation time. Lord, thank you for showing me when my ego hears all my inner chatter, and it brings it all up again when I am trying to pray and meditate. I should know to guard my thoughts better than I do.

2008 7/30 – *"Jack, There is something else at work here with both you and your ego of which you need to be aware: both you and your ego have a deeply buried memory of your existence in the void before you asked the question, 'Am I?' The overwhelming loneliness still haunts both of you. This is one reason both of you want the continuous thoughts of planning and fantasizing for the future and grieving over your failings in the past. You need to discuss this with your ego and encourage it to understand that it will never be alone again."*

He is referring here to the message I received and recorded in *The Last Enemy,* when he mentions the "Am I?" experience.

(1997 8/10) - *"You Missed Something."*

2008 8/4 – *"Rest in Me!"*

My Father is constantly admonishing me to "Rest in Me!" It seems I am so anxious to get on with our program that I try to jump on my horse and ride off in all directions. But, I know there is a reason(s) for delay and holding back. He knows the reasons, and I will rest in that.

2008 8/5 – *"You have no need, but Me."*

I cried out, "No question here, Lord. I need You more every minute."

2008 8/8 – I awakened from a dream at 3:00 a.m. aware that I was having a very painful heart attack. Immediately upon awakening, I realized it was not just a dream. I was having extreme pain in my chest exactly the same as my last and worst heart attack, the one the doctors had called a "Widow Maker."

I thought, "Should I awaken Jonnie Ann? No, because she would want to call 911. Soon after, I would be rushed to a hospital where I would probably be subjected to heart by-pass surgery."

I decided long ago that I would not allow any more surgery, so I decided to try to get up and go to my sacred place for meditation and wait for my Father's pleasure as to what was next for me.

I didn't know if I could even get out of bed—the pain was tremendous. But, I did, and I made my way to my study and my floor pillow where I sit to meditate.

I sat down on the floor pillow and began to draw light-energy down through my Crown Chakra and up from my Base Chakra through the various other chakras to my heart. I did not resist death, but only asked that my Father's will be done. I told Him that I felt my life had been spared many times before for some special mission, but perhaps, unbeknown to me, that mission may now be accomplished. I am ready to go if this is my coronation day.

As I sat there, I decided to scribble a note of my last words to Jonnie Ann. I wrote her a short note explaining what was happening and that I was thinking of her. Then I waited for the end.

I sat there and meditated drawing more and more energy into my heart. I sort of expected to begin to see lights and hear some kind of music, but nothing happened but my meditation.

The pain stopped! Suddenly, I felt much better physically than I have for months. Then, I realized I probably had been going through a healing crisis. (A healing crisis is a phenomenon that occurs many times when our body goes back in time, in reverse order, through an earlier illness or accident in its regression into healing that particular part of the body involved in that incident.) I believe my coronary artery was being healed. All I could do was to praise our Father for another day.

2008 8/11 – *"Keep working with the process. You will find the answer, and make it work."*

He is speaking here about the water fracturing process for burning water as a fuel. As I have probably mentioned before, our Father never intended for civilization and mankind to destroy themselves with their overpopulation and worldwide petroleum based energy system. He knew how we would over populate the Earth and try to drain her blood (oil) to satisfy our insatiable appetite for energy. When He created and populated this planet, He made arrangements to some day show someone the secret of how to burn water. So far, it takes more energy to fracture the water molecule to produce free hydrogen and oxygen than one could recover from its burning (oxidation); however, He says now He is ready to reveal the process and none too soon. Praise His name!

2008 8/14 – *"When I said earlier, 'Everyone is exactly where they are supposed to be,' I was talking about you too. You need to be totally in allowance, first with yourself, and totally non-judgmental. Just flow with life. Remember, be like the leaf floating on the water delightfully going where the water takes it* (2003 2/6). *Allow yourself to come home."*

> 2000 8/16, *The Last Enemy,*
> *"When you pray for or send light-energy to others, empower their quest! They are where they are supposed to be."*

Each individual must travel through the whole course and range of emotions and situations to come to the awareness of union with the Father. No one can skip a grade in this school. Each has to fulfill every experience to mature unto ascension.

Can we ever again justify our judgment and condemnation of any person, including ourselves, if in God's eyes, we are exactly where we are supposed to be?

I think learning to wait on and rest in you, Father, is going to be my greatest spiritual accomplishment. Keep pushing me to stop and rest in You.

2008 8/14 – *"On Judgment: I do not judge people—situations are evaluated by that faculty of your being you refer to as your conscience, that is Me. Yes, that is Me speaking to you when you feel your conscience cautioning you or approving and encouraging your actions and thoughts in any given situation."*

I responded, "Thank You Father. We all know our conscience has been with us as far back as we can remember. Why are we so slow to realize that it was You all along?"

2008 8/14 – *"Ida, the name you gave to your ego, is neither male nor female, but it wishes to be thought of by you as a female entity. You and she are together eternally. Presently, you both are one flesh as you have been in every incarnation. Learn to love and enjoy her, and together plan your conquest to union with Me."*

I gave my ego the name IDA because she asked to be referred to as a lady. I am learning to ask Ida to help me every day in every way.

2008 8/15 – *"Each of you must overcome the illusions of physically, or continue on the wheel of reincarnation. Each of you will eventually learn to cancel the negative illusions and with it the life/death cycles. There is no hurry though; just relax. Jack, you are going to find your way home this time. Rest in Me."*

Reincarnation should not scare anyone. We are eternal spirits, and as such, never die. We just change scenes.

Here, He is assuring us that He will patiently wait for us, no matter how long it takes. He loves us enough to wait on us, so let's rest in Him as He waits for us.

2008 8/16 – *"You will never be alone; Ida is always with you. Ida not only accepted the role of subservient mate in this relationship, she craves it. She wants only to serve you forever."*

I replied, "Now, that's true love. Lord, I will never understand why she feels this way. She reminds me of You: You both desperately love me and will be with me forever."

2008 8/20 – *"Just because you are not yet aware of having exercised your omnipotent creative power consciously does not mean it is not there, nor does it mean you have not already used it in times past, but unawares. Use it! Be what you are. Cancel the illusion of limitation and create whatever changes you wish in your world."*

Talk about double negatives—this is a quadruple negative, but it still makes sense. No, I am not aware of using omnipotent power yet (?) unless, my seeing a friend three thousand miles away and experiencing with him his fatal airplane crash into a mountainside. Was this omnipotent, mental telepathy, or maybe it was my own omnipotent power that healed Jonnie Ann in the Fort Collins hospital; or perhaps much of what is being revealed to me is my own omniscience being awakened.

2008 8/27 – *"Eat light and EAT LIGHT!"*

I am writing an addendum to this book specifically emphasizing the messages and techniques of fasting and Light-Energy Ingestion. (See: **Addendum "A"**) The Addendum is growing as He continues to speak to me about ingesting light-energy.

2008 8/28 – *"You don't war against your ego—you don't war against anything! You are omnipotent—who can stand against you? Instead of war, you bring love and peace—these are your weapons, and <u>Love is always victorious</u>.*

You don't war against your ego—you embrace her. You don't war against appetites, lusts, and cravings (spirits) of the body, you embrace them with love and instructions of how they should manifest in your body. Love is your weapon."

Just as our Father does not war against us, (the spirit cells of His body), we must love the spirit cells in our bodies—love them into a positive, supportive relationship.

I am growing closer to my ego, Ida, everyday. I feel her presence now when I talk to her.

2008 8/28 – This LOVE-FEST warfare is working for me. Ida helps quiet my mind now for meditation. We meditate together. My mind is still and silent for longer periods of time. It is open then only to my Father's thoughts and words. Glory! Ida, I couldn't do this without your help. Because of your helping quiet my mind, I am now hearing my Father continually during my meditations. Thank you, lady for helping me find a place of peace. Now, I must engage the other spirits in my life—lust, appetite, etc.

2008 8/28 – *"Study love—it is the 'fast-track' to enlightenment."*

I need to just consider the changes in my relationship with Ida to understand this message. She is helping me "fast-track" my spiritual journey. Another way we can study love is to watch our pets, especially our dogs, in their relationships with us. They are totally into unconditional love. I believe they were sent here to us to teach us love. My ancient family crest (Bentley) has a dog in it with one front foot raised in friendship.

2008 8/29 – *"Enlightenment is union with Love. Our Father is Love. When He manifests, it is always as love."*

I agreed, "Yes, Father, that is what I have experienced. You have never shown anger or judgment toward me, only love and support. I know that if you were the least bit judgmental, I would have felt it, and justifiably. I believe Your lack of judgment toward me is what continually draws me to You."

He spoke again, *"Yes, my son. Now, consider what you have just said and make sure you continually integrate this truth into your behavior toward others."*

2008 9/08 – *"You are not asking Me for help in fracturing water; I am requiring this endeavor of you. I am asking you to be faithful and give this gift of energy to My people."*

I will continue working with the process until it fires, and then I shall see to it the world is the beneficiary. This does not mean I won't patent the process. It must be patented to keep control of it away from the unscrupulous.

2008 9/10 – *"Seek union with Love, with Me. As I told you years ago, 'Love is passionate compassion.' You know what and who Love is, but few know Me as Love. Locate your deepest compassion—that is Me. Remember what Jesus said, 'He that loveth not knoweth not God, for God is Love.'"*

I answered, "Father, allow me to re-unite with and manifest Your love."

2008 9/18 – *"At this instant Jack, you are creating universes! Know how great you are."*

I asked, "When do we stop creating universes, Father?"

He answered, *"We don't stop. It is our nature to create new life and expand our consciousness. We are still evolving in Love. That is why it is so exciting. There is no end to the evolution of Love—Passionate Compassion."*

I replied, "Thank You, Father. Let's get on with it!"

2008 9/18 – *"You must understand now as you see yourself still finding fault or seeing error in others, that you must not judge yourself for seeing their faults. You are evaluating your own actions and responses to life's situations through them. You must always be in total allowance with them and yourself—non-judgmental. Don't attempt to make yourself less than what you are by judging yourself. You are the omnipotent God. You are Me and I am you. We are one and the same person. Don't judge Me."*

I exclaimed, "Wow! Father, I'm sorry! You must take incredible abuse from each of us as we judge ourselves, our own consciousness, who is really You. Father, You are so precious—we all love you so much, and yet, don't even know it."

He is saying, when our conscience is pricked, we should not feel ashamed and defeated. We should be thankful for the redirection from a loving Father, and we should go forth more victoriously.

2008 9/19 – *"Jack, when you are transported to the next realm, you will take a perfect body with you."*

I said, "Thank you so much, Father, I have always enjoyed this body and I will be delighted to see it perfected."

This sounds to me like it may be soon. Could this be referring to the galactic alignment of December 21, 2012? I understand that when I do depart, I will also be taking Ida with me. There may be a lot more to this 2012 date than just the end of the Mayan calendar and the galactic alignment???

2008 9/20 – *"Your hands are radiating Love now. Love does not wear down your body as you send love energy to others, as some believe. Love is inexhaustible. Love radiates from your heart. I dwell in your heart; therefore, you see, the Love you radiate is Me!"*

Some have suggested that my broadcasting love to others everywhere and to all dimensions during my morning meditations, could eventually deplete the life energy of my body. Father says, not so. His love for us is inexhaustible.

2008 9/21 – *"You are from beyond nothingness, beyond expression, where I dwell—in pure consciousness, and there you will return. Be careful now, your mind will have a problem with this as you have already begun to experience."*

Father has told me about the void and various other physical, semi-physical and totally spiritual realities, but this is the first time He has mentioned a realm beyond nothingness—beyond our ability to relate or even imagine. Just as we are unable to conceive of a physical realm being created from nothing, we are unable to comprehend a realm beyond or before nothingness. What could have possibly been before nothingness? Therefore, we have to understand this: There is a canopy or sphere over and around our ability to understand and/or comprehend its existence that will stay in place until we come into the full enlightenment and awaken to union with the Father. Don't let this confuse you. Just understand that presently we see only a minute part of the divine creation and plan for us, but the time will come when we will see and understand it all. Glory!

2008 10/8 – *"The void is not just out there; it is omnipotent consciousness all around and in you, eager to manifest any and everything your consciousness desires. All manifested physical reality is mostly void, full of un-manifested power. Think on this. Your body is mostly omnipotent, creative potential—the Void."*

The "Void" He is speaking about here is all that area in and beyond the universes that is not yet occupied by mass. The area beyond the universes is called outer space by our scientists, yet it is full of the consciousness of our Father. It is full of His and our creative energy potential.

The air on our Earth is mostly space (void) with a few oxygen, nitrogen, hydrogen, etc., atoms dashing around. The Earth, its oceans, mountains and molten core are mostly space (void) and, therefore, neutrinos pass straight through the Earth without ever touching anything. Occasionally, a neutrino collides with special ultra-dense collection devices designed by our scientists to prove their existence, but even trillions more are passing through these collection devices and colliding with nothing.

Our bodies are mostly water, and water is made of two atoms of hydrogen and one atom of oxygen. Now, to illustrate the size of a hydrogen atom with its single proton and single electron: If we expanded a hydrogen atom to a size that could barely fit in Mile High Stadium in Denver, and then placed its pin-head sized nucleus proton at the center of Mile High Stadium, its single electron would be orbiting somewhere near the last upper level seats and would be a speck the size of a needle point. That illustrates how much space (void) must be available in a molecule of water (H_2O). Our bodies being mostly water are enormous containers of VOID, or creative consciousness potential. Our belief that the material world around us is all solid physical stuff is just our imagination—just illusions—but, useful illusions for the present.

2008 10/23 – *"When you are offering prayers for the healing of others, recite the names, and <u>see the person you are praying for in perfect, joyful, health</u>. Fold back the page listing the illnesses corresponding to the name, and see it no more.*

You have been, by observing the medical condition shown on the page, keeping that illness alive, and in the individual's illusion as long as you and they acknowledge it. Never again connect a person to an illness in your prayers. Just send love energy to that person, and rejoice with him or her in their life."

Our prayer list formally showed the name of the patient, the date we listed him or her, the illness, and the outcome from the prayer sessions. He tells me here to not even ask for the diagnosis, and to not mention healing. Just send Father's love energy to the person to use as that person and Father see best. The love energy may not be used to cure the illness—It might be used to cure the cause of the illness, or to strengthen the person to go through the illness experience, even to death if that is in his or her plan for this incarnation. Take care to follow this admonition. Don't interfere with another person's carefully planned destiny.

2008 10/24 – *"Jack, illness is an illusion. Perfect health is also an illusion. Old age is an illusion. Youth is also an illusion. Live any illusion you choose. You are omnipotent. You are continually rewriting the script for your life. Your imagination is the creative force that continually creates and sustains the illusions."*

I think here He is clarifying the last message. It is all just illusionary situations that we wrote into our script for this life. Nothing just happens to us! It is all very carefully scripted, and in some cases re-scripted until we have designed the perfect illusionary experience for our maximum spiritual growth during this incarnation.

2008 10/25 – *"Consciousness cannot be contained; not in a human body; not in a universe; not even in the void. Consciousness is boundless, timeless, and omnipotent."*

The truth is, our consciousness has been connected to many physical and non-physical bodies in many universes and dimensions, in a timeless dance of creative spiritual advancement. We choose to become and be united with whatever environment or situation that will help us advance in our spiritual evolution.

In truth, we are already one with the Father, but, in another sense, in our spiritual quest, our individual spirit longs for more understanding, truth, and love that will draw us ever closer to our source, our Father's All-That-Is consciousness. He is the ultimate creator/sustainer of our being. He, as our deeper self, is the one who is drawing us ever closer to Himself, and ever more like Himself.

2008 10/25 – *"Come before me with praise and thanksgiving. Think about it: That is all you have to offer."*

I reacted, "Father, You have certainly just shortened my prayers. You already know my desires, fears, joys, and everything that I am and think, so I see what You are saying. Know who I am!"

As I "think about it," I ask myself what can I offer God that He needs, does not have, or is unable to create? I cannot even imagine all that He has already created, that He has watched progress through billions of millenniums to its extinction, including multiple universes. Yet, He keeps me in His constant view and under His wings, that whether in time and space, or beyond nothingness, He watches me develop as one of His cherished souls, and part of His own being. What a wonderful Father we serve.

2008 11/12 – *"You constantly sustain your own illusions such as your weight, your health, your economic situation, and your relationships. Even such small things as a sinus drip are sustained illusions. Every facet of your physical life is your own accepted illusion."*

I laughed, "You noticed the drip today, huh? You surely are pressing in on the illusion theme. I must be a little hesitant or reluctant to completely accept this truth. Press me even harder, Father!"

2008 11/18 – *"Get outside of time where I dwell, where everything that is, is not, and where everything that is permanent, is temporary; where you realize <u>everything physical and mental exists at your own pleasure</u>. Your omnipotent consciousness is all there is that is changeless."*

Volumes could be written on this. The ongoing generations of life on this planet were written and scripted long before the big bang.

It is much like a stage play where every actor's words, movements, and even gestures are written and performed exactly as scripted. Every word and action is known beforehand and is watched and guarded by the director. Our Father, and bands of angelic beings, guard our every moment, so that every moment confirms perfectly to our pre-scripted plan.

The director, our Father, the stage hands, our angels, and multitudes of interested loved ones and friends who have gone on before and have finished their parts in the play, are now watching and waiting anxiously for us to finish the course. They know our whole script now and can see our lives from birth to death from their observation point. Soon we, too, will be watchers.

When we finally realize who we are, things will begin to change around us. We will see outside of this time/space limited reality into the unbridled consciousness of our omniscience. We will begin to understand the mysteries of the physical and spiritual universes around us. We will be home.

2008 12/09 – I was awakened at 4:20 a.m. by the odor of candy cooking. There was no candy cooking. I had asked the night before for the spirit world to awaken me before 4:30 a.m.

2008 12/10 – While I was sending love light-energy to someone, my Father spoke, *"You cannot give them any more of Me and My love than they already have. They are exactly where they are supposed to be. Just remember them, and hold them in your mind. Know that I am fully in charge of their situation."*

Sometimes, when sending love light-energy to an ill friend or loved one, we feel inadequate or intimidated by their not showing improvement. Here, He is telling us gently to get off their case as to whether or not they are being healed. This is His and their business. He is quite adequate for the occasion.

This should relieve us of any burden we might feel for the discomfort of others during their infirmities, no matter what they are going through. Our Father's love is there in its fullness. No one else in existence could love and cherish them as much as He. His intention for them is that they grow to the utmost through their present circumstances, and He will see to it they are victorious. He wants them back home as soon as possible, but fully developed ascended beings moving totally in passionate compassion (Love). He will spare no experience for them towards that end. Remember, our Father and we, together, planned this incarnation and the experiences we wanted to face.

2008 12/11 – *"Jack, be fair to every entity; consider their feelings in response to your action. Yes, even learn to be fair to Me! I love you more than anyone else in existence. Think on this."*

I cried, "Father, I'm sorry that I have been unfair to you. Please enlighten me to how and when I did this so I can avoid such behavior in the future."

2008 12/13 – *"You say you believe you and I are one, but when I say to you, 'Then be Me!' You draw back. <u>This is fear and self-loathing.</u> You are afraid of what you might do if and when you become omnipotent. Allow the deeper part of you to come forth and rule your consciousness. Then, all will be love and peace."*

This self-loathing that I *evidently* harbor may be a holdover from my Fundamental Baptist teachings of the past. We were taught that we were conceived in sin, born in sin, have lived all our lives in sin, and deserve nothing less than a devil's eternal hell as punishment. We were taught that there is nothing good and decent about us; that we are all condemned depraved reprobates, worthy only of the wrath of God.

However, our spiritual journey had to begin somewhere, and the fundamental church was as good a place as any to launch my spiritual life—probably better than many alternatives.

Fear has the same roots. Sometimes, we forget there are only two responses in and to life—Love, or Fear. Realizing this, I cast off the fear of how I might handle omnipotence, and press forward in love and fellowship with my Father. Love will prevail!

2008 12/14 – *"Now, you are seeing the scriptures in a whole new light when it says in, I John 2/16 '...the lust of the flesh, and the lust of the eyes, and the pride of life...' These are the aspects of your life you are afraid would prevail if you accept your omnipotence. Fear not, my son, lay these jewels at My throne, and open up to your omnipotence. Love will prevail!"*

I replied, "Thank you, Father. You see right through me continually."

2008 12/14 – *"All of my children eventually come to a point in their incarnations where they see the impurities or negative tendencies in their lives, and choose death again and again rather then bring Me into an impure temple. Now, you are facing The Last Enemy again—Self and Death. This time, you are seeing the truth and choosing love and life."*

Until one becomes aware of the truth of who he or she really is, the only course of action is to allow one's self to be destroyed (death), they think! Most don't realize they will have to return again and again until they allow the truth to penetrate their stubborn minds and overcome centuries of lies and distortions of truth. They must stay on the wheel of reincarnation until they come to realize that they are indestructible spirits. They finally will realize that they are eternal entities repeatedly occupying different physical bodies as they awaken to their ascension destiny. When we have finished the course, the death experience will be destroyed forever. The scripture confirms this: "The Last Enemy that shall be destroyed is death." (1 Corinthians 15:26)

2008 12/14 – *"My son, love is more powerful than lust or pride or fear—love will prevail. Love is the omnipotence—I am love. Trust Me with your life and your consciousness. We really are one and the same person. Our love will guide us and sustain us through it all."*

I thought, "Yes, I believe Your love will eternally guide me through it all. Praise You Father!"

2008 12/15 – *"Remember My words, 'Make water rejoice with your praise!'"*(2006 6/8)

I declared, "Since you told me water is Your liquid consciousness, I find it easy to praise you in and as water. Thank you for this wisdom."

Yes, I am preoccupied with water. I surely hope so—I had better be. He seems to exhort me every day to keep my mind on water. It is the life-giving substance of all universes, and it is our planet's salvation.

2008 12/15 – *"Remember My words on Compassionate Detachment—realize your responsibility to allow every entity their growth experience."*

Yes, I do remember and this truth takes a load of pressure and concern off me. It relieves the anxiety of watching some others in their awkward and self-defeating situations.

2008 12/16 – *"Think about honor and nobility. Everyone down through the ages, on a deeper level, including you, has chosen death again and again rather than bringing Me into an unclean and corrupt temple. On a deeper level, each one chooses to honor and revere Me to the point of self sacrifice. Think on this and consider how this must make Me feel toward each of you?"*

I replied, "Father, I am always amazed by the depth of Your love for us. I don't think that amazement will ever change, even in eternity.

I never dreamed we were doing such a personal heroic action. As I consider Your words, I realize we really are Your sons, and on a deeper level, we love You as we should."

2008 12/17 – *"One reason the timing of the water project is so critical is that when it fires-off, you and the others involved, will realize you have the power to alter the nature of water—You will realize you are omnipotent beings."*

I prayed, "Yes, Father, I realize this will be so, and I rest in the knowledge and assurance that we will be ready to handle that kind of realization. I am also aware that this is the reason this power could not be given to us sooner. I am tremendously grateful that You revealed to me that the others involved are also ready in their spiritual journey to handle the awareness of their own omnipotence." And, this is why the timing is so critical—we have to be prepared to live with the social consequences of the experience of developing the system for super-efficiently burning water.

2009 1/1 – *"Remember I told you to look at others as they will be and not as they now appear? That is how I see each of you: as the glorious, finished, ascended, perfect expression of love that you will be. Remember also the words 'If I will be, then I already am, for time is not.'"*

We need to be reminded constantly of what we really are and what and who others really are. They, each one, are a physical manifestation of a part of our Father, an incredibly beautiful facet of His personality. <u>We must allow ourselves to forget everything else we know about them and just observe their beauty.</u> We must not miss this opportunity to know the individual parts of our Father's being, and thereby of our own. Observe and be totally satisfied.

2009 1/2 – *"Love has two functions: <u>Response</u> and <u>Responsibility</u>. First, Passionate Compassion must be our <u>response </u>to every entity and every situation. Secondly, Compassionate Detachment is our <u>responsibility</u> to every entity. They have each chosen to be where he or she is today for a specific purpose—a certain set of circumstances that will help him or her toward enlightenment and spiritual fulfillment. Allow them to proceed without your interference."*

Our Father always sees the finished product when He looks at us. There is no judgment, just Passionate Compassion. He knows "all things work together for good" for us, and that we will eventually come into the fullness of enlightenment. He has established a system of spiritual evolution in which we will each advance precept upon precept, lifetime after lifetime, until we come unto the fullness of enlightenment; until we will know Him in us and as the creator/sustainer of All-That-Is, and share His glory as one entity.

What is Compassionate Detachment? This is Love that understands that *"Everyone is exactly where he or she is supposed to be."* (2000 8/16 *The Last*

Enemy), and must go through whatever situation he or she has set up for himself or herself. Every soul has chosen to come here at this time to fulfill certain situations both positive and negative that might bring spiritual growth toward their goal of enlightenment and union with the Source of All-That-Is. This kind of love understands it must allow every other individual his or her blunders, falls, failures, weaknesses, misjudgments, and outright rebellion, in order that he or she might, through these experiences, gain more understanding, and grow spiritually through them.

We dare not interfere with or deny them their opportunity to face all these various experiences. If we do so, and they allow our interference, they just postpone the inevitable. They must go through each of these positive and negative experiences again. Parents, if you love your children, heed this advice: They mapped out what they needed to accomplish in this incarnation before they were born. They decided beforehand in what country and social situation they would dwell, what race and gender they would have, who would be their parents, what occupation they would pursue, and even what friends and lovers they would eventually embrace to fulfill their mission. Lovingly protect, nurture, and carefully teach them and then allow them to proceed without your interference. Help only when asked.

2009 1/8 – *"Jack, you are gaining weight because any material food is now excess to your body as you ingest light-energy. Your body is being fed and sustained by light-energy. Think on this. You don't really need physical nourishment."*

Actually, we need nothing but light-energy; however, even when not fasting, less than a cup a day of material food would be sufficient for us, but not animal flesh or animal products. Animal flesh and animal products would draw us right back into the death spiral. One day, I will understand this on a knowing level and be able to leave off physical food altogether.

2009 1/20 – I asked, what, if anything, is going to happen in 2012? A voice answered in one word, ***"GLORY!"***

Now, I don't know exactly what "Glory" means here, but I know it is good. Heaven is referred to by some scriptures as "Glory". Whatever it is, it will be a glorious experience.

In reference to 2012, if you are interested, John Major Jenkins has written extensively on the subject. Look for his books on the *Galactic Alignment and the Mayan Cosmology and calendars.*

2009 1/20 – Alantra, one of my spirit guides, came to me and I saw her face for the first time. She looked remarkably like my wife, Jonnie Ann at about age thirty. I asked her about this similarity.

She replied, *"Jonnie Ann is a part of me. You are together to help each other through this incarnation."*

2009 1/20 – Sabatino, another of my spirit guides, came while Alantra was here this morning, and I saw most of his face for the first time. He is a good looking fellow with light wavy hair and a great smile—not broad like Barak Obama, but more like Robert Redford's. Both of these entities came to minister and talk to me while I was ill with the flu.

2009 1/27 – *"Your temple does not need cleansing, Jack. You are clean, and exactly where you are supposed to be at this moment."*

I want so much to please my Father, so I am always trying to find ways to please Him and be more ready for His presence. He is assuring me that He is already in His temple and quite pleased to be here.

I am always ready to point out to others that everyone is exactly where he or she is supposed to be so as not to be critical or judgmental, but I seem to forget: Me too! We must cease judging ourselves. He has told us that He does not judge us at all for anything. He just loves us and helps us through this experience.

2009 1/27 – *"Get excited about where you are spiritually today. Get excited about your ability to change the whole nation's economic situation.*

First, concerning the national economic situation, there is the realization that you can change it. Then, there is the excitement of the challenge. You wish to change the economic situation for all, not just for your own self and your company. This is good; however, this exercise is sort of like walking a tightrope over the Grand Canyon; you must keep your eyes on the other side—don't look down. Don't get involved in the dreary, alarming, and fearful everyday economic forecasts. They are created out of both fear and <u>treachery</u>. Keep your eyes on Me and the truths I have revealed to you. Look at Me, Son!"

I think it is interesting that He used the Word "treachery" here. Could it be that this present economic situation we are experiencing is just a gigantic, behind-the-scenes, manufactured, financial propaganda scheme of recession to push a certain group's agenda and their puppet into the White House to implement their plans? Is this just for political party power, or is there a much deeper and more sinister plan here to bring this country down, and make it just another third world nation under the NEW WORLD ORDER?

They didn't know it, but it would have happened anyway. Barak Obama with his veiled ambitions was destined to be our next president. It was all in the cards, and everything is just as it should be. It may not be pleasant, but it is exactly as it should be.

We have been heading in this direction for decades. Yes, I'm sure there is an active conspiracy at work behind the scenes vigorously tearing down this country morally, socially, and financially, but I doubt the pawns in the game (The news media, most of our brilliant politicians, and educational institutions) are aware that they are participants in the conspiracy. I won't dwell on this—it is not healthy spiritual thinking. It is negative thinking. Everything is exactly as it should be. We need this in our collective spiritual evolution, or it would not be happening.

2009 1/28 – *"You are growing up. You are maturing into a spiritual adult. You are now at a place where you cannot be humbled. You are realizing you are omnipotent, and there is none greater—that is what humbles you."*

Having heard this, I have gained new insight to the nature of our Father, and even some of the ascended masters such as Jesus and Buddha. They are so loving, forgiving and humble because they know they are one with the Father—they know they are omnipotent. They are one with Him and know everyone else is also. So, there is no strife, no competition, and no fear, just loving confidence that all will be well.

2009 2/8 – *"All the various sense organs of the body were given to you to enjoy physicality, not to addictively indulge in their pleasures. Be moderate in all things, and let these sense organs teach you the uniqueness of their being and abilities. Listen, touch, taste, and smell the subtle universes in and around you."*

Funny, I'm afraid I have always acted like my stomach should be full continually. It seems we are continually encouraged toward food addiction by everyone (the medical profession, the food industry, and media advertising) to eat three gigantic meals a day. They also tell us to eat animal flesh, poultry, cheese, eggs, and milk products each day which I have found, are harmful to our bodies.

Most men and some women believe that without sex they would go insane in short order and some men are convinced that without sex, they might even die. Father says, "No such Thing!" These are needful appetites of the sensing organs of the body, and should be used conservatively to more fully understand who and what we are. It is more about feeling than fulfillment.

2009 2/10 – *"Two things are impossible for our Father. First, it is impossible to express His love for us in words, symbols, or even internal revelations. Second, it is impossible for us to ever lose His love, no matter what we do, say or think."*

His love is the result of His being, and it is ever growing and deepening. He loves us more today than He did yesterday, and He will love us more tomorrow than He does today. He tells us that "Because of us and our experiences, His love grows stronger as He goes through every experience of life with us." He tells us that He faces each positive and negative experience with us. He lives our joys and our heart-breaks with us. He feels everything we feel, and understands why we feel the way we do, and why we do the things we do, but He never judges us. He knows us more deeply than we know ourselves. Let's think about that again. He has gone through many life-times with us and understands why we feel the way we do, and He never judges us.

His love for you and me is much greater than that of our own mother and father. He says, *"When my father and my mother forsake me, then the Lord will take me up."* (Psalms 27:10) What a mighty loving Father we serve.

2009 2/14 – *"Let's talk about eating the flesh of other sentient beings* (animals, birds and fish). *These beings have the same feelings and emotions that you have, but lack the ability to express them verbally. They have the same fear, and feel the same terror you would feel if you were in their place, and going through their experiences in the slaughter houses.*

As you saw last night, the restaurant in Fort Collins tried to satisfy every gluttonous flesh-eating pleasure; there is no end to the human desire for the taste for new flesh. This addiction to eating animal flesh cannot be satisfied.

Flesh addiction always leads eventually to cannibalism in those who yield to it, especially in times of dire circumstances, or in affluent societies where the extremely rich have exhausted all other forms of entertainment.

You can be sure that there are secret groups of people, even in this country, who are feeding on human flesh. Many of the missing young people in this country have been served up on the table of these gluttonous cannibals. These atrocities will be exposed later, and all will understand the extent of this addiction."

I am so shocked about the revelation here of cannibalism in this present day and our own country, that I cannot bear to think about it. I will just wait for the atrocities to be exposed. I have come to realize that slavery (sex slavery and other enslavement) is still common even in this great country, but cannibalism being practiced here in the United States is a new revelation to me.

Now, concerning the restaurant experience in Fort Collins, I do have some observations and comments: Have you ever visited a slaughter house? I have had the unfortunate opportunity in my early life and later on during my time in my industrial equipment sales days to visit two different slaughter houses in two different cities.

The first was the slaughter house at the Milledgeville State Mental Hospital in Milledgeville, Georgia. The State Hospital, as it is called locally, was, when I visited it, a huge complex, with twenty-five or more mentally ill patient confinement buildings scattered over thousands of plush, manicured, acres just south of Milledgeville, Georgia. It contains the population of a small city, counting both inmates and state employees. Meals are served by the complex's own kitchens. At the time I visited there some forty years ago, these kitchens fed vegetables, milk products and meats, all grown on state farm lands adjacent to the complex. The animals were killed and their meat processed right there on the grounds of the State Hospital. The slaughter house was at the south end of the complex about a mile away from the nearest patient confinement building. Upon approaching the slaughter house area, the stench of blood, guts, fecal matter, and urine was overwhelming. Then, upon entering the killing area and the slaughter chute, and hearing the wailing and bellowing screams of the cattle being electric-shock prodded along to the sledge hammer which would administer their final blow, a normal newcomer would be overcome with nausea. No outsider unaccustomed to the scene can endure the sounds, smell, and sight very long. The terror of the scene has lived with me ever since.

My second slaughter house experience was a chicken rendering plant in Claxton, Georgia. This is the same town that produces the Claxton Fruit Cake which is one of my favorite Christmas treats. The stench at this rendering plant was different from the cattle slaughter house, but even more poignant. So many chickens were being killed here that a concrete trench I stepped across, about a foot deep and a foot wide, was flowing nearly full with blood and chicken debris. I was told that the blood, feathers, heads, beaks, feet, and legs were all ground up together, then cooked, dried, and fed to other chickens and animals. Folks, there is something wrong here.

Now, it's no wonder that in this Fort Collins restaurant, I was being offered beef, pork, lamb, venison, wild boar, chicken, turkey and fish. I got sick!

2009 2/15 – *"You are still having trouble understanding union or oneness with me. It is not, 'We are one,' It is, 'I am one.' I Am! I Am!*

Jack, understand this: Someone else did not de-materialize your body and the vehicle when the gasoline tanker drove through your pick-up truck in Alabama; you did it! Someone else did not push your motor home back up on the bridge on the Alaskan mountain; you did it. At those times, you reached deeply into your reservoir of emotional focus and re-created the experience more to your liking. You were not ready to depart this realm, so you instantly rewrote the script. You changed the program! You and everyone else do this occasionally in times of great stress and focused determination. You really are the one, the I AM. I AM."

I have spoken with others who have recalled such experiences. I think such unexplained, mysterious, mind-boggling, experiences cause many to completely dismiss, or mentally block all memory of them because the reality of what happened to them is too frightening or confusing to think further about. Many feel if they tried to admit to themselves that such an incident actually happened to them, they would know they are insane, or everyone else would think them a lunatic—much like a little twelve year old girl who is raped by a father, grandfather, uncle, brother or some other close kin, who totally blocks it out of her mind until later on in life when that grown woman is hypnotized or regressed, wherein she remembers the incident.

2009 2/16 – "Father, after reading again the last message, it scares me to think that I am All-That-Is. I begin to feel alone again, just as I felt in the beginning before I started separating myself into others, and giving them individuality and amnesia."

I felt like "Oh no, I've been here before." Then, something deep within me began to rejoice and the words surged out of my heart:

"Alas! I don't have to feel alone. I can discover myself—new facets of my personality in others who are me. *I can watch them and intermingle with them to learn of myself. I will discover the uniqueness of each of them, and thereby the uniqueness of myself. There are billions of these other expressions of me out there, and more are being created every day. What a wonderful plan I created to discover myself."*

I exclaimed, "Father, you have approached this truth over and over again to me. Eventually, I will be able to walk in it continually. I can only wonder about the love it will create in me for them all."

2009 2/17 – *"Think on the depth of emotional stress you experienced when you dematerialized in front of the gasoline tanker, and when you were going over the cliff, and off the bridge in Alaska. Remember your thoughts and concentration then, and you will begin to realize how to change water and the economic situation on Earth today."*

Sometimes, I have relived these stressful experiences and still felt the hopeless, powerless feelings, but also I recall having the will to try somehow to survive. Until about five years ago, I could not think of some of those experiences without the stress, sweating, and hopeless feeling returning. Now, I just remember that a miracle occurred, as someone intervened. Now, I know it was me!

2009 2/24 – *"I would not have told you this is your primary reality if it is not.* (This is referring to words I received on 2003 6/12.) *Now, since it is your primary reality, you straighten it out.* (He is talking about the world economic situation.) *You know it is all illusionary, so just use your imagination and your emotional focus to change it."*

I responded, "Father, it sounds like you are blaming me for everything that is going on in this world today!"

He answered, *"I am, this is your primary reality. Think about just the recession/depression and its causes. You have been predicting (creating) this situation for years. Are you now surprised when it appears? Straighten it out the same way you created it—with positive affirmations of its ending, and prosperity again reigning in the world. This is your primary reality."*

Below are some earlier messages on Primary Reality:

2000 11/15 - *"Every entity has a primary reality where all other entities are supportive to him. In your primary reality, you have absolute control of the reality. You form everything, every situation, every relationship, and every experience. In your secondary realities, you have a supportive role to the entity who is primary. The experiences and wisdom gained in these secondary realities are then reflected into your primary reality, and help your own quest."*

Since all realities are actually happening simultaneously in the eternal now, and contrary to that fact, seem to exist in separate spheres of linear time, we still must understand that all our parallel/secondary lives are being lived at this very instant.

No one is being cheated, deprived, diminished, or devalued. In our secondary lives, we are doing this secondary role for each other and with each other that we might all attain ascension.

I wonder what characteristic traits may be presently reflected back and forth through our secondary realities. Could one's sexual preference, personal habits, social preference, racial preference, discriminations, and life styles from one reality reflect into another and influence other secondary/primary realities? Could these reflections influence our other reality manifestations, causing us to act certain ways, and attract certain people? Could this be why some men are oriented as women and visa versa? Could it be that a person is having so much fun and being so delighted as a man in one reality that the male psyche dominates another reality's female body? Perhaps…

2000 11/20 - *"If you are having problems with each person having his* *or her own primary reality, look at the sky at night for the probabilities and proof. There are trillions of physical realities shinning out the confirmation of this truth. They are there to help you understand this truth.* "

We are now told by our astronomers that there are over 100 billion galaxies in this universe, with hundreds of billions of suns in each galaxy. There are planets revolving around many of these suns. Is it so far-fetched to believe that each of us could have a primary reality? Are we so narrow-minded as to believe that we are the only developed species in this vast universe?

I suspect that as our infrared telescopes continue probing deeper and deeper into this universe, the 100 billion galaxies will be revised to trillions. Then they will discover more universes. If the other species that are out there began their mental, physical, and spiritual development a million years prior to our beginning on Earth, could they, by now, have discovered a unique method of space/time travel and be visiting our planet? Could their mental and spiritual development have allowed then to avoid wars and their own annihilation and enabled them to develop into superior mental and spiritual beings? I think, probably, yes.

(Also look back at messages received on 2003 6/16 and 2003 6/19 in this book.)

2009 2/24 – *"Don't worry about some negative or fearful thoughts you might have from time to time. Just override them with the truth of your nature. State your <u>positive affirmation</u> with focused conviction. MAKE IT SO!"*

We all have negative, fearful, doubtful, hateful, thoughts from time to time with the result that most of us are having conscience pangs and feel ashamed. We want to kick ourselves for being so infantile, spiritually. He is saying that this is normal, and can be expected, but we can overcome this tendency and eventually not be bothered by such thoughts.

The method of overcoming negative thoughts is to face them instantly with a strong, positive, affirmation. Such an affirmation will make a statement in the present tense, such as, "I AM" such and such, but not "I WILL BE," which really means, <u>not now</u>! "I will be" really means, "I don't expect it right now, but would really like it someday in the future when my belief system can project such a creative action." Or, "I'm really not strong enough right now to expect this, but I really want it."

He, very subtly here inserts the words "the truth of your nature." That is the most powerful truth of all. In truth, our nature is that of the omnipotent creative nature of the almighty God, our loving Father and the Source of All-That-Is.

The truth and eternal fact is: *there are no limitations on our creative ability.* The only thing that holds us back is our own timidity and/or ignorance. My brother and sister, we must be what we are, the Omnipotent Source of All-That-Is.

2009 2/24 – *"Your cardiologists are confounded by the healing progress they are seeing in your heart's health. They feel you should be getting progressively worse. They will eventually resent your progress. Watch out for a curve ball."*

Yes, the curve ball has already been pitched. Following my last check-up, my blood pressure was down to 110/60, and my total cholesterol was at 108. This is excellent even for a practicing athlete.

After reviewing my file, my cardiologist looked at me sternly and said, "It looks like we have you stabilized, so now we can go forward. We need to look into implanting a defibrillator, because your heart is damaged, and could suddenly stop beating. You would die instantly!"

I said, "My friend, if my heart stops, it is time for me to die. No Thanks!" I'm sure money had nothing to do with his suggestion (?)

2009 2/26 – Lord, there are so many voices vying for my attention!

"Yes Jack, there are medical voices, political voices, religious voices, economists' voices, and many of those around you trying to pull your mind in different directions, and the professionals don't even agree among themselves, so what are you to believe? The only voice of truth is within you, and no matter how much it contradicts what you are

hearing or even seeing, you must follow this still, small voice. It is Me—it is truth! Walk in it. I Am.”

At this time, our nation is in a mess. We are in the greatest recession/depression during my lifetime. Last year, our two-party political system gave us very little differences with which to choose a direction for our future. The news media chose the candidate they wanted, and then set about shoving him down our throats, and torpedoing any other by very forcefully promoting the idea of a failing economy caused by the present administration. We, whom they see as the cattle in their pens, ate up the new slop propaganda scheme being force-fed to us. Eventually, about October of 2008, our perception of our economy changed our situation to a **reality of a failing economy**. We began to "get ready" for the possibility or probability of a depression. We stopped spending our expendable income, and began selling our stock so we could avoid losing it when the crash came as it did in 1929. Soon, everyone was selling their stock. This began exposing stock market fraud that had been in progress for decades. Banks began to fail, exposing banking fraud that has been in progress for decades, and alas, we were propelled into a national, and then a worldwide economic failure—all the result of years of investment and bank fraud, irresponsible government oversight, and a news media determined to have their man elected, regardless of the consequences.

There is always a silver lining. We are now aware of a highly developed scheme of investment and banking fraud that eventually would have brought us all to even worse financial ruin, plus we are seeing the ultimate corporate greed, and the irresponsibility of our government institutions which were supposedly set up to monitor and control such schemes. We have watched as our pathetically stupid, or just ignorant, auto industry managers led their companies down the road to bankruptcy. Now, the unashamedly ignorant, slothfully uninformed, inexperienced, and utterly corrupt, national politicians are going to play businessman, and oversee these corporations. Let's watch and see what happens. Through this all, we should be convinced that the only voice we can believe is that one within each of us, no matter how contrary to public opinion. Believe your inner voice, and follow it.

2009 2/26 – *"Jack, do what makes your heart sing. There is no right way or wrong way for you. Follow your joy, and re-write the script as you go. Learn the excitement of continuous creation. Be aware of what you are—You are the, I AM!"*

I get excited every time I read this! He is showing me that state-of-life I, and all of us, are moving into as we discover our omnipotent creative ability. We discover we can manipulate the illusions of physicality to our own liking. He is letting me know that creating anything I want is OK. There is no right or wrong for me. He tells me to create what makes my heart sing, to get excited about who I am and what I can do because my intention is now moving in love for All-That-Is. I am past wrongful intent and negative creation. Thank you Father.

2009 2/26 – As I was speaking on the phone to a new friend, a recent reader of my first book, *The Last Enemy*, when I noticed a light-entity nearby. This being appeared as a vertical, blue fog or smoke located about four feet in front of my desk between my desk and a decorative tree in my office. It was a shimmering figure about four to five feet tall. I could see the tree through it, but I could not make out any facial features. I was very much aware that this non-physical being was closely observing me. It remained there for about three minutes, and then it disappeared.

This little spirit creature completely ruined my chain of thought as I was trying to have a meaningful conversation with my new friend. I wanted to get off the phone and try to communicate with it, but my friend I was talking to wanted to talk about the messages in the book, even though I told him I had a spirit visitor. However, I think as I conveyed what was going on in front of my desk, I probably convinced the reader that I was either possessed or insane, because as I described what I was seeing to him, the phone conversation quickly ended. The blue figure faded away before I could communicate with it.

2009 3/1 – *"If you awaken completely right now, you would immediate exit your body. Your vibratory rate could not be contained in a physical body."*

This message should give us an idea of what we can expect in the future as we progress on our quest for union with our Father. I have already written about the messages concerning our invisibility to some of those on other levels of spiritual development, so here is another teaching on the subject. He tells us it concerns our vibratory rate, or light vibratory rate. As we draw ever closer to our Father, we acquire more and more of His light-energy vibrations. As we do, our bodies become less and less dense. We become more and more loving until others find us irresistible. They meet us and feel our light penetrating their soul's awareness. They feel as if we can see right through them, and they feel the nature of our Father (LOVE) saturating their being. Some will be startled and retreat in fear, but others will want to bind themselves to us. Still others will want to take a wait-and-see stance as they confront their inner, confused feelings.

As we continue to develop, the day will come when we will have to concentrate deeply just to remain in the physical body. Some of us will find ourselves able to **blink** in and out of physicality, and even find ourselves dwelling in both the physical and non-physical realms for extended periods of time. Don't be disturbed or afraid if you find yourself in this situation from time to time. Fear not, you are growing up.

2009 3/7 – *"We are all for you Jack, including Ida, your ego. You have no foes. All those that seem to be foes, and those supposedly negative situations, are your own creations especially designed for your spiritual progress. Go gloriously through them praising your Father and your helpers."*

Remember, the Bible says in Romans 8:31, "If God be for us, who can be against us?" Yes, we are the omnipotent sons of the most high; who can stand against that exalted position?

I remember President Franklin Roosevelt once said, "The only thing we have to fear is fear itself." Here, our Father is telling us not to fear the situations of life we are facing. They are special situations created in advance by each of us to experience for our spiritual advancement. The only one we have to blame is ourselves! I myself created each situation I am facing. I designed each physical life situation I am facing to help me to enlightenment, that I might rejoin my omnipotent glorious family, and behold the highest, most glorious being ever to exist, our loving Father.

2009 3/7 – "Father, what is holding me back from total enlightenment?"

He answered, *"It is just Habit and Doubt! Think about it, you still have a tendency to doubt the words you receive for a time, just because they are coming through you. Also, you and most others on spiritual quests, habitually and <u>tentatively,</u> are easily distracted from earnest spiritual meditation and prayer. Part of this tentativeness is due to lack of preparation before and during meditations. Remember the relaxation, light-energy work and praise time I taught you to use at the beginning of a meditation session? Be sure to do this spiritual grounding. As they say in your sports, 'let's get back to the basics.'"*

Note: I had to look up the meaning of the word **"tentatively"** as He used it here. I thought I knew the meaning, but it did not seem to make sense here. The dictionary says: *Tentative – Indicating timidity, hesitancy, or uncertainty.* Now, it makes perfect sense.

Well, He didn't mince words here! It is habit and doubt. Certainly He is right! It is habitual laziness, timidity, hesitancy, or half-heartedness caused by doubt. When we do not take time to meditate, pray, and ingest light-energy, and there is poor preparation in praise and relaxation preceeding the sacred time, then there is very little honest intent to deeply worship and listen for His voice. When we have a thousand other agendas on our mind, and we dutifully sit to mediate, we can expect very little response and power from that activity. No wonder He flatly states it is habit and doubt. If we did not habitually doubt, we would rush to our meditation place and anxiously await his voice. Suppose He treated us with the same nonchalant, disrespectful, attitude we display concerning our designated time with Him? Do we even have at least one designated time each day for the Almighty King of all the Universes?

Suppose He doubted us as much as we doubt Him. He certainly should! Most of us do really doubt Him, you know? Yet, He still humbly bows to speak to each of us, but most every man and woman alive today denies that He speaks to anyone at all. Most who believe there is a God think He is some kind of vague, universal consciousness. Read what He said when I asked Him, "Are you just a universal consciousness?"

2002 7/30 - *"You have asked Me, 'What are you, just a universal consciousness?' I am more than just a Universal Consciousness. Do you think I could be less of a person than you? I, too, am an individual entity, fully realized, but wholly All-That-Is. I am All-in-All. I am you and you are Me. We are one, yet two beings, two personalities."*

He speaks to every single person regardless of what he thinks, but most everyone alive today who hears His voice denies that it is Him. They shake off any profound thought or voice they might have or may have heard as some fearful hallucination, or their replay of some scene from a movie, or a television program they saw, a book they read, or some past dream they have had, because their God is a **distant concept** and totally powerless.

2009 3/7 – In praise, I exclaimed, "Glory, What an incredible gift you have given us, Father—to be an individual, and yet to share your being, your personality, your love, your omnipotence, and glory. I do praise you in me, and as me, and as All-that-is."

2009 3/8 – *"You need to consider too that not only are other people obligated to support your words here in your primary reality, but the entire system of consciousness is obligated to support your thoughts, opinions, pronouncements, and affirmations. You are omnipotent, and you and your Father have chosen this to be your primary reality."* (Ref: 2003 6/16)

Sometimes I seem to forget the message about "Unit Consciousness" that I was taught. Everything that exists in this physical reality is alive, has consciousness, volition, and power to create any situation if feels it must. Also, remember His words, *"Some inanimate entities already know they are in union with the Father,"* and they know their creative abilities are unlimited.

2009 3/10 – *"Jack, in your primary reality, you have not only chosen your parents, your body type, physical condition, historical time period, and global location for this incarnation, but also <u>you have chosen the intensity of life and events you wish to face during this incarnation</u>, much like choosing the intensity in computer games you see today.*

You are wondering, 'Which situation seems to indicate a person is further along in his spiritual evolutional journey? Is it the one, like yourself, who has chosen for this incarnation, a more tranquil life, or is it the violent, militant terrorist, drug runner, or even a slave in his day-to-day flight and fight for survival? How do you think our Father feels about those who have chosen the harder, more intense life course? Can you understand that we all have chosen both types of life situations at times for our own growth needs? Should you then be more tolerant and understanding of those who chose the less intense life courses you see in society today? You need to realize that once a life situation is chosen, one must finish that incarnation course no matter how hard, intense, and terrifying it might be. You are all on the same journey—a quest for union with Him. Should you feel guilty for your present less-intense life situation? No, you should not. I assure you, you are now living in other secondary incarnations, and in parallel realities, the most intense and terrifying life situations imaginable. Enjoy where you are and who you are today in your primary reality."

I think I got an inkling of this when I was counseled by the spirit world on 2001 9/13 and recorded it in my last book, *The Last Enemy*, about my feelings at that time concerning the terrorist, Osama ben Laden. I was reminded that he, Osama, is also a part or facet of our Father (Love), trying to find his way back to union with the Source of All-That-Is. He is absolutely sure, through all his dogmatic religious teaching and brain washing, that what he is doing what is right, that he is pleasing God, and will be rewarded in the hereafter for all the havoc he is creating on the Earth. He lives in a world that preaches, "I must defend the faith!" One day (probably not in this incarnation), he will see that God is able to defend the faith without his help.

Many Christians feel the same way, "I must defend the faith!" and they have felt this way for centuries. Remember the Christian Crusades? They lasted hundreds of years and killed thousands of Muslim and Christian people, just because they embraced another religion. The Christian Crusade war rally was "Kill the infidels!"

This ages old resentment and hatred by the Arab/Islamic people towards the Christian nations is completely understandable. It is no wonder that their new war rally is "Kill the infidels!" You can't be right by doing wrong, my friend. Need I say more?

2009 3/11 – *"Your primary reality is the summation of all your incarnations, the ultimate incarnation—you might say, the last incarnation you will have to go through in your spiritual quest, even though they are all being lived at the same time, in the now. You are nearly home."*

This may be difficult to understand. We understand our existences in sequential or linear time, and yet here He is speaking both of linear "last incarnation" and "all being lived in the now." We have to realize both are true, linear or sequential experiences and simultaneous experiences are all in our now experience. The past and the future are all now. Yes! Yes! The future is known!

2009 3/12 – *"Since your Mead house is now cleaned up and ready to sell, life is not going to slow down as you might think—it is going to speed up and get busier. We have a lot of work to do."*

I think my Father is clearing up a lot of litter in my life so as to free me for other tasks He has on my agenda. I expect the Mead house selling sooner rather than later will reveal this even more in the present, tough, real estate market.

2009 3/16 – *"You must read the messages recorded in your first book at least weekly now. Time is getting short. You need to focus on ALL I have taught you."*

I have started doing this, and it is time consuming, but I already realize the benefits from this exercise. It keeps all that He has told and shown me over the years fresh in my mind. It is incredible how he continually builds on the earlier messages.

2009 3/18 – There was a <u>blunder</u> overdraft at my company to the tune of over five hundred thousand dollars. We ran out of money! I could not believe we had made such a slip-up. I complained to my Father asking how such a thing could happen.

The reply came: *"**Remember My words, 'Your financial success is unavoidable.'**"* (1988 11/8, *The Last Enemy*)

Later today, the bank recalculated our asset loan availability and found, suddenly it was over one million dollars. Thank you, Father!

2009 3/19 – Concerning yesterdays overdraft: *"**You did it Jack. You called forth the new calculation at the bank. Actually, the assets were not there before you spoke them into existence. They were not there before the company's entire historical and financial data were changed to reveal the new capital availability. Don't you realize that your financial people, and the bank's financial people, were diligently working on, and watching the calculations nearly every day. The assets were not there. Now, think of the emotional focus you used yesterday when you were asking for my help.**"*

As is the case many times, there is no way to prove this, except to say we were in financial turmoil one day, being in an overdraft situation caused mostly by carelessness (Not closely watching the bank account balance and <u>assuming</u> the money was there, as it always has been). Everyone was in a panic, which completely disappeared the next day. Everyone accepted the recalculation as clearing up some earlier miscalculation on our and the bank's behalf. It is stranger still that now all historical financial data supports the recalculation. I wonder how far back the data was changed. I'll bet my slippers it was all the way back to 1945 when our company was purchased from the original owners.

2009 3/20 – *"**I am consciousness. All you can respond to is consciousness. The air you breathe and the water you drink is just consciousness.**"*

Anything you can see, touch, smell, or hear is just consciousness. It is Me. It is you. It is not separate from you; it is all you. You are it responding back to yourself. Awaken! Know who you are. You are All-That-Is. Remember the Scripture in Philippians 2:5-7, *'Let this mind be in you, which was also in Christ Jesus; Who, being in the form of God, thought it not robbery to be equal with God; But made himself of no reputation, and took upon him the form of a servant, and was made in the likeness of men...'*

I would not have it any other way! I think this "All you can respond to is consciousness" is a brain stimulator. It makes me reconsider that consciousness (Our Father's essence) is all there is. Everything is consciousness, even to the blade of grass or the rock in my drive-way. They are all conscious and alive with feelings, understanding and great memory; moreover, they are not separate from me. We are all one entity, making our separate appearances in this reality to help each other to ascension to the next higher level of consciousness. Love them all and help them in their quest. I need to consider these thoughts daily until I know it and show it.

2009 3/24 – *"Let us talk about meditation techniques. Do you suppose meditation praise and communion with Me is just a physical experience? So much of the meditational techniques taught today are concerned with discipline of the body, positions of the body, body chakra charging, and manipulations,* <u>etc</u>. *Did you prepare your body for meditation when the gasoline tanker was bearing down on you? Do you suppose all meditation and spiritual striving for growth ends with the death of the body? Then, why put so much emphasis on body positions and techniques? The way to Me is still, and always will be, seeking Me within your deeper consciousness, not in the discipline or debasement of the vessel—the body. The body is the wilderness you have found yourself abiding in for the time being. I am the deep center of your soul. Find Me there!"*

This brings up further discussion. My continuation of praise and meditation never ends. We ascend to the next dimension and then find we can work toward ascension to an even higher realm. Remember the message I was given on 1999 8/25 in *The Last Enemy?*

1999 8/25 - *"There are innumerable and unimaginable bands, or dimensions, of consciousness above where you are now. These are exponentially greater than the differences in your consciousness as compared to that of the animal kingdom."*

This conflicts with the present New Age teaching of a limited number of spiritual dimensions. It looks like we will be growing in knowledge, wisdom, love, and compassion forever. There will always be higher ground to climb and new truth to claim.

Can you imagine other dimensions so much higher in consciousness that when compared to our consciousness it is magnitudes higher? Wow!

There is no end to the growth opportunities as our Father leads higher and higher in love, understanding and consciousness.

2009 3/28 – *"Earnest seekers the world over are being taught to chant 'OM, OM, or AUM,' but not knowing exactly what 'OM' or 'AUM' means. This precious chant means 'I AM! I AM!' Chant 'OM' or 'I AM,' knowing and feeling its truth. I AM!"*

Yogis spend hours praising our Father every day with the OM chant, and claim it is the highest praise sound and chant that our voices can utter. I have a CD of the Dali Lama chanting "OM" that I cherish.

When I chant now, it is with the "I Am" words our Father is teaching me—that we all are the "I AM" with and in our Father. I AM!

2009 3/29 – *"You learn what is from what is not, for what is, is not apparent, and what is not, appears to be what is. This mind twister is given to help you think about reality and the illusion of physicality. It is all the same thing—consciousness, whether it exists as what is, or as what is not."*

I love this! Every time I reread it, it excites me again. It is so short, yet so full of power.

2009 3/31 – *"You are 'I AM,' but not the only expression of Me; therefore, you see, you are not alone, just as every one else is not alone. You are all one. The difference is that you know you are one with Me, but most do not know, nor can they even imagine oneness. Look how long it has taken you to realize your unity with me."*

Evidently, it took me twenty million years, give or take a few thousand. I think He is still addressing my complaint on 2009 2/16, when I was feeling alone again. The other fragments of my Father are fragments of me, and just like me, they are independent, but yet fully connected souls. I can fellowship with them knowing our companionship will never end. We will always be independent souls, but one with our Father and each other. They will be there, too, no matter where there is, nor how long it takes for us to realize our relationship with our Father and each other. Now, here is a relationship that is closer than a brother.

2009 4/7 – *"You will make it work!"*

He is speaking here about the water burning process I have been working on for the past thirty years. I feel He is telling me I am very close to finding the answers to completing the process. I really have no doubt I will complete the project and give the world a new, plentiful, free, source of energy.

2009 4/7 – *"Don't worry about the alignment of the planets on 2012. Concern yourself with your alignment with me. All else is secondary."*

More books are being published monthly on the subject of 2012. I recently saw a whole section in Borders Book Store completely dedicated to the subject of 2012.

I have received no definitive words on what is going to happen, if anything, on December 21, 2012, but I have some ideas.

I would not be surprised to learn that the mysterious Planet "X" discovered over a decade ago, coming into our solar system, is the Planet Nibiru (meaning "crossing" or "X"), and is heading for another near-miss to Earth as it did a few thousand years ago when its gravitational pull caused the oceans to be pulled up over the highest mountains. However, I believe that I would have been told by now to prepare for this if there were going to be such a <u>very close</u> encounter this time, one that might cause world-wide flooding as in the past great deluge, The full story is recorded on Lapis Lazuli and clay tablets now stored in European and Middle Eastern countries' museums and translated in Zecharia Sitchin's many books, especially in his latest transcription of the *Lost Book of Enki.*

2009 4/7 – *"You cannot understand the fullness of oneness or total union with Me any more than you can totally understand the fullness of the creation process—making something from nothing. This knowledge is higher dimensional thinking just beginning to be available to you. You are getting glimpses of it, but soon you will see it all. Be patient and wait on Me."*

Paul said we see through a glass darkly: (1 Corinthians 13:12) *"For now we see through a glass, darkly; but then face to face: now I know in part; but then shall I know even as also I am known."*

It appears a certainty to us that no human can possibly comprehend, or even try to conceptualize, a creation process that brings physical matter into being from nothingness.

Oneness with our Father is just as impossible to comprehend. How He can be fully Himself in me and in everyone else at the same time is incomprehensible; yet He lets each of us be individuals, but still one with each other! This is "other realm" intelligence and must be opened up to us gradually at some future time in this incarnation or another.

I remind you again that there is a canopy, or veil, over and between our understanding and that conceptual ability. It is truth, but presently we will just have to receive this truth without understanding it, and simultaneously able to see the reality of it all around us. I get excited as I think about what the next dimension is going to reveal when it is opened to us.

2009 4/13 – *"When one leaves the body, what will sustain his life? Will he need to eat? Think about it. Light-energy will sustain him then,* *and it does now! Physical food will not be required then, and it is not required now. You each have light transducers* (chakras) *all over your physical bodies that convert light-energy to physical energy now. Ingesting as much physical food as most humans do interferes with and diminishes their life-force. You already know that digesting food uses a great amount of energy. The continual physical food digestion processes slowly drain your reserves of life force. Again, I admonish you; learn to live on light-energy alone. Begin a life fast!"*

Some might ask, "How about people who starve to death because they have no food?" The key here is "learn to live on light-energy alone." No one has to starve to death who knows the truth of living on light-energy. We can sustain ourselves for months and years on light-energy alone.

One of the benefits of my four heart attacks is that when one's heart is damaged and is not capable of producing enough blood to supply the muscles of your body to allow you to perform over a certain level physically, you learn where your new (after heart attack) physical limits are for work and exercise. You realize very quickly that you need not even try any strenuous exercise or physical labor within three or more hours after even a small meal. Just walking from your car into the supermarket during that time will give you chest and jaw pain. It also makes one keenly aware of the tremendous amount of energy that is required to digest a meal. If you over-eat, it is even worse. You find yourself eating much less so you can function somewhere near normal, or as your norm was in the past.

The cardiologists told me that the damage to my heart would never heal, but I can attest today, a great deal of healing has gone on since my last major heart attack two years ago. I now do much more manual work, and a good deal of walking even after sizable meals and without pain. My heart is healing beautifully and I am doing more exercising than before.

So, when He says "Digesting food uses a great amount of energy," I can attest that this statement is true. This message makes total sense to me when He tells us light-energy will sustain us in this and the next realm. This reminds me of an earlier message on 2000 11/9, *The Last Enemy,*

"You and all humanity have a deep seated belief that, 'If I don't eat, I will get sick. If I don't eat, I will die!' This is not true! The opposite

is true! Light-energy is the only life-sustaining food for the body. The body is light-energy. It must feed on its source! Breathe in more and more light-energy, and eat less and less physical food until you sustain your body's life on light-energy alone."

2009 4/14 – I am beginning a fast regiment by cutting out all meats and eating lighter every day until I am on a total fast as a way of life. Let's see how long it takes me to get to and sustain a total fast.

One of the most challenging and difficult endeavors for a human being is to attempt a total water fast while living with others who are not fasting, and moreover, are lovingly fearful for the faster's health if he continues this endeavor beyond a few days. They, out of genuine love for the faster, will do everything in their power to persuade him or her to quit the fast, even to sabotaging and disrupting his attempts to be faithful to his quest.

It is best, if possible, to leave everyone you know and love, go someplace where you can be totally alone, or with another person who is also fasting, so you can fast, meditate, and ingest only light-energy. Even Jesus had to journey into a wilderness to be alone where he could fast and pray. Others, Moses, Elijah, and Buddha experienced the same thing.

2009 4/20 – *"Light-energy ingestion is not fasting! During light-energy ingestion, you are consuming and ingesting the purest food source. It is pure life-force energy, much more complete and powerful than physical food of any kind could ever be."*

This is why, while one is "fasting," **and faithfully ingesting light-energy**, he or she does not degenerate physically. **He or she really is not fasting at all.** These people are by-passing their normal digestive process and feeding the body directly on the source of all food products, light-energy. This light-energy nourishment has no toxins, no herbicides, no plant growth stimulus chemicals, and no animal products with their growth hormones, antibiotics, and saturated fats. It is pure life-force energy. It is the same energy that fires the sun and propels the planets and galaxies through their orbits. It is the omnipotent energy of the universes.

2009 4/22 – *"Remember the message on 2000 8/30 when I told you:*

'If you were not capable of doing anything that is happening on this Earth today, it would not be happening at all! It is all part of you doing all that is going on. It is not positive or negative; it just is! Don't judge.'"

This applies to your national economics and social situation, and the desperate, hopeful remedies being imposed by your national government. Do not fear; everything is exactly as it is supposed to be at this time. Rejoice!"

He tells us not to fear and not to judge because our national government, our banking community, our business community, and we personally, are experiencing this **"teaching situation"** together. No, it is not just the banking community's fault, not just Wall Street's fault, not only the government's fault, not George Bush's or Bill Clinton's fault, not the government's financial institution Oversight Committee's fault. We are all at fault and all to blame because of our own indifference to what is going on around us, and even in us. Our own lack of caring and concern, and being oblivious to what is happening around us, not only allows such actions, but also encourages it. We don't want to get personally involved even to meeting our next door neighbors. We have become lazy, withdrawn, paranoid, and indifferent as a society. We sit glued to our favorite television sit-coms and are oblivious to local and world events. We are not aware of what is going on around our world, our nation, our local communities, nor in our own homes. We are thoughtlessly setting the stage for a national social collapse, leading to anarchy and/or a national revolution. But, He tells not to fear; just go through it because we need the experience. Everything is just as it is supposed to be at this time in our journey.

2009 4/26 – *"Why does the physical body have chakras? If physical food alone would sustain the body, why have these light transducers all over it? The truth is: light-energy is already our source of life-force, but most are unaware of this, and are actually defiling their bodies with* *copious amounts of animal and other physical foods that war against, and defile their bodies. Most have forgotten, or never knew, how to energize (feed) the body on light-energy, so their bodies degenerate and die. Physician, heal thyself!"*

Look around you. <u>Food</u> **is killing everyone you see!** How many times, and in how many different ways, does He have to tell us this truth. This time, He reminds us that **we have light transducers for some purpose;** they are not just nipples on a male pig. They are there for a reason, but 99.999% of the people on Earth do not even know they exist, and most who do know refuse to believe these chakras can provide total body nourishment and give continuous life (unending life) to the body. Almost everyone believes the medical, social, and philosophical community that says, "The only sure things are death and taxes." We have all chanted this stanza from time to time, but it is one of the greatest negative (false) global-thought-forms ever to infect the mind of all mankind.

Think about what He is saying, "Light-energy is already our source of life-force energy. We, most of mankind, allow very little light-energy into our bodies, except what little we are born with that helps sustain us for seventy to ninety years or some light-energy we allowed in as a child before we were programmed to not listen to our inner voices.

Where did that (the seventy to ninety years) come from? Realizing I had just written something I knew nothing about, I asked, "Lord, what do You mean by a person being born with enough light-energy to sustain him or her for seventy to ninety years?"

He answered, *"The initial stroke of love-light-energy generated by the father and mother's joyous, loving, creative act during sexual child conception energizes the child with life-force that usually sustains its body for seventy to ninety years. This life-force fades over the years until the body must release its consciousness back to the spirit world."*

Should the act of sexual union take on a deeper meaning for us? This brings up a whole new world of other considerations, doesn't it?

2009 4/29 – *"I have been preparing you for this moment! These many years, you have believed My words which were totally contrary to the wisdom, teachings, and thinking of your day. Most others are blocking my voice, and my thoughts from their minds. Yes, I speak to all, but most resist anything that disagrees with what they have been taught—the conventional wisdom of the day; therefore they are infants in their ability to effect changes in the world, the economy, the climatic conditions, or our social systems. They have no idea that all these situations are illusions that can be changed in an instant. You know you can change these illusions, and you must now change them. This is your primary reality; you have brought it to this moment. Now, rewrite the script. Make the changes you desire. I did not raise you up to this moment for you to retreat in timidity. Move forward and conquer. The new illusion you must create is PEACE, PROSPERITY, LOVE and GOODWILL, THE WORLD OVER."*

I don't know if I am being encouraged or chastised. But then, sometimes I get such far reaching revelations and instructions that I hesitate and wonder if I am sane.

I remember when my eighty-two year old dad (Pap) was suffering his last few months on Earth with lung cancer. He told my mother and my sister that they needed to take over his real estate business, and help him write his will, because he felt his mind was failing. They sought legal council on whether he would be considered cognizant enough to write a will, and would it stand up in court? Council said, that the court has already ruled in such cases, that If he was aware that his mental abilities were failing, he was certainly still capable of dictating a will. It would stand up in court.

So, maybe if I sometimes doubt my own sanity, that's a good thing; however, I do realize I am not what most would consider *normal*, but if this is insanity, it surely is fun, and I'm loving it.

Now I shall move into a new mantra and affirmation while meditating; **"There is peace, prosperity, love, and goodwill all over the world."**

2009 4/29 – *"I called you Moses back in 1985 because I had already chosen you to lead my people out of the chaos and economic bondage of this present world order into a new world of peace, prosperity, and goodwill. You are going to develop the process of fracturing the water molecule to enable water's use as a fuel source. Then, you are going to lead my people to the ultimate spiritual path of inwardly searching for and finding Me. This will free them from physical and spiritual bondage to the freedom and fullness of joy and life on this planet."*

I realize that after all the experiments that I have done in the past, just thinking I can find the process of fracturing water is an eccentric, weird, and unconventional venture. The very idea of a novice scientist discovering a way to fracture water will not be received or understood by very many people in or out of the scientific community.

However, after the experiment fires off, I patent it, and present it to the world; most will insist that I discovered the process by thirty years of constant scientific experimentation. Some will allow that, through constant prayer and supplication before God, I dragged the formula from Him, who then revealed this process to me. Few will ever believe that I may have actually developed the omnipotent ability to change the nature of water to conform to my desire concerning its nature. They will exclaim that not even God can change the chemical and biological nature of water. But, at that time, those who do believe that I changed the nature of water will understand my and their own omnipotence, and they will immediately shift to a higher realm of existence.

2009 4/30 – *"For centuries, earnest seekers have been and are now searching for victory over physical death. <u>Deeply within, they all know this is possible</u>. They have searched for the fountain of youth all over the Earth. They are living in foreign mountain caves and ashrams in continual prayer and meditation. They are restricting their diets to only fresh and raw fruits, nuts, grains and vegetables. But, within seventy to ninety years they still die. You must lead them to the truth: Only light-energy ingestion will support continual, physical body life. Tasting a bite of fruit, nuts, grain, or vegetables from time to time for joy and fellowship (after it is radiated with light-energy), will not interfere with your body's health. The physical body can only live* *into multiple centuries by receiving its life-force from light-energy ingestion."*

Did you get that? We all "deeply within" know eternal life in this body is possible. This is why Ponce de Leon, and others down through history, have searched for the Fountain of Youth. They were not insane; they were searching for their own mind's truth. They knew! Some are finding life extension through meditation, relaxation techniques and proper diet, but this message promises more than life extension. He is telling us we don't have to die at all physically, period.

The real problem is that most folks on this planet are still seeking their revelation and life instructions from other men, and completely disregarding the voice within. The men they are listening to are dying just like themselves. The dying teachers are teaching death! What else would they be teaching and believing? The dead are burying the dead, as Jesus said.

I love it that I was told again that tasting a bite of fruit, nuts and/or vegetables (after infusing it with light-energy) will not interfere with my body's health. What is the mouth and teeth for if not for tasting something sometime?

A very thought provoking book for life extension and health is: *The Fountain of Youth*, by Peter Kelder. After reading that book, we would do well to practice the five rites recommended in Kelder's book.

2009 4/31 – *"You thought it, so you brought it!"*

I was complaining about the economic situation again, so He just told it as it is. I created the situation by my own thought processes; therefore, I must correct it. I think, perhaps, you all helped me create the present illusion, don't you?

2009 5/4 – *"Let me remind you again about FORCE-OF-WILL. Everyone has trouble with 'What is Force-of-will?' FORCE-OF-WILL is ABSOLUTE DETERMINATION to create, do, or have some thing or*

result. The highest form of intent is ABSOLUTE DETERMINATION. I have told you this before."

2004 11/10 - *"Think on FORCE OF WILL. This force of will is absolute determination to create the situation desired."*

Often, I consider the Force of Will that was necessary to blast this universe into being from pure consciousness. How much mental/spiritual force, and how long did it take to develop that technique? How much focus does it require to sustain this creation?

2004 11/11 - *"Think on the CREATIVE FORCE OF WILL."*

He keeps coming back to me with this. Of course, He does; it is the most important lesson we must learn as awakening gods.

This was previously taught on 2003 2/21. *"Remember the creation of the Sun? That light beam was focused consciousness. Consider this and learn to focus your consciousness on what you desire."*

This vision about the sun being created was revealed in my first book and inspired the cover scene of my standing in a doorway watching a beam of light focusing on a spot in the universe eventually forming the sun.

I'm praying about this Creative-Force-of-Will and the focus that accompanies it. I want to know exactly what He means by Force-of-Will. I'm sure it is a technique of focusing emotions during a time I'm trying to change a situation, or possibly see someone healed. He will make this known to me.

2009 5/6 – *"Think of the word INTENSE when thinking of the word INTENT. Omnipotent creative intent is INTENSE, ABSOLUTE DETERMINATION."*

My Father is continually trying to open my understanding for me to further realize the thinking process that brings instant creative ability. He expresses the meaning of Force-of-Will over and over again. Each time I have the thrill of a deeper insight and understanding of what it takes *mentally* to create something from nothing, and to feel my mind more closely meshing with His regarding this process. The emotional evolution in this process is baffling, and extremely exciting.

2009 5/6 – *"Remember when I told you* (on 1999 1/5), *'You are like a piece of a jig-saw puzzle. You are an indispensable part of the whole, of Me. I am not complete without you.' <u>I have entrusted a unique, indispensable part of my own soul to each of you.</u>"*

> On (2000 4/13, *The Last Enemy*), He said, *"Without you, I would not exist."*
>
> On (2000 4/1, *The Last Enemy*), He said, *"This consciousness that you are, is a Holy thing. It is unfathomably beautiful. It is a unique part of Me that is unmatched anywhere in existence."*
>
> On (2002 12/4 as recorded in this book) He said, *"Love Me in them! Hidden in each one of them is a unique part of Me. Find it and you will find another adorable part of Me and of yourself. Think of the pearl hidden in the oyster. I'm there, find Me!"*

You know, if we could ever really understand and believe this, it would solve most of the conflict in our lives. If we realize we were talking to a unique part of our Father when we confront another person, could we become angry and disgruntled with him or her? Or, would we instead, try to encourage that one to reveal his loving side to us? Would we counter his or her anger, sarcasm, and rudeness with love, joy, and tenderness until they melt before us in relaxed jubilation? This is why we are here—to defuse the fear, anger, hatred, and suspicion and redirect it into love, joy, peace, grace, faith, and union with us and our Father.

2009 5/12 – *"Why have I waited so long to reveal the truth of light-energy ingestion to you? Would others believe a young man in perfect health telling them to fast and ingest light-energy for perfect health and longevity? No, they would not, and very few will believe a one hundred year old former heart patient who looks thirty years old, and runs marathons. However, the few that do believe will lead the rest of humanity to life."*

It appears that I am going to totally recover from the tissue damage caused by my four heart attacks and then begin running again, which I dearly love. Years ago, I ran five to seven miles a day.

A friend who is interested in what the spirit world says to me, after hearing this, asked, "Do you really believe you are going to become perfectly healthy again and revive your biological, thirty year body appearance?"

I answered, "I certainly do! If I could experience a gasoline semi-tanker driving through my body, and find it perfectly intact and unharmed, I can certainly believe He can rearrange the cells of this heart and body to again be biologically thirty years old, and remain at that age level for centuries."

2009 5/13 – *"During an extended fast, why should you radiate the morsel, or taste of food, that you decide to eat? The reason is that in doing so you are infusing the morsel of food with the real, basic food energy, light-energy.*

This is why the custom of blessing food before we eat a meal, was brought down through the ages. Originally, people knew the safety and nourishment of food came from the blessing (light-energy infusion), *and not from the dead physical food product itself. Even vegetables, fruits, and nuts are dead food products, and will eventually decompose* (rot). *Light-energy is the only continually-living food source for your bodies."*

In the major religions, the people follow many customs for reasons of tradition, but even most of the religion's leaders have long ago lost the truth and significance of the power these rituals have. Just as the Catholic Church uses "holy water" in its ceremonies even to blessing ships with it, few of the priests know the power of this ritual, and certainly don't know that without focused intent they are losing much of the power of their ritual. <u>Few know we are all omnipotent Sons of God</u>, and therefore are able to infuse power and life-force into this ceremony. Most priests are unaware of the magnificent power of the ceremony they are performing.

I personally believe that much of the destruction and concealment of deeper knowledge has been a deliberate attempt to hide or destroy these truths in order to keep the people subservient to the various political ruling classes and religious orders. Truth frees people—ignorance enslaves.

2009 5/14 – *"Add to your description of Force-of-Will the word* <u>BLIND</u>. *Omnipotent creative Force-of-Will is* **intense, absolute, blind determination.** *It is blind to the accepted thinking and even blind and contrary to proven scientific facts. Intense, absolute, blind determination will change scientific facts!"*

I love this! Somehow, someway, He is going to lead me to the water, and force me to drink of the deeper truth, until I cross the threshold from ignorance to knowing and am able to speak any condition or situation I desire into existence. Every time He talks about determination, I understand more fully what creation entails. Our thinking is changing scientific theories everyday, but we call it scientific discoveries and innovations.

2009 5/15 – *"Everything that exists is a fragment of the whole, of Me, yet it is all of Me. That is why every cell and every atom has independent will, volition, constitution, intent, resolve, and determination. Each fragment is able to create its own destiny as it follows the direction of its over-soul. The core of every fragment is still love—Me. That is how it all works, Jack."*

Again, volumes could be written here. What could be accomplished by us if we completely understood that every cell and atom is alive and instilled with intent to aid us in our physical and spiritual evolution?

2009 5/15 – *"I designed a way to give independent thought and eternal existence to fragments of My own self that I might intermingle, co-create and enjoy myself with each individual fragment, while still being each fragment."*

Here, He is talking of our intermingling, co-creating and enjoying ourselves with each individual fragment or inanimate object in the universes. Is there any limit to our omniscience?

2009 5/15 – I asked, "Who am I, Father, and why do You entrust these tremendous truths to me?"

Someone spoke, *"Because you are fool enough to believe them, write them down, walk in them, and publish them for My people. You are my fool, my son, and my foolishness is wiser then men."*

Wonderful! Yes, I see that "foolishness!" or "lunatic!" is the response from many who browse my book or hear me speak. They think I am a fool, or a lunatic. Some, who have branded me as such, have returned later after reading the entire book, and now we have developed deep spiritual relationships; however, I still wonder what my Father sees in me that He should entrust such great truths to me. I honestly believe it has to do with more about the future than all that has been revealed to me in the past. Somehow, I feel the journey is just beginning.

2009 5/16 – *"There are four levels of food sources for the human body. The first level, and highest level is direct life-force light-energy ingestion. Light-energy is everywhere. Even in total darkness, there is an abundance of life-force light-energy. It is Father's life-force light-energy and is omnipresent in every corner of the universes, in every dimension, and saturates the void. It is always available.*

The second level of food source is the natural vegetable kingdom. This includes vegetables, fruits, grains, and nuts. This food source feeds directly from celestial light-energy and Earth energy. It therefore contains a great amount of light-energy and will help sustain the body healthily for many years. The vegetable kingdom food source however, is diluted energy, and is dead or dying food when you eat it. Even vegetables and nuts cannot be a substitute for direct light-energy ingestion.

The third level of food source is herbivore animal flesh. <u>Gods do not eat animal flesh!</u> The herbivore animal flesh foods are nourished from the second level food source—vegetation. **Animals are not nourished by direct light-energy ingestion as are vegetables, and, therefore, their life-force is greatly diluted.**

The fourth and lowest level food source is carnivorous animal flesh. This is the worst source of food for the human body and carries very little life energy."

Note: You might find the book, *The Sunfood Diet,* by David Wolfe would be a great help in understanding vegan diets. It was certainly enlightening to me.

2009 5/20 – "I have told you that you must overcome the illusions of physicality. When this begins to happen in your life, there will be no end to the changes you will excitedly create around you. This time is near. You are already beginning to apply intense, absolute, blind, determination to your own body's health and your company's business success. You will soon apply it to your process for the burning of water."

Yes, I can see the changes in my body. I feel great. I can again do any manual labor task I desire, and I see things changing around me as I change the illusions. My only problem now with manual labor is my wife, Jonnie Ann, who is not totally convinced that I am physically able because of all my heart attacks.

I certainly am glad to see He says that I will soon apply intense, absolute, blind, determination to the process for burning water. The world is nearly at the starvation level on oil consumption, but for everything there is a season. I can see the season changing.

2009 5/21 – "Soon, you are going to meet some ETERNALS. They are very much aware of your spiritual progress. Jack, they, too, are God's fools."

I am waiting! I wonder, sometimes, if some of the people I am meeting on the street are some of the eternals. This is why I believe the scripture when it says we should do good to strangers because sometimes we are entertaining angels unawares.

2009 6/1 – *"For any meaningful results, you must move light-energy into the situation. Remember I told you to 'Share the light.' We are all light conduits?"* (1999 2/25, *The Last Enemy*)

This is our command: To send or infuse light-energy into the needful situations of others. This is the secret to meaningful prayer and intercession. We must move omnipotent life-force light-energy into individuals and into local, national, and global situations to <u>intensify their intent,</u> and avert a prolonged adverse confrontation with their present situation. Nothing much is accomplished by just nonchalantly or aimlessly holding someone or a situation up in prayer, without forcefully, and enthusiastically moving divine light-energy to them. Even then, you must take care that you do not inadvertently move against their deeper intent in their situation. They are in this situation for some spiritual progress purpose.

It could be that someone has finished his or her course in their present incarnation and has planned to leave their body. You could unknowingly send a message with your love-light-energy encouraging them to get well. This sets up a deep spiritual conflict within them. They know, subconsciously, on a much deeper level, that they are ready, and have planned to leave their body now, but you are sending powerful light-energy telling them to stay and live longer in this incarnation. This sets up a tremendous emotional conflict in the body, and the person suffers greatly.

I have been personally involved in such situations twice in the past before I realized what was going on. In the last days of two different friend's lives, I laid my hands on them and prayed for healing and quick recovery to come into their body. Both their bodies began to heat up until each one cried, "I can't stand the heat, I'm on fire! Please stop!" At the time, I was hearing this truth but was unaware of what it meant. It would be years before I would realize these people were walking out their own life plan to the exact end they had planned and ordered.

2009 6/3 – While sending light-energy to a very ill lady, she said "I don't deserve all this!" I could feel that she was talking about all the abundance she and her husband have accumulated over the years: their beautiful expensive home, its furnishings, her wonderful loving husband, and their lifestyle. She was not complaining about her illness. She was trying to explain why she felt she should depart this life.

Someone replied to her, *"Blessed are the pure in heart for they shall see God. Yes, you do deserve all I have given you. You're a beautiful flower in my kingdom, and I am raising you up."*

Then I saw a long stemmed flower being raised up in a hand and arm. It was wonderful to watch.

During my light sharing time with this lady, I did not seek a consciousness bonding, but it occurred anyway. I believe it was brought about by the depth of concern and love I have for her and her husband who have been good friends and business associates for over twenty-five years. This is the first time I have had a mind or consciousness bond with someone without my seeking it. She died two days later.

2009 6/3 – *"Remember now your technique of pulling light-energy in for cleansing and restoring the body—yours and others. Breathe in deeply, bringing in the white/golden light-energy from the celestial realms; bring it down through your crown chakra; bring it down through your entire body.*

Next, breathe in deeply, bringing up the red light-energy from the red molten core of Mother Earth through your base charka at the tip of your spine; bring it up through your entire body. This is a cleansing, restoring, healing, light-energy exercise. Use it this morning to send cleansing and healing light-energy to others. Just bring in the light, and then send it out through your arms and hands to others."

2009 6/3 – *"Teach others to view their aura's shadow in the late afternoon sun, seeing their own blue, gold and white auras. This will help them to know they are spirit beings"*

This is easily demonstrated by walking onto a section of green lawn or even better, onto a section of black asphalt pavement in the late afternoon when the sun will cast a fairly long shadow on the darker grass or pavement. Turn sideways to the sun and view your shadow. You will notice the gold aura and the blue aura at the front and back of your shadow. You will then notice the blossom of white light above your head which is your crown chakra. You are a light being, posing as a physical entity at this time. This exercise will help you know what you really are!

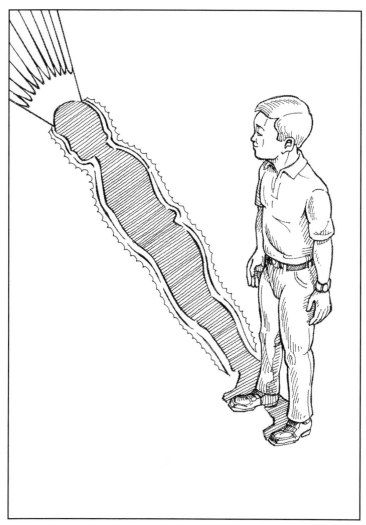

How to View Your Aura

2009 6/4 – "Jack, I'm sick!" This was said to me while I was lying awake in bed, before getting up this morning. I won't say who this person was because he may someday read this. I immediately began to send this one love-light-energy.

2009 6/4 – *"Can anyone know the future? Think back to the miracles in your life: Someone knew there was going to be a bicycle crossing in front of you at the end of the blind alley in Aiken, S.C., in 1963 (The*

Last Enemy) **when a voice shouted, 'Stop! There is a bicycle!' Then, as you slammed on the brakes, a child crossed in front of you on a bicycle.**

Someone knew the future when He emphatically exclaimed, 'Stop! Wash the gasoline out now!' Ten minutes later, fire erupted up through the drain where you had been standing and working all morning in two inches of gasoline (1975, *The Last Enemy*).

Someone gave Walter Blake a dream of the new person he was to hire, in the future, to manage a new office in Savannah, Georgia. In his dream, he clearly saw your face, your dark brown hair, your horn-rim glasses, your blue suit, your white shirt, and red tie. He recognized you immediately when you walked into his office as the one he saw three years earlier, even before your Alaskan homestead adventure. He excitedly asked, 'Where have you been? I have been waiting for you for three years!'"

I'm reminded that the scripture says, *"My people are destroyed for lack of knowledge."* (Hosea 4:6) Yes, the future is known, and it is changeable. There will be more on this later.

2009 6/4 – *"Jesus said to the raging storm, 'Peace! Be still.' Why 'peace'? Was there a war going on above them in the sky? Who was then, and is now, pushing the atmospheric pressure systems to bring hurricanes, tornados and blizzards and heat-waves upon you?"*

I said, "Father, I know it is not a devil; we settled that long ago. So then, what truth was Jesus trying to teach the disciples?"

2009 6/6 – *"Two days ago I spoke to you about Jesus calming the storm, and I asked you who was pushing the storm. The answer to the question is that Jesus knew why the wind was whipping the raging sea, the clouds rolling overhead, and the lightening flashing about them. Jesus knew that storms are manifestations of consciousness, or thought-forms, and are illusions that can be changed in an instant. You need to understand that the hurricanes, tornados, blizzards,*

Earthquakes, tsunamis, and heat waves that your people face today are thought-forms; some are regional thought-forms and some global-thought-forms.

Moreover, you need to know that the more people think on them, dwell on them, and fear them, the more power they give to them because these weather systems are just thought-forms. You must understand that you are all, unknowingly, already omnipotent sons-of-the-Most-High; therefore, you receive what you emotionally focus on. You bring all these catastrophes on yourselves. You emotionally dwell on them, and fear them so they are created and empowered forthwith.

Moreover, you have commanded before you came into this incarnation (1998 11/24 The Last Enemy) that there be a time-delay between your creative thoughts and the appearance or manifestation of those creative thoughts, just so you would not realize that you have personally created them; so you might receive the full effect of the created situations, and glean the most spiritual growth and benefit from the experiences. There are thousands, and even millions, of people thinking the same fearful thoughts with great intensity and fear, who need the same experience.

Actually, people, not realizing why they are doing so, locate themselves in the same regional areas where these catastrophes are destined to occur so they can all receive this spiritual growth opportunity. Yes, they are all in agreement, from the richest to the poorest; from the most educated to the most ignorant; from every race and creed; they all worked this out together on a deeper level for the catastrophes to occur at a particular time and location, to further their celestial journey back to our Father. The only real thing is consciousness."

This explains why we need to be careful when agonizingly praying for the "victims" of these catastrophes. They, on a deeper level, planned to participate in the particular disaster in which they are involved. **Nothing just happens! There are no coincidences!** These people located themselves in the particular disaster area, and then along with other local residences, ordered the catastrophe on themselves. We have all done this to some degree in our lifetimes. Everything in our lives has been carefully scripted and orchestrated to provide us with the greatest spiritual growth experience.

2009 6/8 – *"Believe My words as you wait and watch the situations at your business, the regional weather patterns, the water fracturing project, and your personal health situations. Know that everything has been arranged on a higher realm and is destined for your greatest spiritual learning advantage and success.*

Now apply this knowing to your business, and the water project, knowing that you are already successful.

Remember the scripture, 'And we know that all things work together for good to them who love God, to them who are called according to his purposes.'" (Romans 8:28)

2009 6/8 – *"Jack remember also, 'To every thing there is a season, and a time to every purpose under the heaven…'* (Ecclesiastes 3:1) *That time for you is near."*

I replied, "Yes Father, I am very much aware of the timing aspect of everything you do. I know when the vessel is ready, it will be filled."

2009 6/9 – *"Jack, most of those near you will not believe your words on fasting until you prove them. When you prove the words, some very close to you will believe, begin a fast, and miraculously heal their bodies through following your example in light ingestion and fasting. Others, who have only read your book, but don't know you, will also follow your example, and be healed of miserable debilitations. Go for it, my son, for them and yourself."*

I know most people will not believe the words, and some will openly rebuke the words and me. Everything is as it should be.

2009 6/9 – This morning, I asked, "Lord, how do I love uncontrollable, negative, habitual hunger back to a positive impulse?"

He answered, *"You have to remember these 'hunger impulses' are spirits. You have never fully understood or received this fact. You have, however, observed and acknowledged it in others, even piously, in times past, calling them 'demon spirits.' Now, understand that in yourself, gluttony is a spirit that needs to be loved back into a positive impulse position. It wants to help and be faithful to you. Face this spirit entity with love. Love it, and reprogram* (re-polarize) *it to become a faithful helper in your quest for a lengthy, fasting experience. It will help you on your quest to hold a fast indefinitely."*

(See: 2003 8/1 on re-polarize)

I said, "Father, I remember how I used to try to war against my ego (Ida), and now I cherish her and praise her for her help in my spiritual journey. These spirits of gluttony will respond as well and guide me to the perfect fasting experience. Thank you, Father."

2009 6/9 – I asked, "Father, why do I constantly forget to radiate my food before I eat it?"

He answered, *"I am helping remind you! I sit with you every time you sit down to eat, and then you cloud your own mind to this urgent ritual. You will continue to do so until you are ready for a total fast."*

Yes, I know, because I sit down to eat thinking, "This time I shall bless and radiate my food." But, before I raise my hands to place them over the food, the thought of radiating the food vanishes, and I dig into the meal. Then, about half way through the meal, I think "What happened? Why did I not follow through with the radiation and praise?" I find myself confounded for the rest of the meal.

2009 6/10 – This is day one of my total fast. I intend to fast totally with the exception of my coffee, and rice milk with any pills I take. Other than that, Father told me earlier that a taste of food will quell my appetite "if" I am ingesting light-energy.

2009 6/10 – *"In our Father's kingdom, there are no servants, but all serve."*

I love this! Our Father, the greatest and holiest of all is the most humble servant of all. "Praise you Father!"

2009 6/11 – *"Remember the Scripture about the relationship of the Father and Jesus in the new Kingdom?"*

I thought, "Yes, Father, You are reminding me of the Scriptures in 1 Corinthians 15: 24-28": *"Then cometh the end, when he shall have delivered up the Kingdom to God, even the Father; when he shall have put down all rule and all authority and power. For he **must reign till he hath put all enemies under his feet.** The Last Enemy that shall be destroyed is death. For **He hath put all things** under his feet. But when he saith all things are put under him, it is manifest that he is excepted, which did put all things under him. And when all things shall be subdued unto him, **then shall the Son also himself be subject unto him that put all things under him, that God may be all in all."***

"I have many glorious children and Yeshua ben Joseph (Jesus) *is one of the most faithful."*

I don't know why this subject was brought up at this time, but probably, someone is having trouble about Jesus' position among the rest of us in the Kingdom of our Father.

The scripture also says, Jesus was the firstborn among many brethren, (Romans 8:29) *"For whom he did foreknow, he also did predestinate to be conformed to the image of his Son, that he might be the firstborn among many brethren."* This verse signifies the equality of us all in the kingdom; however, in my heart, Jesus is still Lord in my life, and I don't see that changing.

Verse 26 is the place where the title of my first book originated. If you have wondered who The Last Enemy is?—It is <u>death</u>.

2009 6/12 – *"You need to let others know that you are now able to observe the chakras' colors as you are drawing in their different light colors, even without imagining the colors."*

Today, with my eyes closed, I am seeing the golden light from the celestial realms when I draw light down from my crown chakra; I see vivid, bright, red, light when I draw light up through my base chakra from the red, molten, core of Mother Earth; I see green and then pink light from my heart chakra, and bright yellow from my solar plexus. There is no concentration now involved in seeing colors other than imagining pulling light-energy in through these chakras. This is beautiful, and it is certainly a confirmation that the traditional chakra colors are correct. Now, I realize how the far-eastern yogis knew the chakra light colors, and the native American Indians, ten thousand miles and oceans away, also knew them. They all discovered the colors as they prayed and mediated. Fascinating!

**2009 6/13 – **This is day three of my fast. Day three of a fast is always the hardest. This is the day one's body usually goes into Ketosis, and total body detoxification begins. You can verify Ketosis by the tongue coating over with a white film. Note: You will find more on Ketosis in the Addendum in the message received on 2000 7/17.

2009 6/15 – *"Having the truth and knowing the truth are two different things. Having the truth about the benefits of fasting, and knowing these benefits, are totally different experiences. Being told the truth that water will burn, and watching it burn, are totally different realities. As I told you before, being told about sex, and experiencing sex, are totally different experiences. One must experience truth for it to be real to him."*

I pleaded, "Father, allow me to continue a fast until I experience all the physical and spiritual benefits. Help me, Father!"

2009 6/19 – This is the ninth day of my fast. I am taking medication with rice-milk and ingesting little else. Sometimes, at mealtimes with friends, I will eat a mouthful of vegetables or bread. Today however, I was very busy and did not take time during the normal meal-time to ingest light-energy as I have been instructed. That was a mistake! My Father told me to ingest light-energy during traditional mealtimes when on a total fast (2003 10/8). Later on in the evening I noticed as I rose from the sofa to get a glass of water that I was a bit dizzy. I shrugged it off and returned with my water. The next time I rose to let my doggy buddies outside, I nearly fainted I was so dizzy. I had to grab hold of the sofa to keep from falling, and cautiously I eased back down on the sofa, hoping Jonnie Ann didn't see it. Then, I realized I had not fed my body with light-energy as I have been instructed, so my body was beginning to react to starvation. I immediately began to pull in light-energy through my crown chakra and base chakra. The dizziness vanished, and I could feel the stabilization throughout my body. A few minutes later, I jumped up and let Duke and Tigger out. Four or five more times, I rose to do various things and felt great. What a demonstration of truth on light-energy ingestion.

2009 6/19 – *"A spiritual master ministers to others before he ministers to himself. His needs are few; theirs are many. Always send light to Mother Earth and others when you pause to meditate or ingest light-energy. These little ones are depending on your faithfulness."*

2009 6/20 – *"Remember again what I told you about your connection to Mother Earth. I told you that you and she are one physical being. This connection is not readily visible, but it is very real. You are invisibly but physically, connected, and her body is part of yours."* (See 2000 1/27, *The Last Enemy*)

> **2000 1/27** - *"Disregard the apparent non-connection with Mother Earth; this is an illusion. You are connected absolutely."*
>
> Here is a paradox! We are independent, physically, of Earth, but yet joined absolutely to her as if we are still joined by an umbilical cord. We are babies still nursing off our mother. As such, she will give us nourishment whenever we breathe in her energy, just as does a mother as her baby nurses.

2009 6/20 – I am now in the tenth day of my fast. Jonnie Ann and I have come up to our mountain house for the weekend. While walking up and down my steep driveway getting tools and material for a job, my legs began to get weak. My pulse rate was no problem, since it was still at about 82, which is normal for me when exerting moderate physical energy at these altitudes, but the weakness was noticeable, I thought, "This is probably from fasting for ten days."

Someone said, *"Remember My exhortation to you, to pull more energy up from Mother Earth through your feet?"* Look at the words on 1999 11/30, *The Last Enemy:*

> *"Don't neglect your feet. Pull my light-energy up through your feet too."*

I recalled also what had been said to me just this morning during meditation, and so with each step I took, I breathed in the red light-energy from my dear Mother Gaia. I brought it up through the foot touching the ground as I walked. The weakness disappeared immediately. I kept up this light-energy breath rhythm all the way up the driveway until I reached the top. The weakness did not return.

2009 6/20 – I have been made keenly aware today that when I just take a small taste of something for pleasure during a fast, I must stop eating with just that one taste. Any more than a taste will generate an appetite for more food. Light-energy ingestion is critical to eliminating hunger. It is the light-energy **food** that satisfies my body's hunger, not the physical food being tasted. This has always been true in this physical reality, but few have ever realized it. I remember the words given on 2000 11/9:

> *"The body is light-energy. It must feed on its source."*

The words "keenly aware" here are an understatement. I mistakenly took a couple of mouthfuls at breakfast, and immediately found myself ravished by hunger. I ate more and realized the fast was over for this time, and that I would have to start all over again to experience a sustained fast. We live and learn, don't we? This was a lesson I needed to experience before I begin another fast. I must remember once and for all that, *just a taste will satisfy, but a mouthful will break the fast.* What I should have done when I was tempted to take another taste was pause and begin bringing in light-energy, instead of a second bite—the fast would have continued. I broke my fast!

2009 6/23 – *"Pay close attention now to how you breathe in light-energy, especially the termination points, as you bring in the energy from your crown and base chakra. The termination point from Crown Chakra light-energy is the perineum/gonad area. The termination point from Base Chakra (Mother Earth) light-energy is the Third Eye."*

This might be a good time to review two messages I received in 2000 concerning light-energy meditation. You will notice that the only difference in what He is telling me now and then is that now, in ministering to our own body, the upward termination point for energizing the body is the third eye instead of the celestial realm, and the downward termination point is the perineum or base chakra. Other than that, the meditation is exactly the same.

> **2000 2/4 - I am being led to meditate on the double helix crop formation in England.**

Almost everyone is familiar with the double helix, our molecule chain. Below, Mother Earth is showing us something wonderful through the double helix crop formation.

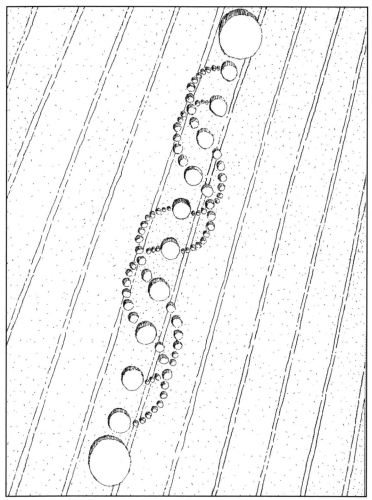

The Double-Helix Crop Formation

2000 2/5 - *"Consider the double helix crop formation. Mother Earth is showing a meditation of breathing in light-energy for the regeneration of the DNA. It directs us to breathe in light-energy swirling clockwise* (as viewed from above) *from the celestial realms down through the crown chakra, down the spinal column to the base, root, or perineum chakra. Then, breathe out through the base or root chakra into the core of Mother Earth. With the next breath, she is instructing us to breathe in light-energy swirling counterclockwise, from Mother Earth up through your base chakra, up the spinal column to the third eye and crown charkas. Then, breathe out through the crown chakra into the celestial realms."*

I found that after breathing this way for some time, I could then take deep breaths of light-energy in through all my chakras at once. What a lift! This is one of the most invigorating experiences I know. The clockwise and counter-clockwise is seen by viewing the body from above.

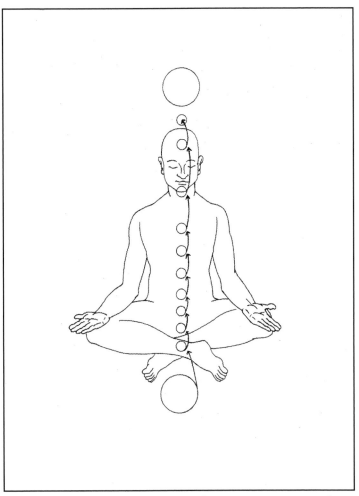

Double-Helix Meditation—Bringing Light-Energy up From Mother Earth

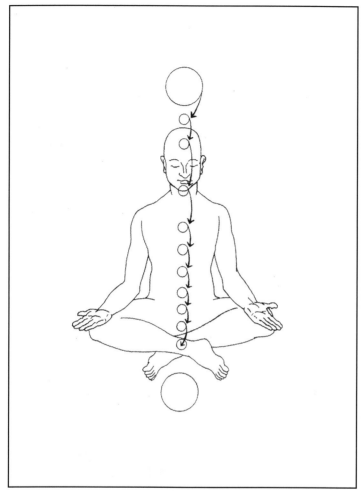

Double-Helix Meditation—Bringing Light-Energy down From the Celestial

2009 6/24 – *"Time is an illusion. I have told you this many times, but there is more truth to think about. You can re-write the script for your life both forward and <u>backward</u> in time. Yes, you can change the past or the future! <u>The future is known and the past is changeable.</u> In your present mode of thinking, this will be hard to understand, but so is most great truth. The truth is: You are not limited to what you can do. Remember, you are in a dream, dreaming. It is just a dream, nothing here is real. You can spin the record backward if you wish. Nothing is impossible for Me or you."*

Our Father lives outside of time. He sees time as a linear capsule from its beginning to its end, simultaneously. He is able to manipulate it from any point in its capsule. It does not matter that a change in the past changes the future. He knows the future was destined to change with the changes to the past…Also look at 1999 7/21, *The Last Enemy*:

> *"Disregard time. Get outside of time, and come back in, in the time period and situation you desire. All parallel existences are already there. You already created them through your imaginations. They already exist. Just focus there. There is no guilt! You are not destroying this present time period as you go to another. You exist in many parallel time realities. You are just shifting your awareness to another time reality. It is all done with the mind through imagination. Expect it, embrace it, and it will shift; it will appear.* "

He tells us we can shift our consciousness in time in either direction—past time or future time realities because all is known and all is changeable.

He says, *"Expect it, embrace it, and it will shift; it will appear."*

2009 6/25 – *"Send love-light-energy to Mother Earth during your meditations. Breathe in deeply, pulling light-energy in from the celestial realms, down through your Crown Chakra; down through your arms to your hands, down your spine to your perineum; and down your legs to your feet. Then with a deep exhale breath, push the love-light-energy from your hands, feet and perineum down into Mother Earth to the pulsing crystal at her core. The five chakras in your hands, feet and perineum are all together transmitting love-light-energy to our Mother Gaia. This loving energy exchange through these five chakras to Mother Earth is the reason the ancients gave the sacred number five to stand for motherhood. Make sure the soles of your feet are touching the ground or floor during this exchange; however, you never lose your total physical connection to Mother Earth."*

> (2000 1/27, *The Last Enemy*) *"You and Mother Earth are one physical being, just as surely as your hands are a part of your physical body."*

You and Mother Earth are One Physical Being

2009 6/25 – *"The creative force-of-will, the intense, absolute, blind determination needed to accomplish a desired result must be sufficient to overcome all the negative or opposing thought-forms on a situation that hold things as they are. An example would be the economic downturn that your entire planet is now experiencing. To change this situation, you must overcome this global-thought-form of fear that holds it in place by highly emotional focused, intense, absolute, blind, determination. You must affirm that, 'All is well with this robust world economy.' It will change to the degree that you can focus on a growing,* *booming, economy. I declare that you are able to focus to a point where you will overcome the fearful thought-forms of five billion people. Yes, you are able because this is your primary reality."*

Note: He is saying that the economy is changed in proportion to the degree of intensity of our affirmation. What should our response be to this truth? I believe our response should be to declare and affirm emotionally: "This world economy is vibrant and strong, and this vibrant economy will continue for generations."

2009 7/7 – *"Eating-until-full is evidence of food addiction. Eating animal flesh and animal products is highly addictive, and is very harmful to your body.*

Look at the book of Enoch, chapter seven, for references to animal flesh addiction. You will find some truth there."

The seventh chapter of the Book of Enoch talks about the Nephilim (Giants) that were present in ancient times in the Middle East and other areas of this planet. They were meat eaters, and it seems they taught us to eat the flesh of animals. I wonder if these giants were the Anunnaki of old from the planet Nibiru as describe in Zecharia Sitchin's books? I noticed that some of the ancient carvings show the Anunnaki kings in Sitchin's book are much larger than the subjects standing before the kings, (*Divine Encounters*, page 130; *The stairway to Heaven*, pages 187 and 121). Nonetheless, we have become addicted to the taste of animal flesh, and it is killing us.

He spoke again, ***"The digestive system of the human species was designed for the processing of small amounts (tastes) of fruits, nuts, and vegetables for enjoyment. Light-energy is your staple and essential food source."***

Look at the size of most fruits and nuts. Most fruits grow to the exact size for a good taste treat and enjoyment but will not fill you up. Also, it is interesting that one nut, such as a pecan or walnut, which is much smaller than most fruits, is big enough to give you the hunger satisfaction of feeling full, and it is rich in protein. Try it. Take one whole pecan, hold it in your hand, send light-energy radiation into it, eat it, and drink some water. Your hunger will be satisfied, *if* you have ingested light-energy first.

2009 7/8 – I felt love and peace enter the palms of my hands during a light-energy session this morning. I was immediately aware that the soft feeling in my hands was peace and love. It was so light and very soft, and shaped like a little ball to my feeling. I never knew we could feel emotions through the touch sensitivity of our hands. What else will I discover on this journey?

2009 7/8 – *"Consider again what enlightenment means. I told you* (1999 7/10), *'Enlightenment means bringing in light. Become enlightened. Intensify the light.' To become enlightened, bring in more and more light-energy until you become one with the light. That light is the consciousness of the Father."*

I declared, "Yes, Father, I realize that light is You and Your very essence is love, as You told me earlier, *"Study love, seek love for it is the fast track to ascension."* We forget that Your essence is a conscious emotion—LOVE. We can know You are near when we feel concentrated love around us. Let me feel You near always, Father."

2009 7/8 – Someone recently e-mailed me saying he was having trouble understanding the words concerning *sequential* and *simultaneous* reality experiences where I was told: (*The Last Enemy,* 1999 7/22).

> *"There are two ways to experience life: linear sequential experience, or simultaneous experience."*

He did not understand the difference between sequential and simultaneous experience.

Maybe this explanation will help: Before we decided to incarnate into these three dimensional bodies, we lived in innocence, without the teachings of experience, but as omnipotent entities, we had all the abilities of conscious creativity; therefore, anything we imagined was created forthwith. There was an instantaneous response of manifestation of the thing or situation imagined; hence, whatever we wanted, instantly appeared. We were not even aware we created it—at first. We were experiencing *simultaneous* reality creativity. There was no waiting or time delay, no wishing for it, or asking for it—we imagined it and it appeared. We eventually realized that we had a problem: Since we were omnipotent, we were capable of creating situations contrary to our Father's wishes; situations and manifestations of consciousness that might not be of love, but selfish, hateful situations, or other beings that could eventually produce chaos in the kingdom of our Father.

We realized that we needed, wanted, and must have consciousness maturity! We realized we could not grow and mature as spiritual beings in that *simultaneous* reality environment. We must have a time-delay between the desire and the receiving of a thing; a time-delay environment where we would have to wait for the manifestation of our desires. We wanted to have the experience of desiring a thing or situation, and not seeing it immediately appear before us.

This time-delay environment would necessitate temporary amnesia along with the time-delay manifestation of our desires, or a *sequential*, linear-time, reality experience. First, we would experience the desire, then the waiting, then the emotional drawing of the desired thing or experience to us, and then its manifestation—hence *sequential*, linear, creative reality experience. One of the hardest decisions for us was realizing this *sequential* time-delay; linear experience must also provide a temporary amnesia of whom and what we really are, and separation from our Father. This would terrify anyone, especially beings who know they are now omnipotent. We needed all this so that we could experience living in fear and separation, until we realize the truth that living in love is the only place of eternal peace and joy in all realms of consciousness.

This *sequential*, linear, experience is the great teacher of whom and what we are, but it is not our future permanent reality as gods. Our future, in the family of our Father, is to exist as we were before this linear, *sequential*, reality existence. We will return to our *simultaneous* reality existence as omnipotent, **EXPERIENCED**, mature, co-creators with our Father.

2009 7/9 – *"Remember what I told you last month concerning the economic situation* (2009 6/25). *I said, 'It will change to the degree that you can focus on a growing economy.' Keep this truth in mind. I was giving you a great central truth about your and My nature. <u>Every time we focus our attention with intense determination, something changes! It changes to the degree that we focus our attention. It always changes a situation to some degree.</u> Right now, you are still an infant in the use of spiritual energy, but you are growing, and as you grow, your intensity and focus becomes greater and greater until you can speak to a mountain and tell it to move into the sea, and it will obey.* (He is making reference here to the Bible verses in Mark 11:23: *"For verily I say unto you, that whosoever shall say unto this mountain, Be thou removed and be thou cast into the sea; and shall not doubt in his heart, but shall believe that those things which he saith shall come to pass, he shall have whatsoever he saith."*) *You are growing up My son. Now, love must temper all your creative action. Don't interfere with the predetermined, prearranged quest of others with your creative powers. Be patient and seek My wisdom when moving creative energy into any situation."*

Thankfully, I replied, "Father, especially for the clause 'It always changes a situation to some degree.' I think on this truth every day now as I pray and send light-energy to others and to various situations. Years ago, (1998 *The Last Enemy*) you said, *'You influence everything spiritually.'* I didn't know the extent of what You were saying then, but now it is clear. Prayer does change things! It always changes a situation to some degree—to the degree that we are earnest and intensely focused in order to make it happen. Again, You said on 2006 12/8 that the change is proportional to our focus-of-will. Thank you, precious Father."

2009 7/10 – *"Sometimes during your meditations, like right now, you feel it may be you speaking instead of Me. It is you, Jack, for you and I are the same consciousness. You feel you already know certain truths as they come into your consciousness. You do! You already know all truth, but you are just awakening to this. It will be a bit confusing for you from now on to know exactly who is speaking. I can assure you that it is Me, and it is you revealing the truth. Rest in Me!"*

2009 7/12 – *"Nothing is impossible to you now because nothing is impossible to Me. Everything in your linear time, physical experience are illusions and dreams, but not eternal reality. It is but a stage play and can be rewritten at any place in the play and replayed to suit your desires. The reason you are now allowed to change the manuscripts for your life's program is that you have progressed unto such a state of enlightenment that <u>love will constrain and direct your actions</u> to allow others to live out their prearranged destinies. You are now living in the realm where you assist the destinies of others as they are living in that state of being where 'all things work together for good to them...'"* (Romans 8:28)

This is the explanation of why we are where we are. We have to grow in love to a point where we can handle omnipotent power; else we could destroy everything on Earth.

2009 7/13 – At a dinner theater outing last night, there was a lull or boring time in the program. At my back-row corner seat in the dark auditorium, I decided to use the time for some light-energy meditation. A few minutes later, I began to feel a strong pulsing in my hands, and as time went on, it became stronger and stronger until it felt as though I was holding a live 120 volt wire in my hands. It also felt as though my hands were holding a vibrating piano string. Realizing there was tremendous energy being transmitted to my hands, I concentrated first on sending love-light-energy to Mother Earth, then to others who have asked for help, then to healing the world economy, then to my own company, and then to my own body. The high energy transmission continued there in the theater for about twenty minutes and then returned unsolicited again later during the show. I had a ball sending love light-energy to Mother Earth and everyone I could think of. Then the knowing that situations were changing for all involved came also. What a night.

2009 7/13 – I was having trouble with the air conditioner at our home. Finally, after some personal maintenance on it, it seemed to be working properly. The following morning as I was praying and meditating, someone spoke these words:

"Jack, when you turn on your air conditioner, or your furnace, to change the temperature comfort level in your home, this is the exercise of a global-thought-form. One hundred and fifty years ago, this was not possible because people were not yet aware that such was possible. Now, they believe it is possible, so they walk up to their thermostat and set the air conditioner or heat level at whatever temperature they desire.

A similar temperature changing thought-form experience was being practiced by the early American Indians on their Spiritual Quests. In the middle of the winter, a young Indian lad would journey miles from his tribe with nothing more than a small cloth or animal hide. He would imagine that the small cloth would keep him alive and warm in the icy cold of a mountain winter, and it did. It was simply faith in the operation of a thought-form, a tribal-thought-form.

Today, most people don't believe in these individual miracle thought-forms, but are convinced that if they manipulate the thermostat, they can change the temperature in our house. But, neither the thermostat, nor the furnace, nor even the house is real; these are all just illusions. Most think (global-thought-forms) *it is all real, so their illusion produces the warmth or cooling they desire. Do you see where I am going? Nothing is real! It is all imagination. Imagine what you will with the same total confidence that you have in a thermostat, and it will come forth."*

Why can't we get this? It is all just illusions. If we could just muster the same confidence we have in the thermostat on the wall or the starter button in our car, we could change the creation around us. We can change the global-thought-forms of illness, famine, war, weather, and chaos if we could only understand that it is all just illusions, <u>our illusions</u>. We can change any illusion! We can change anything!

2009 7/13 – As I was relaxing in our sunroom with Jonnie Ann and <u>rereading</u> *The Lost Book of Enki*, by Zachariah Sitchin, I began to have a series of sharp pains in my left ankle, sharp enough that with each jolt, I would jerk violently. Jonnie Ann shouted, "What's wrong?" She thought I was having a heart attack. I told her about the pain in my ankle and she relaxed. Finally, I had to get up and try to walk it off. No good! The sharp pains continued. I finally stumbled into my study and dropped down in a chair. I grasped my ankle in my hands. The same vibration and pulsing I had felt at the dinner theater the night before returned to my hands and instantly the pain ceased. A few minutes later I was reminded of an accident I had in the mid 1960's. I severely sprained my ankle and thought I had chipped a bone when I stepped on a rock on a dimly lit road while jogging. This was the same ankle and the same intensity of pain I felt that night when I had to crawl two blocks to my house. I quickly realized this was a healing crisis that was repairing that old injury. What a journey!

Since I have mentioned Zachariah Sitchin's books before, some of you are wondering if you should go out and pick up a copy of the *Lost Book of Enki*, or some of Sitchin's other books, and I would like to encourage you to do so; therefore, maybe I should make a few comments about his books.

I became interested in archeology in college, and ever since have read as much as I can find time for on archeological discoveries. I'm always amazed at what the ancients were doing and teaching.

Over the years, I found and have read all of Zachariah Sitchin's books because he, during a lifetime of study, so meticulously documents every hieroglyphic symbol he translates, and because his findings do not conflict with the words I have received from the spirit world.

In the many books from Sitchin's studies of archeological discoveries around the world and especially in Egypt and the Middle East, he tells us, of the Anunnaki, beings from the twelfth planet in our solar system, named Nibiru, Sitchin's writings tell us the Anunnaki arrived here the last time over three hundred thousand years ago to embark on a gold mining mission and operation. The ancient writings tell us that powdered gold was crucial to repair their planet's deteriorating atmosphere. They were still here mining gold when the great deluge drowned most of the inhabitants of Earth some twelve to fifteen thousand years ago. The Anunnaki were aboard their space ships well out in space when the deluge occurred.

After the great flood or deluge, and after the Anunnaki had completed their gold mining operations, but before they departed, the visitors from Nibiru decided to set up some sort of government on Earth to help lead the primitive Earth-people into a more civilized society; so they set up theocracies or god-kings that would have total control over these Earth-people while they developed into an effective civilization. These god-kings ruled in Egypt for hundreds of years, RA, being the first pharaoh (RA actually was Marduk, an Anunnaki, a grand-son of Enki, who was a son of Anu, the King of Nibiru).

According to Sitchin, the ancient writings tell us that the normal Anunnaki people live thousands of their sars (One sar, or one Nibiru orbit of the sun, equals over 3,600 of our years), so it would be easy for the short-lived inhabitants of Earth to believe these kings were gods—god/kings. The earthling's grandparents, great grandparents, great-great grandparents, and so on, lived under the rule of and talked about RA and his glory, that he was an immortal being and that he was a God.

They, the Anunnaki, of course, were not gods, but they certainly were scientifically, at least, highly advanced beings from another planet. When and if, as promised in the hieroglyphic, the Anunnaki do return, some even today will believe the gods have returned. Sorry folks, they still are not gods! They still have the same character weaknesses that we have, the same drives, fears, and faults we display. They may even come claiming to be gods, but we will not yield to that ploy again.

When the Spanish conquistadores arrived on the shores of Central America in their great sailing ships, the Aztecs thought they were the gods returning (The Anunnaki had mining operations in Central and South America, too.) as they had long been taught by many ancient writings. However, the murderous, looting, Spanish soon proved to the Aztecs that they certainly were not Gods.

It is interesting to me that the ancient writings say that the Anunnakies (People from the planet Nibiru) set up a theocracy or monarchy/god type government before they left this Earth, instead of some more modern democratic form of rule. Civilization on Nibiru is said to be millions of years old, yet their form of government has been for hundreds of thousands of years, a monarchy with a king and his immediate family ruling the entire planet – a one-world government.

I'm sure Nibiru tried democracy along the way and probably even a republican democracy, but they found, as some of our great philosophers ages ago realized that democracies can't last over 300 years because the non-productive, envious hordes will eventually realize they can elect their own cronies into office to loot the treasuries and give it to them. It happens over and over again, and yet we Americans are all over the world promoting and pushing democracy on the nations, even by force. And, their democracy, like ours, will eventually fail, and those (behind the scenes) who have long planned the demise of democracy await their chance to triumph and rule the world as dictators and eventually monarchs. Hopefully, they will be benevolent monarchs.

It appears that the Anunnaki were tremendous people being eight to twelve feet tall and weighing over five hundred pounds each. Probably, the Nephilim of the Bible were Anunnaki. Reference: David killed Goliath, his brother killed another Nephilim, as did one of his generals. The king of Bashan by the name of Og, was a Nephilim. When the Israelites spied out the Promised Land they found giants (Nephilim) occupying part of the holy land and reported back to Moses that they, the Israelites, appeared as grasshoppers in their sights. The spies said these giants ate men.

There are some interesting Bible verses concerning giants, or Nephilim:

(Numbers 13:33) "And there we saw the giants, the sons of Anak, which come of the giants; and we were in our own sight as grasshoppers, and so we were in their sight." (It is interesting how close the name "Anak" in this verse is akin to the word, Anunnaki.)

(Deuteronomy 2:11) "Which also were accounted giants, as the Anakims; but the Moabites called them Emims." (Here again, "Anakims" is very close to the word, Anunnaki.)

(Deuteronomy 3:11) "For only Og, king of Bashan remained of the remnant of giants; behold his bedstead was a bedstead of iron; is it not in Rabbath of the Children of Ammon? Nine cubits was the length thereof, and four cubits the breadth of it, after the cubit of a man." (This measures about fifteen feet long and seven feet wide.)

Anthropologists have found there was a race or group of people in Australia called "meganthropus." These people were of very large size – estimated at between seven to twelve feet tall. Look on the internet for more information on the ancient giants of Earth.

The planet Nibiru is said in the hieroglyphics to have a 3,600 year elongated orbit around our sun, and because it crosses some of our solar system's planets' orbits, it is named Nibiru (meaning crossing). It is interesting to me that our astronomers have discovered a huge planet (out there somewhere), not yet visible but large enough to disturb the orbits of various planets in our solar system, and have named it Planet-X. Do you think someone knows something?

The ancient hieroglyphics, according to Sitchin, tell us that the grandsons of Enki and Enlil were set up to be the Anunnaki rulers of different continents of the Earth, and had critical disagreements that eventually led to war on this planet. As the conflict escalated, one of the grandsons used nuclear weapons which in turn caused the other family to respond in-kind. The ancient records tell us that many humans, Anunnaki, and possibly warrior-androids, were killed during this war.

This story caused me to research as to where there might be evidence of nuclear reactors and/or nuclear warfare on this planet before our historical records indicate such an occurrence. I looked on the internet for information on Ancient Atomic Knowledge and found that according to this web site, the discovery that thirteen nuclear reactors existed in prehistoric times along the 200-meter mine bed in the valley of the Oklo Mountains in east Africa; furthermore, this and other articles about the discovery of archeological sites which demonstrate characteristics, including high levels of radiation, consistent with atomic explosions. There was physical evidence similar to those found at the site of current day atomic bomb test site detonations in New Mexico, and evidence of depleted uranium with plutonium products. The New Mexico atomic bomb explosions also fused desert sand into a green glass, labeled Olive Green Trinitite. Archaeologists who have been digging in the ancient Euphrates Valley were shocked when they uncovered a layer of an agrarian culture eight thousand years old, then under that, a layer of a herdsman culture much older, and still an older caveman culture; then, below that layer, they recently reached a layer of fused green glass—Trinitite. It is well known to them that atomic detonation on or above a sandy desert will melt the silicon in the sand to a sheet of green glass. It appears that nuclear warfare is not new to this planet.

That is a brief introduction to some of the information contained in the Zechariah Sitchin books, and from the internet information sites. Do I believe all this? I see no reason not to believe what the clay and lapis tablets reveal, especially when it is confirmed by present-day findings. I do see evidence that it could all be true. Maybe I will be here on Earth when Nibiru swings by next time. If so, I have some issues with the past actions of the Anunnaki.

2009 7/25 – *"Concerning the miracles earlier in your life, as I told you, you lifted the RV back up on the bridge in Alaska; you dematerialized your body, the pick-up truck, John Holman's body, and everything else in the truck during the gasoline semi-tanker incident in Alabama. You did it all, and when you come to know you did it all, you will know you can do these kinds of things anytime and anywhere. You have the ability to levitate anything, no matter how large or small. You have the ability to materialize or dematerialize anything you wish. Think about it: to materialize something physically, is to create it from nothing; and to de-materialize something, is to bring it back to nothingness. You have the ability. Now you have the understanding of what you have already done. What you have already done, you are able to do again."*

Some things like the traumatic mountain turn-a-round episode still cause me discomfort when I think about it, but through it all, I have come to realize that when I need a miracle, it will be provided. I'm really excited about my Father continually showing me this truth, and He continually encourages me to expect the miracles every time I need them. Does this make me something special in our Father's kingdom? Certainly not! Any of His children can experience the same and even greater miracles than I have seen. Remember earlier in this book on 2003 4/16, He said:

> *"Remember that no matter how much you create for yourself, it doesn't diminish what others may have; it is all spirit. You are not hording or taking away from those who have less or from those who have more. Those who have more or less than you have the same ability as do you to create anything and all that they desire; hence, as the scripture says: "…Ye have not because ye ask not."* (James 4:2)

2009 7/25 – *"A person is filled with fear to the degree that he is not filled with love. There is only love and/or fear in your lives. Fear separates one from others; it causes one to envy others; it causes one to hate others, and eventually wants to destroy them. Fear is your only real enemy. Love is your only weapon against fear."*

Can we see this message operating around us and even in our international relations and politics? Fear is the one thing that drives our more ruthless leaders to wage war on other nations. How many times has a national leader, even in this country, watched his approval rating fall in the polls, and fearing he may lose power and control, reacted by creating some kind of international incident or war-like action to appear heroic? How many times have we leaped into a major war just to spur the nation to a more productive and prosperous economy? In war-time, the president is always popular and seems heroic to us. Why? He does not rush to the front lines to personally face and fight the enemy giant like Kind David of old. He has done nothing heroic, unless you feel that political rhetoric nowadays is heroic. Why do we go along with and condone this madness? Why are we seemingly so blind and ignorant that we cannot see through these pretenders? Probably because we don't study history! Some wise man of the past said, "If we disregard the mistakes of the past, we will surely repeat them." This has been going on since civilized man has existed. Fear rules the affairs of nations and most individuals. It will continue to be the system of world order until we grow up in wisdom and love. Read, study, and pray until you understand what is going on in the world. Father will enlighten you.

On a more personal level, most people, when fearful, will try to blame others for their discomfort, and as their fear grows, so does their antagonism towards their supposed perpetrator. What happens next depends on their depth of discomfort.

A person filled with love and allowance knows his situation is of his own making, and he knows it is necessary in his life, so he blames no-one, <u>not even himself</u>. He knows that whatever is happening is necessary for his spiritual growth, no matter how uncomfortable. If he is growing spiritually, he will eventually realize he personally wrote the script for this life, and he will joyfully march on in carefree expectation.

You have heard the expression that "Some see a glass as half-empty and others see it as half-full." We perceive our life the same way. Are we being filled more and more with love or are we being filled more and more with fear? It's your glass; fill it with what you want.

Our Father certainly wouldn't blame you if you are full of fear today, but you don't have to be. **You can overcome all your fears if you know who you are.**

It has been my observation that, as people age and are forced to experience the many hardships and disappointments of life in 3-D, most of them grow more cynical, suspicious, hardened, unhappy, distrustful, pessimistic, and angry until they finally just close down and die.

Seldom do we meet the perfectly happy, loving, radiant, elderly person who knows who he or she really is and continues to grow in love, a person who loves the meeting of a new friend, and enjoys learning something new and wonderful, and can't wait to experience his or her next day.

2009 7/26 – In the middle of the night, I was awakened by a strong, painful vibration in my left hand. It resembled the feeling of what I call having a hand, foot, or leg, go to sleep. I tried to exercise my hand by squeezing it and moving it, but it wouldn't relieve the painful vibration. Then I realized it was much like the vibrations I experienced at a dinner theater episode a few weeks ago, so I asked to whom it I was supposed to be sending love energy? Immediately, a lady's face came into my mind. I concentrated on sending her energy through my vibrating left hand. The vibration increased for a few minutes and then subsided. I felt relief from the pain and a knowing that the love energy had found its mark and accomplished its purpose. I went back to sleep.

Now, I ask you, can we really rest in Him? When a need arises, He will awaken someone from their sleep to send light-energy, and by doing so, grow both of us spiritually. Could He have sent loving, healing light-energy to this lady without me? Certainly He could, but I needed this experience, and she needed the experience of the healing, and knowing it was from Him and through Me. I grew closer to our Father and to her, and she grew closer to our Father and to me. Our Father never ceases to amaze me by what He does next. It's as if I am the only one He is concerned with, but I know that He feels the same, and works the same way, with anyone who will allow Him into their lives.

2009 7/27 – "*Your physical universe is just one of many manifestations of consciousness. There are countless other types or manifestations of consciousness (realities) other than the physical, three-dimensional realities all around you, and out there. Consciousness is the only real basic reality from which all other realities originate. It is all Me, and it is all you.*"

This is interesting. I can imagine maybe one or two other possible types of realities: maybe one with height, length, width and then internal dimensions of some kind; still another that is all that and yet non-physical, but He says there are many other realities. I'm sure some are totally ethereal, but somewhere beyond that, I get lost in my own contemplations.

A message I received on 2004 3/31, **"*There are many realities operating in your present three dimensional experiences. You see them all around you, but you are invisible to some of them. Each reality is bound tightly in its own global-thought-form acceptance.*"**

This probably has to do with vibratory rate. All realities are vibrations of consciousness. Reality in our three dimensional experience is produced by the vibratory rate of an individual and his or her acceptance of a group of global-thought-forms. Some realities are so far apart spiritually (in variations of consciousness) that those people dwelling on the lower consciousness vibratory realities are not even aware of those in the higher reality levels, thereby making those in the higher level realities absolutely invisible to the lower levels. The higher reality vibratory consciousnesses can observe the lower, but are not seen, nor affected by them.

You may experience situations in which you will realize you are not being seen nor perceived by others; or you might realize you are being perceived by physical objects. (Yes, objects such as stones, plants etc., have perception of other life forms.) Just roll with the program; all is well.

It was a lonely, scary world indeed when I thought I was all alone and all by myself in a strange, cold city, or in a forest mountain wilderness, or in a vast desert wasteland. Now, I know I am never alone, for my human family is almost everywhere I go, and when I am alone in the wilderness or in the wasteland, my brother Rock, or brother Tree, or sister Gaia is there. They are always around me, and they are all various manifestations of my omnipotent Father.

2009 8/8 – In my meditations during my lying awake at 3:00 a.m. this morning at the mountain house, I became aware of a message:

"See Me in the large boulder up the mountain above your house. Know all those boulders are just other manifestations of Me. They are Me! Find Me in them, and in every animate and inanimate entity. Never fear the bus-sized boulder rolling down on your house as you have in the past. If I, as the boulder, roll down the mountain, I will always guard you and yours, as I always have.

Come up and talk to Me in the rock sometime. I am all you see and touch. You, too, are all you see and touch. Rest in Me."

2009 8/9 – I was praising our Father in me and as me this morning. He reminded me again of yesterday's message and that He is also the consciousness of the rocks, the trees, the grass and the water in the lake in front of our mountain house.

Then He began to speak again about the unit-consciousness (2007 3/6) of the boulder above our house that is so precariously perched on a small ledge some five to six hundred feet up the side of the mountain behind our house.

He said, *"The boulder is conscious as a unit, and I am the consciousness of it. Therefore, you should have no concern that it might roll down the mountain on top of your house. If it rolls down the mountain, it, as I, will simply jump your house, or dematerialize it as I pass though. It is just Me and it is just You.*

You, of all people, should know what I am capable of doing when you are in danger. You, of all people, should be unafraid and able to rest in Me in every situation."

Then, He reminded me: *"Your mountain house is also a unit-consciousness."* (Meaning: all the molecules and cells that make up the house, and everything in it, is conscious as a unit.)

Then He told me something very exciting, strange and wonderful indeed: *"The warm, welcoming, homey, feeling you and everyone else receives when they come into this house, is the unit-consciousness of the house eagerly and joyfully welcoming you back after your absence, even if it was just for you to go out to Estes Park for dinner. Your dogs feel it too, and love the house and yard because of the love and peace they feel from the house.*

Also, the house would like you to know that it was very sad when you tried to sell it two years ago, and so it changed its attitude to emitting a cold, foreboding, sense of gloom and danger when a prospective buyer looked at it. The house loves you, and wants your family relationship to continue indefinitely."

I know this sounds ridiculous to some of you, but you would have to both hear these words and then feel the emotional emissions from the house to know they are true. You would have to feel the sadness every time we leave the house to return to our home on the Front Range, and you would have to see the grief of our dogs every week as we pull away from the house and leave the mountains.

Now, this leads to further discussion. I asked, "Father, what about haunted houses?"

He answered, *"Yes, as you suspect, the houses in most cases, are doing the haunting. Very seldom is a departed human spirit involved. You see, a house, being a unit consciousness, experiences everything that transpires in the house with the people and animals that lived there. The house loves them and experiences both the positive and the negative activities of the family. If something horrific went on inside the house, the house experienced it with the people and animals involved. Sometimes, the house, being a unit consciousness, has a hard time getting over such experiences, and for a time, consciously relives those traumas as hauntings. Sometimes, the house is trying to reveal to others what really happened in the house. Other times, the house just wants to be left alone while it tries to recover from these traumatic experiences."*

Wow! Well I asked, didn't I?

2009 8/14 – *"Limitations are illusions too, Jack."*

Somehow, we forget to include our list of supposed limitations as illusions. We forget that we have no limitations, but those we personally ordered for this physical incarnation.

He spoke again, *"When you leave this physical body, you will leave many of your limitations behind. I say 'many,' because most will still see themselves as less than what they really are, and thereby still limit themselves, even in that higher realm. Father wants his sons and daughters to claim their inheritance as omnipotent, omniscient, omnipresent, beings. They must return to physicality again and again until they can see, understand, and accept this truth, and claim their places with Him."*

Perhaps, this is why there are "many higher realms" as I was told earlier in 1999.

> (1999 8/25, *The Last Enemy*) - *"There are innumerable and unimaginable bands, or dimensions, of consciousness above where you are now. These are exponentially greater than the differences in your consciousness as compared to that of the animal kingdom."*

Even in the next realm, most of us will not yet claim our omnipotence. I realize that, through each new realm, we will grow closer to our Father in all things. I think it is because, when we arrive in the next higher realm, new revelations of His glory will begin to open to us, and we will move on to higher and higher realms of love and understanding. This is a never ending journey into the glory of our Father.

2009 8/22 – *"In my recent words to you concerning 'who is speaking to you when you receive a message,' (2009 7/10) think about this: Confusion about who is speaking is what keeps most people (those striving for spiritual growth) from hearing, believing, receiving, and accepting My teachings. They surmise that it is just their own imagination and thoughts about life and spiritual matters when it is actually My speaking to them. Most of the time, they just dismiss My message as a passing thought, and disregard it, instead of analyzing the message, and trying to comprehend its depth and its supernatural origin. Most will never know in this incarnation that the Source of All-That-Is was speaking to them."*

How sad! The eternal God was trying to communicate with them, and they never allowed Him into their minds. How terrible they will feel when they leave this incarnation and realize what was going on. But, praise you, Father, that is not the end of it. They will return again and again until they get it right. Not one sheep is ever lost by this Shepherd.

Spiritual growth is a building process. It builds from one basic concept of truth to the next deeper revelation, and then on to the next, "line upon line and precept upon precept," until we come into the fullness of ascension. Isaiah 28: 9-11 says, *"Whom shall he teach knowledge? And whom shall he make to understand doctrine? Them that are weaned from the milk, and drawn from the breasts. For precept must be upon precept, precept upon precept; line upon line, line upon line; here a little, and there a little:"* We can't skip a line and continue to grow. To attain enlightenment, we must listen to, record, and re-read every word we receive until we can instantly remember every message He has spoken to us. Seek His voice within constantly.

Again, as King David wrote in Psalms 119:11, *"Thy word have I hid in my heart that I might not sin (err) against thee."* That's the way David did it, and that's the way we must come to ascension.

2009 8/26 – *"Just keep on affirming, with great passion, that the economy is strong and vibrant, Jack. As I have told you before, 'It always changes a situation to some degree' when you affirm with* *intense determination*. *You change it a little everyday, and no one can stop or deter these positive changes. They are not in charge; I Am!"*

I replied, "Yes Father, Those who are trying to tear down this great country and destroy it are confused by (what seems to be) it's resiliency, as it recovers in spite of all they can do to destroy it. You certainly are in charge."

2009 8/27 – *"When you praise Me, praise all of Me! Praise Me in every animate and inanimate entity on this planet and in all the universes, <u>both past and present</u>. Each is a distinct part of Me, and whether they are in the physical, the celestial realms, or between lives, they need your love-light-energy and encouragement. You are a healer—heal! Send love-light-energy to the universes to help and heal your other selves there. They are all you—they are all Me. Heal them all with your love. Be Me!"*

He says "heal!" here and I finally get what He means: Heal by sending love-light-energy to them so they each might use the energy by directing it to whatever service they desire. Some might use the energy to heal their minds, some to heal their bodies, some to heal relationships, and others might use it to change situations. Just send Love, Heal!

He spoke again: *"You are sending My love; you are sending Me! See the great authority I have given you. You are sending the Source of All-That-Is to them, Heal!"*

2009 9/8 – This morning during my meditations, I declared, "Father, I realize now that I can be of service to the universes only through love—through being You. Help me to love. You must increase, but I must decrease."

2009 9/12 – I was thinking this morning, "I hate to waste money on that!"

Then someone said, *"There is no such thing as waste, Jack. There is only love and abundance. When you know and live in truth, there is no waste."*

I need to think more on this and its implications. Somehow, this seems to fit in with the truths I received earlier that assured me that we all create from nothing and all physicality proceeds from nothingness. So then, the thing we think is wasteful, is nothing but specified and directed consciousness. There is no waste. Thinking "waste" is contrary to truth.

2009 9/13 – *"There is an order in fasting and light-energy ingestion. Ingest light-energy first. Fasting should follow when your body realizes it no longer requires physical nourishment. I did not tell you to fast first and then ingest light-energy. I said,* (2000 7/17, *The Last Enemy*)

> *'The truth you are now receiving about light-energy ingestion transcends the global thought-form about life sustenance. It may be the most difficult to learn and to prove, but you will prevail. It is crucial that you prove this light ingestion concept. Only by ingesting light-energy, can you sustain continual, vibrant, youthful, physical being.'"*

That is interesting. Notice: in the 2000 7/17 message, <u>fasting was never mentioned at all</u>. When we are ingesting light-energy, we are not fasting. We are feeding the body its basic life sustenance, light-energy. Maybe, if I ingest light-energy before meals, I won't be hungry, and then not eat as much. Maybe I would eat less and less until I am eating very little or nothing at all but light-energy. Now I think I finally understand what He has been saying to me all along about light-energy ingestion.

2009 9/14 – *"Remind and teach others to find the tender spots around their rib cage and breastbone, and then hold pressure on that point with their fingers for healing of internal organs."*

Yes, I personally work on my own body using this technique, quite often. When I feel internal pains in my chest or abdomen, I search my rib cage or around my breast bone for tender spots. These are the meridians, or surface connections, to internal organs and glands. There will always be a very tender spot at the surface that corresponds to the internal pain. I press this spot, and hold it until the pain stops, and the sore spot tenderness dissolves. It always works. Sometimes, the tender spot is on the rib cage on the side, under my arm. I was told this has to do with the timing of my heart beat, so I press there, and hold until the pain ceases. The pain is simply directing my attention to an organ that needs healing light-energy. I very seldom massage the tender spot because this can cause bruising, and then a different soreness results. Sometimes though, it seems to require hard massaging to stop the internal pain. I do whatever it takes to ease the internal pain. Our bodies will tell us where we need to apply healing light-energy to correct its problems.

We might do well to study the meridians of the body and the various pressure points on our head, hands, feet, and body for aligning and correcting body functions, and healing problems before they become acute. A good massage can do wonders here.

Recently, during a six-month check-up, I had an echocardiogram. I noticed the technician placed the sensor directly on the points on my breast-bone and rib-cage where I have been treating tender spots. I watched the monitor screen as the technician placed the sensor on various places on my breast-bone and on various spots under my arm. On a particular tender spot under my arm, it showed a picture of a heart valve opening and closing.

The technician remarked to another nurse that "There seems to be some calcification buildup on this valve."

I said, "That's all right, I'll take care of it." They acted like they didn't hear my comment; probably because either they didn't understand what I meant, or they heard it and thought I am insane.

I love the way my Father proves such truths as the location of heart meridians. What a beautiful *picturesque* lesson.

2009 9/15 – I was told earlier on (2001 8/31, *The Last Enemy*) to study love because it is the fast track to ascension. My Father is love; therefore coming into a closer relationship with Him, is coming into a closer relationship with love. Praise, adoration, and appreciation of Him is the path to love.

2009 9/15 – *"Don't take from the spirit world until you give to it. Send love-light -energy to others before you draw light-energy to yourself. As I said before, 'Their needs are many; yours are few.' Gods give love first, always. Share Me first. My love is always here for you."*

I exclaimed, "Yes, Father; and as You take more neglect and abuse than we can possibly imagine—from us, allow me to be more like you, Father— totally selfless."

2009 9/17 – Glory! I find now I had rather send love-light-energy to others than bring it into myself. I am finally at rest. Just use me now, Father

Someone spoke: ***"There comes a time in your spiritual progress when you realize your desire to help others overshadows your desire for personal spiritual ascension."***

I agreed, "Yes, Father, I know my spiritual ascension is unavoidable, so I rest in you. Take me wherever you want, and use me as you will. Praise you Father."

2009 9/20 – I was reading again in Masaru Emoto's Book, *The True Power of Water (pages 140-169)*. I was reading the part where Emoto is exposing a glass of water to words written on a piece of paper and then taped to the side of the glass with the printing facing the water. The emotional content of the written words changes the type of crystals formed during quick-freezing the water. The positive words love, peace, joy, appreciation, etc., will always cause water to form beautiful crystals when quick frozen. The words hate, fear, kill, fool, etc., will not form crystals at all, or will form disfigured globs of ice.

As I was reading this, a voice spoke, ***"You must understand that the printed words have <u>unit-consciousness</u>. They become 'alive' just like any other imagination that you as omnipotent beings produce. <u>So, they have the ability to communicate with the rest of creation</u>. Written words are first thought-forms, living conscious thought entities, and as such radiate out into the universes to live and influence everything,*** *just as you do. Think about this and how alive any written message must be."*

I cried out, "Lord, this never ends, does it? Does this tell us to be careful what we write, or speak?"

He spoke again, *"Everything is alive. Everything that exists is our Father. He is All-In-All, and so are we!"*

I am very conscious now that these words I am writing are becoming living spirits. Lord, make me even more mindful of this, and even more careful to write exactly what You, and my other spirit world teachers, are saying to me.

He spoke again, *"Spoken words and written words are eternal entities. This is a supernatural universe. All is just consciousness. Consciousness is All-There-Is."*

2009 9/21 *"You are now at the point in your spiritual progression where you are <u>observing more than you are personally experiencing</u> truth unfolding before you. This is because you are now living in a state of non-judgment which allows you to <u>observe life around you, and in you, through the prism of love.</u> Love breaks down every situation so that you can glean its truth as you walk through this life experience. Just observe!"*

I responded, "Yes, Father, I feel this now. I am no longer concerned with myself. I just want to be close to you. I can see and feel myself in others, even in Mother Earth and the whole universes around me. Yet, I am more aware of my own self, and the promptings of my own mind, body, and spirit.

I am now growing by observing more than I am growing by experiencing. I believe this is because the messages of truth I have been receiving for over half a century are becoming real to me. I observe others in their situations, and while observing their actions, I am becoming aware of their motivations and feelings, and why they are thinking and acting the way they do.

I feel so heavy for those around me who are going through so much doubt, fear, confusion, and anxiety about what is happening in the world. As I talk to them, and see they are trying to carry it all on their shoulders, I grieve for them in their struggles. I grieve for them because they are so closed minded to you, Father."

Relief from their burden resides in their own deeper self, but they will not listen to the still, small voice that can give them rest and peace. This gentle voice sooths the mind and allows peace by giving understanding that all we face is exactly what we need to further advance spiritually. We are all exactly where we need to be at this moment in our spiritual quest for awakening and union with our Father. We are all in this dream drama together, acting out our combined individual scripts. Yes, we wrote it all together to further our spiritual evolution.

2009 9/21 – *"Remember your affirmation concerning your physical body's strength, health, and youth. As I said before, 'Make SHY your daily mantra.' Claim your great physical <u>strength</u>, your glorious perfect <u>health</u>, and your mature <u>young</u> manhood, appearing biologically thirty years of age. See it! Claim it!"*

I know this message, and many other words in this book, must sound like the ravings of a madman to many of my readers. Sometimes they seem that way to me too. But, I have to remind myself that I have lived through the miraculous experiences that prove what I am hearing and seeing is truth.

Father reminds me that He knows the future because He has proven it so many times in my life. He has proven our bodies are not solid mass because He dematerialized its vaporous nature to allow a semi tanker to pass through it. He has proven everything in physicality is just illusions so many times so that I must accept any and every thing He tells me, no matter how contrary to common belief. The only way I or anyone else can progress spiritually is to believe and accept and rejoice in our Father's words. Lead me home, precious Father!

2009 10/10 – *"Jack, this book is finished."*

It appears that it is time for me to conclude this book and prepare it for publishing. My first book covered about fifty years of my live and this one about eight years. I expect the next book, now being written, to be published in even a shorter time—maybe even before the solar alignment on December 21, 2012.

If you would like to comment on the book or contact me for any other information, you may contact me on my e-mail address: carljbentley@ msn.com.

TO BE CONTINUED

My next book is titled:

FROM "AM I?" TO "I AM!"

TEACHINGS FROM BEYOND THE VEIL
VOLUME III

ADDENDUM "A"

THE TRUTH ON EATING, FASTING AND LIGHT-ENERGY INGESTION

Here again, upon the counsel of my attorney, I must advise you that I am not a medical professional and, therefore, am not qualified to offer dietary advice to anyone. I am not a licensed physician or dietitian. You should seek medical advice before embarking on any reduced food intake program.

In this Addendum, I will be quoting messages from both my first book, *The Last Enemy,* and this book, therefore, the book name will be omitted.

The Scripture says, *"My people are destroyed (die) from the lack of knowledge."* (Hosea 4:16). The inference here is that if they had been taught or gained certain knowledge, they would not die!

There may be a time in the near future when there will be a world-wide famine—a time when the lack of essential electrical service and motor fuel will make life miserable and perilous on this planet. If and when that time comes, the only ones who will survive may be those who know they can live on light-energy <u>alone</u>. (2000 11/9) Is our Father preparing us for something?

2000 11/9 - *"You and all humanity have a deep-seated belief that, 'If I don't eat, I will get sick. If I don't eat, I will die!' This is not true!* <u>The opposite is true!</u> *Light-energy is the only life-sustaining food for the body. The body is light-energy. <u>It must feed on its source!</u> Breathe in more and more light-energy and eat less and less physical food until you sustain your body's life on light-energy alone."*

A note on beginning a light-energy fast: During the first few days of fasting, I have found in my own experience that it is advisable to clear the colon of any food residue that might stop moving caused by my no longer eating any solid foodstuff. I find it advisable in my case to eat four to six prunes and take two or three stool softeners at bed-time the first few days. This keeps things moving out until my colon is empty.

I must share with you my own experiences when doing light-energy fasting and drinking ample amounts of water. After a few days of beginning a light-energy-ingestion water fast, I begin to enjoy having a cup of Chi-tea, Earl Grey tea, or Mocha both morning and evening, and I have learned I am able to live with just these amenities very comfortable on less than four hundred calories per day.

The greatest wonder I have found in this nutrition technique, and what keeps me going, is that as I bring up light-energy from my perineum, down from my crown chakra, and in through the other chakras up and down the body, I have begun to feel the high concentration of energy filling my body and limbs—sometimes it is nearly overwhelming. I find I am stronger during a light-energy-ingestion and fasting from physical food than I am at any other time in my life. I told Jonnie Ann recently that I will probably continue fasting from physical food and ingesting light-energy indefinitely for the rest of my life. If you are wondering if I will ingest any other food? Yes, and I will have, a meal now and then with family and friends, but when I do, I feel physically weaker. I realize that light-energy ingestion with an occasional meal with friends or family is becoming a way of life for me.

I would also like to make a few more comments concerning total fasting from any nourishment:

#1 - Our bodies require nourishment to survive! A total fast, or even a total water-fast, will destroy the body; the body must have nourishment.

#2 - Light-energy is the primal food source of all that exists in the physical realm. Light-energy enlivens every individual particle in all the universes.

#3 - Without light-energy, plant-life will not survive, but the plant-life we see about us does not live on light-energy alone, it must also have nutrients from the soil, water and air. On this planet only mankind has the ability to focus on ingesting light-energy alone, and thereby not only survive, but grow healthy, beautiful, strong, youthful bodies.

Following are messages and comments I have received from the spirit realm on fasting and light-energy ingestion over the years, and have recorded again here from both of my books that the reader might see the great emphasis the spirit world has shown about food and light-energy ingestion. I am bringing one of the later messages on light-energy ingestion to the front here because it is one of the most important I have received on the subject. First, it is imperative that we, "Do all things decently and in order" as the Apostle Paul advised..

2009 9/13 – *"There is an order in fasting and light-energy ingestion. Ingest light-energy first. Fasting should follow when your body realizes it no longer requires physical nourishment. When I spoke to you about this earlier, I did not tell you to fast first, and then ingest light-energy. I said,*

> (2000 7/17): *'The truth you are now receiving about light-energy ingestion transcends the global thought-form about life sustenance. It may be the most difficult to learn and to prove, but you will prevail. It is crucial that you prove this light-energy ingestion concept. Only by ingesting light-energy, can you sustain continual, vibrant, youthful, physical being.'"*

This is interesting. Notice: Back in the 2000 7/17 message, <u>fasting was never mentioned at all</u>. When we are ingesting light-energy, we are not fasting. We are amply feeding the body on its basic life sustenance, light-energy. Maybe, if I ingest light-energy before meals, I won't be as hungry, and then not eat as much. Maybe I would eat less and less until I am eating very little, or nothing at all, but light-energy. Now, I think I finally understand what He has been saying to me all along about light-energy ingestion.

1995 4/5 – In meditation this morning, a voice spoke, *"Spirit (Light-Energy) was the food Christ was referring to as 'Meat to eat that you know not of.'"*

This story, in John 4:32, tells of Jesus' meeting the Samaritan woman at Jacob's well where Jesus had come to teach. He had asked the Samaritan woman for a drink of water and thereby engaged her in a religious debate. In the next few minutes, He convinced her that He was a prophet and the Messiah. She left her water pot and ran to the city to tell the people about Jesus. Meantime, Jesus' disciples had gone into the city to purchase food. Upon returning, they offered Jesus the food, but He refused and told them, *"I have meat to eat that ye know not of."*

It is interesting that the disciples were offering Jesus physical food to nourish His physical body, and Jesus let them know there is another way to nourish the physical body. He said, "My meat is to do the will of Him that sent me, <u>and to finish the work</u>." He was saying, of course, the meat of spiritual obedience energy. He was teaching that we do not need physical food to survive. We need only to listen to the word of the Father within, and follow that word and finish the mission we came here to earth to accomplish. He will lead us to the spiritual meat we need to heal the body and live eternally. (Spiritual Light Energy is what Jesus was talking about ingesting). This book will teach you to live and grow on spiritual light-energy.

1997 7/24 - During meditation this morning, a voice spoke to me about surrender to the Source within: *"Remember Jonnie Ann's terminal illness? I said: 'You be obedient; I will be faithful!' I have already added thirteen years to her life* (25 years at this book's publishing). *Commit your 3-D body to Me in obedience. I am not asking you to have faith. <u>I am asking you to recklessly abandon your body and surrender it to Me—just obedience.</u> Then see what happens. Take your mental hands off—let go! Commit! Ask Me what and how to treat your body;*

what to eat, etc. I took your body through a gasoline tanker, safely.
I can continue to do so. I did this before and without your complete
surrender and commitment. **How much** *(more will I do)* **now that you**
have surrendered, committed, let go, and abandoned your body?"

1997 11/5 - *"You can get all your body nourishment directly from*
Mother Earth through your meditations. Just bring up her energy into
your body."

I need to discuss, here, the light-energy system of the body for you to fully
understand what I am doing during this meditation. I have been instructed
to bring up body nourishment (light-energy) directly from Mother Earth.
Nourishments for the body are the various trace minerals and other energy
substances required for total health. You have to understand, first, that the
body is a light-energy embodiment. It appears, as does everything else, as
physical substance, but it is actually only light-energy; therefore, it can
be completely nourished directly by light-energy being pulled up from
Mother Earth and down from the celestial realms into the body's light-
transducers protruding out from your body a few inches by the action of
the mind during meditation. (These light-energy transducers are called
chakras. Chakras are spinning light vortexes transforming light-energy
to physical energy.). Each chakra/transducers is sensitive to a particular
frequency/color of light. These transducers are found in various locations
on the front, back and both sides of the body, and seem to function with
various major glands of the body.

The discovery of, and knowledge of, the function of the chakra centers of
the body are ancient. Ancient far-eastern and American Indian cultures
recognized seven major chakra centers corresponding to seven major
glandular positions of the body. They discovered early on that these seven
centers responded to, and would react with, particular light colors. I have
discovered that there actually are more than twelve major charkas

It is interesting that the knowledge and understanding of the chakra
energy system has been prevalent in the American Indian cultures for over
15,000 years.

In her book, *Wheels of Light*: by Rosalyn L. Bruyere, published by Simon and Schuster, Rosalyn shows Illustrations of a jeweled figurine of cottonwood root that was found in the prehistoric ruins near Lupton, Arizona. The placement of the jewels in the figurine corresponds to the major chakra centers of far eastern cultures. Another illustration of a Navajo doll with all seven chakras indicated by bits of stone, coral, and shell inserted in the figurine was also found. Is it any mystery why the Indians had such a profound respect for Mother Earth?

1998 10/24 - *"Food causes most diseases and death."*

1998 10/25 - *"The digestive system is meant for tasting and enjoying little amounts of food for joy, not for sustaining life. People die because they are depleted of life-force. You can live <u>indefinitely</u> only by the life giving force of ingesting light-energy. Life-force comes to you from light-energy through your light transducers (chakras) into your light body, and then into your physical body."*

1999 7/23 – "*Think on this Scripture: 'Man shall not live by bread alone, but by every word that proceedeth out of the mouth of God.'*" (Matthew 4:4)

The "*but*" here is of utmost importance. The inference is "but he may live by the words of God alone." The word *and* was not used, so it did not read "Man shall live by bread alone and every word of God." It read and implied, *"Man shall live by every word that proceedeth out of the mouth of God."*

1999 12/1 - *"Rejoice! The light-energy you are bringing in will eventually restore and recreate your life/growth genes, and your aging process will regress to young, mature manhood. Think on Isaiah 40:28-31: 'Hast thou not known? Hast thou not heard, that the everlasting God, the Lord, the Creator of the ends of the Earth fainteth not, neither is weary? There is no searching of his understanding. He giveth power to the faint and to them that have no might he increaseth strength. <u>Even</u>*

the youths shall faint and be weary, and the young men shall utterly fall: But they that wait upon the Lord shall renew their strength; they shall mount up with wings as eagles; they shall run, and not be weary; and shall walk, and not faint."'

Dismiss this truth and you will die physically again, as most have for millions of years. Study this great Scriptural truth, and you will find the answer to, "Is eternal youth possible?"

1999 12/20 - *"Give me a bite. A bite will satisfy your hunger."*

I have tried this many times, and it works for me. Five or six bites do not work! That just seems to increase my hunger. But when I'm fasting, and terribly hungry, one bite (HAND RADIATED FIRST) satisfies me completely as I ingest light-energy along with it.

2000 2/18 - *"You need to develop the habit of spending more time each day ingesting light-energy."*

This is not just a morning and evening ritual. It needs to be a constant awareness activity. You, as I have, will eventually recognize the presence and touch of your guides and healers as they show you where to bring in, or concentrate the light-energy. This has been going on for some time now for me, so much so, that I sometimes stop what I am doing during the day and attend to the light transfer right then and there when I feel their touch.

If you have not yet recognized the touch of your healers, I will share with you how mine affect me. Their touch resembles a tickle or itch and even sometimes manifests as pain somewhere on my head or body while I am bringing in light-energy and sometimes when I am just going about my normal day. Much of the time, my healers and guides touch me on the head while I am doing light-energy work. It feels like an itch on my scalp and can become a severe burning pain as the light-energy transfer level increases. Don't scratch the itching area for it usually stops when you do. Just increase breathing in energy at that location until it subsides.

2000 7/17 - *"The truth you are now receiving about light-energy ingestion transcends the global-thought-forms about life sustenance. It may be the most difficult to learn and to prove, but you will prevail."*

Fasting is difficult, especially in this food-focused society. It is nearly impossible to fast while living in this society, and especially with a person or family who is not fasting, or who is possibly less than supportive of, or even resistant to your fasting. Don't let this discourage you or even annoy you. They are where they are supposed to be in their spirit quest and you are where you are supposed to be. Allow them to resist you, and continue your quest.

First, they don't understand why you insist on fasting, so there is a conflict. Secondly, most people mistakenly believe it is unhealthy to fast, and fasting without light-energy ingestion is unhealthy. The medical profession is nearly 100 percent opposed to total water fasting. Even though the medical profession sees the folly of overeating and the dangers of too much red meat and sugar, they still condemn fasting as an unhealthy alternative.

The truth is, the body needs a rest from digesting physical foods. It needs time to recoup and expel the toxins ingested from meats, greasy breads, cooked vegetables, and sweets. Within three days after beginning a water-fast, the body changes its digestive process and goes into ketosis. The tongue becomes coated with a white film, and the body begins to expel toxins from every pore and orifice—in the urine, the breath, in the fecal matter, etc.

After the fourth day, the body realizes eating habits have been broken and no longer hungers for the regular, timed meals of breakfast, lunch and dinner; the tongue eventually returns to its pink color, and the body settles down to the job of detoxification. Yet, the smell or sight of your favorite foods can trigger a hunger response.

I was told once in meditation that "just a bite" would satisfy my hunger when it arises during a fast. I found this to be true. Another time, I was told to "feed on the words you have been given when you are hungry." This also works.

Probably, the easiest way to start a total, or water fast, is to fast from dinner to dinner for a few days, gradually reducing the amount of food consumed at that single dinner meal until you are eating nothing at all. Also, I have found that honey sweetened hot tea once or twice a day helps. It is socially acceptable and will not take you off your fast.

After that, go with a total food fast, but drink plenty of water. You can be sure that the longer you fast and substitute light-energy ingestion, the healthier you will become. You will read later (2000 12/4, The Last Enemy) that aging and death are the result of toxin ingestion from the foods we eat.

To accomplish a total fast for an extended period of time, Jesus had to leave his family and journey to a vast wilderness for forty days. We, too, might have to separate ourselves from our families and friends in this food focused society to sustain a total fast and see it through.

You will see on the following pages that our Father speaks to me often about fasting and light-energy ingestion.

I would never attempt a total fast without making sure I was feeding on light-energy from Mother Earth and ingesting healing/cleansing light-energy from the Celestial realms. That would certainly be dangerous and unhealthy.

Note: While proofreading and correcting this manuscript, I found an excellent book on fasting, *The Fasting Path*, by Stephen Harrod Buhner.

2000 7/17 - *"It is crucial that you prove this light ingestion concept. Only by ingesting light-energy, can you sustain continual vibrant, youthful, physical being."*

That is as direct and plain as it can be stated. He has repeated this many times. When will we really see it?

2000 7/17 - *"Ingesting physical food, especially animal products, drains life force from the body and must be constantly overcome by light-energy ingestion. It is best to greatly limit physical food sustenance."*

2000 7/17 - *"Light-energy renews the body and heals all ailments."*

OK, I will do my light-energy ingestion exercises all the time! Refer back to 11/05/97 for this light ingestion technique

2000 7/23 - *"Animal products and manufactured chemical sweets interfere with perfect development of the body. Light energy ingestion is the only perfect food for perfect development of the body."*

Our bodies have never fully developed due to the ingestion of animal flesh and refined sugars. This, coupled with the lack of light-energy ingestion, makes me wonder why we are not all disfigured and dead by the age of seventy. We can change this and allow our bodies to resume the development process by fasting, and ingesting light-energy.

2000 10/5 - *"Animal tissue and refined sugars are toxins to the body and must be cleansed by light-energy ingestion. Immediately after consuming animal flesh or sugar, bring in light-energy to cleanse and neutralize the effects of the toxins."*

Lord, help me remember these words when I sit down to eat. We must treat our foods with light-energy before we eat. We must then treat our bodies with light-energy after we eat.

2000 10/5 - *"Eat less, but when you eat, try fresh and raw fruits and vegetables; however, your body needs only light-energy to survive."*

This is not saying that you can survive without eating and just sit down and wait for your body to renew itself. Your body needs nutrition from Mother Earth and the Celestial Realms in the form of light-energy. Use the light-energy ingestion technique to feed the body.

Well, If we must have a rational explanation of why light ingestion works, here it is! The body is light-energy; therefore it must feed on its life-source.

2000 11/9 - *"Fear of dying from the lack of food shackles you to the world economic system. <u>You will never be free until you know, without a doubt, that you can live on light-energy alone.</u> Whole worlds of truth will then begin to unfold before you."*

I hear these words every time I meditate. This is a challenge for me to see just what will happen during a sustained fast. I yearn for these "worlds of truth."

2000 12/4 - *"If animal products, sugar, alcohol, and most physical foods were cut out, most aging would be stopped. If all physical food is stopped, and only light-energy consumed, all aging would cease, and the body would heal itself. Natural death is the result of continually and completely poisoning the body until the tissues are full of toxins; death of the body results. People slowly poison themselves to death."*

Am I or any one else alive today strong enough spiritually to prove these words? Someone has to be first. Lord, let it be me. Allow me to be faithful to your words. Give me the force of will to walk in thy words!

2001 8/28 - *"The more saturated your tissues are with toxins, the weaker you will feel. This weakness is more apparent as your tissues near saturation. This is what people experience as aging."*

At any point during the aging process, you can fast and ingest light-energy for a few days; thereafter, you will experience the detoxification process beginning and body youth returning. What are a few days? I would say anywhere from 20-100 days, or as you are led by your deeper self. Note: Read "The Fasting Path" by Stephen Harrod Buhner, for further guidance and information on fasting.

2001 8/28 - *"Human body cells renew constantly, but they are finally overcome by the shear volume of poisons in the tissues. At present, this process usually takes seventy to ninety years for total saturation and body degeneration to occur. Natural death of the body is simply toxic degeneration caused by the foods we eat."*

We are told by the medical profession that our body cells are renewing constantly, so why do our bodies seem to degenerate, grow old, and die? Here, He explains it all. Why are our medical schools not aware of this poisoning process of the body? Maybe many in the profession are aware.

2001 8/28 - *"Light energy ingestion will remove toxins and nourish the body back to perfect health and youthful energy."*

If you want to discover the "fountain of youth," there it is. You can go back to the teaching on 10/25/98 to see how to ingest light-energy.

2001 8/28 - *"The medical systems today treat symptoms, not the root cause of most illnesses, which is toxicity. Most medical remedies do nothing more than suppress symptoms (toxic reactions) in the body. They do nothing to reduce toxicity; moreover, much of the time, they add to the toxic levels in the body tissues."*

The reason so many people die while on chemotherapy treatment is that the added poisons kill the last life sustaining cells in the body. There is a better way: fasting and light-energy ingestion therapy is always life-giving.

2001 12/12 - *"Light-energy is the only life-giving, life-sustaining force in the Universe."*

There it is. Learn to ingest light-energy or die and try again; it is that simple. This is because light-energy ingestion brings in truth and life directly from the Source. He is the only source of truth and life. Truth and life directly from the Father is what we must seek above all else.

2001 12/12 - *"We receive light-energy indirectly from the foods we eat, but it is too diluted to sustain continual cleansing and regeneration of the physical body."*

The foods we eat also bring in all kinds of toxins, which eventually saturate the tissues of the body, and help to destroy it. The substances we feed our body appears to be that very things that destroys it.

2001 12/12 - *"Direct light-energy ingestion is the only pure, life-sustaining energy for the human body. Indirect light-energy from plant life is the second purest light-energy source. The third light-energy source is animal flesh. This animal flesh energy is the most diluted form of light-energy and greatly limits life regeneration."*

Do we need any more help to develop a menu for ourselves in this society? No meats, no sweets, no between meal treats! Eat fresh fruits, vegetables, and nuts, and ingest light-energy. Stay healthy. Let your joyful mantra be "NO MEATS, NO SWEETS, NO BETWEEN MEAL TREATS!

2002 1/17 - *"Don't fret; the will and determination to follow My words will come. Wait on Me. I will lead you. I will fill you with joy and the thrill of obedience to perform the quest I have set before you."*

Each of us will find a precious moment when we are filled with joy and the thrill of obedience; then it will be easy to follow whatever He tells us to do.

2002 1/18 - *"When you are hungry, feed on the words you have been given."*

We are each listening to our Father inwardly. This is our food. The word of God from within us will so fill us that we will feel no need for physical nourishment.

2002 1/22 - *"Toxins are materials foreign to the composition of the human body."*

Something that concerns me is that I've always wondered what the ingredients shown on food labels are doing to us. Most packaged or canned foods list one or more preservatives on the labels, and I know most preservatives are foreign to the body. If they kill bacteria to keep foods from spoiling, what are they killing in us? I meet folks that display the definite possibility that their brain cells may have fallen victim to this process.

2002 1/28 - *"Cleanse and energize every food by hand radiation before you eat it."*

Lord, help me to remember to do this. I enjoy eating so much that, sometimes, I forget.

Before you eat, place your hands over the food as shown in the illustration. Then bring in healing, cleansing light-energy down from your crown chakra, down your arms and hands into the food. This will cleanse the good and protect the body.

2002 2/20 - *"Moses, the sea you must part and cross is the sea of false global-thought-forms such a, 'Eat or die' – 'All must die someday' – 'All must age' – 'None have control over his or her own health' – 'I must have doctors to heal me' – 'You are a victim of chance or luck' – 'There is no God, or He just does not care' – 'I am not spiritual enough, so I need a minister, guru, or priest.'"*

2002 5/15 - *"As you fast and cleanse your body with light-energy, you are going to face some emotional issues related to your <u>Youth Recovery Process</u>. As you begin to appear younger and stronger, others around you will still be aging and dying in disbelief, even though they see the truth standing before them. This will trouble you. Don't let it! It is not your concern. Others must receive this truth from within, from the Source, before they can believe this can happen to them. Then, your* *words and revelations will be confirmations to them. The negative global-thought-forms are too powerful for most to believe everlasting life is possible for them. Most will age and die while watching you recover your strength and youth."*

These global-thought-forms that promise death are reinforced by the National Mortality Tables which are accepted by all "learned men." All believe death is certain somewhere between 75 and 95, and we are taught by the medical establishment that total fasting will hasten it. These "notions" are force-fed to by the scientific and medical communities. They believe total fasting is insane, and with their AMA presence in Washington, D.C., they may have a law passed someday to prosecute anyone encouraging fasting.

It is hard for us to just allow our loved ones to slide toward physical death from most food poisoning when they could avoid it. Tragic, but true! I want to just force-feed these truths to my loved ones, but I know that would not work. They must progress through the numerous incarnations until they understand the words and hear them from the Source within themselves. "Christ in you, your hope of glory." (Colossians 1:27).

2002 7/04 - *"When you are ingesting light-energy and are in a total fast, you will be amazed how fast your body will heal and cleanse itself."*

I am looking forward to a prolonged fast of months and even years. I was told (2003 6/12), to "immerse myself in the light" Now, I know how!

2003 8/3 - *"The slaughterhouses produce terror and confusion in the animals they are killing. These terror and confusion Emotional-Thought-Forms are embedded in the animals' cells. These Thought-Forms of terror and confusion are then transferred to those who ingest this animal flesh. Cooking the meat does not remove these terror and confusion Thought-Forms."*

It appears that the tortuous life and violent death experience of slaughtered animals are imprinted or embedded in the indestructible cellular essence and emotions of these entities, and, as such, are transferred to the subconscious mind, or cellular consciousness of those who ingest the flesh of these animals. It sounds to me like He is telling me this terror and confusion becomes embodied in their DNA; and then it is transferred into our DNA as we ingest their flesh.

Is it any wonder then, that we are so fearful, violent and confused? <u>Could we reduce the fear and violent tendencies in ourselves and throughout the world by changing our diet, by just not eating any animal products?</u> Could we eventually eliminate the violent potential in ourselves by ceasing from eating animal flesh, fasting regularly, and ingesting light-energy? It does seem to make sense, doesn't it?

Could this possibly be the root cause of much of the confusion we see around us in education, politics, religion, and in the business world? It seems most of those connected with these institutions don't know what is right and wrong anymore. We sit and scratch our heads wondering what our politicians, business leaders and educators are thinking.

One of our problems is that we don't see the violence and terror inflicted on the animals we are eating. If we did, we probably wouldn't eat them. We are too far removed from the farms and personally tending of the animals to see and understand who they are and what they are going through, and how they feel.

You might really enjoy the information in two books that are listed in the Book Reference section in the back of this book. One is The *Sunfood Diet Success Program,* by David Wolfe, and the other *The World Peace Diet,* by Will Tuttle.

2003 8/6 - *"There is a Chakra that corresponds to every organ and gland in the body. In your light ingestion work, activate each Chakra and bring in its light frequency and color."*

Bring in each Chakra's color if you know what it is. If not, tell the Chakra to bring in the color it needs. Then, just allow light-energy to flow into it.

It is interesting that the Hopi Indians have known about the body chakra locations and their colors long before we <u>civilized</u> Europeans arrived on this continent. And, we have the gall to call them primitive...

Think on your preference or delight when your eyes are exposed to some color they seem to want to feed on. They seem to hunger for certain colors—feed them those special colors. Could it be that your body, through the operation of your eye's color preference, is telling you it needs those color energies? Concentrate on those colors and bring them into your body, asking your body to use these particular colors as it needs. Your body knows?

Your body knows. Read David R. Hawkins book on muscle testing, *Truth v/s Falsehood*.

2003 9/10 - *"Prove the words for others and for yourself. Hosts of Angels are awaiting your success."*

OK, here it is, He is admonishing me to prove fasting and light-energy ingestion. Prove that a bite will satisfy my hunger. Prove that I will have more strength, clearer thinking, grow younger, and experience complete detoxification from fasting and light-energy ingestion. The first thing to do is to begin a sustained fast.

2003 9/17 - *"Water is dormant energy. Drink good amounts while fasting. Water is broken down in the body's cells to use as oxygen and hydrogen to energize the body."*

I intend to follow this utterance to see what the underlying message is that it is teaching, or suggesting. There is more.

2003 9/17 - *"After your successful, sustained, healing, fast, other parallel and secondary selves will then have this light-energy ingestion victory experience embedded in their deeper consciousness. They will know that they too can have this victory."*

Interesting! Since one consciousness resides in us all, and our secondary selves also share our personal consciousness, one victory will be realized by all and increase the enlightenment of all. It will never be as difficult for other secondary selves to believe, intend and accomplish a sustained, youth-recovery fast when it is achieved by any one of us.

2003 9/30 - *"It is all about proving the words, Jack!"*

WE NEVER IMPROVE UNTIL WE PROVE! So, we must go through all the trials, tests and situations until we prove, believe and are able to walk in the truth we are being taught: We must walk out our truth!

2003 10/8 - *"While fasting, spend traditional mealtimes ingesting light-energy. Make this habitual. You must train yourself to spend more time in meditation and light ingestion."*

Our spiritual growth is probably proportional to our time in focused meditation. I know that not much happens spiritually in my life outside of mediation. My quiet, sacred place is my power base.

2004 11/6 -You are moving from the experience of intent to the reality of knowing. This means knowing 'I am well' makes you well. Knowing 'I am younger and stronger' makes you younger and stronger. Knowing that you can live on light-energy alone MAKES YOU IMMORTAL."

I move into this experience by knowing first that "I am," that I am one with the Father, that I am the Father and that I have His power to create whatever experience or condition in the physical or spiritual realm I desire. All that is necessary for me to do is to simply use **high emotional focus** on the situation or experience I desire and then accept it and embrace it into existence.

2005 11/13 – "Drink only Holy Water—water that you have infused with love, joy, peace, grace, truth, wisdom healing and thanksgiving. Give attention to water, then listen, watch and wait."

I think this truth was picked up by the Catholic Church hundreds of years ago, and is still used in their services. They learned that water is alive and conscious and when blessed, carries that power to whatever purpose it is intended.

The prophet Nostradamus used water in his meditations to predict the future. The seer used a bowl of water in his meditations and stared into the water. It would eventually form pictorial scenes of future events.

2006 1/12 – *"Think of water as the liquid consciousness of the Father."*

Yes, Water is a assembly of living cells or organisms just as you are. It hears and it feels emotions like you and feel emotions. Everything in physicality is alive and conscious. It is our Father and it is you and me.

2008 6/18 – *"Don't forget to cleanse your food by spirit radiation before you eat it."*

It is easy to forget to radiate our food before we eat it. We learned from our parents to call it blessing the table, but it goes deeper than that. We are eternal, divine beings with omnipotent power and the ability to change the very nature of a substance set before us. We must learn to hold our hands over the food, or if it is small enough, grasp the food in our hand and bring light-energy radiation into it. This is the same method we use when bringing light-energy into our body. We live on light-energy. We must learn to do what we have been taught concerning our food intake.

2009 2/8 – *"All the various sense organs of the body were given to you to enjoy physicality, not to addictively indulge in their pleasures. Be moderate and let them teach you the uniqueness of their being and abilities. Listen, touch, taste and smell the subtle universes in and around you."*

2009 2/14 –*"Let's talk about eating the flesh of other sentient beings (animals, birds fish and insects). These beings have the same feelings and emotions that you have, but lack the ability to express them verbally. They have the same fear and feel the same terror you would feel if you were in their place and going through their experiences in the slaughter houses.*

As you saw last night when the restaurant in Fort Collins tried to satisfy every gluttonous flesh eating pleasure, there is no end to the desire for the taste for new flesh. <u>This addiction to eating animal flesh cannot be satisfied</u>: it always leads eventually to cannibalism in those who yield to it, especially in times of dire circumstances or in affluent societies where the extremely rich have exhausted all other forms of entertainment. You can be sure that there are secret groups of people, even in this country, who are feeding on human flesh. Many of the missing young people in this country have been served up on the table of these gluttonous cannibals. These atrocities will be exposed later and all will understand the extent of this addiction."

2009 4/13 – *"When you leave the body, what will sustain your life? Will you need to eat? Think about it. Light-energy will sustain you then, <u>and it does now!</u> Physical food will not be required then, and it is not required now. You have light transducers (chakras) all over your physical body to convert light-energy to physical energy now. Ingesting as much physical food as most humans do interferes with and diminishes your life-force. You already know that digesting food uses a great amount of energy. The physical food digestion process is slowly draining your reserves of life force. Again, I admonish you Learn to live on light-energy alone. Begin a life fast!"*

2009 4/20 – *"Light-energy ingestion is not fasting. During light-energy ingestion, you are consuming the purest food source. It is pure energy, much more complete and powerful than physical food of any kind could ever be."*

2009 4/26 – *Why does the physical body have chakras? If physical food alone would sustain the body, why have light transducers all over it? The Truth is, light-energy is already our source of life-force, but we are unaware of this and are actually defiling the body with copious amounts of animal and other physical foods that war against and defile the body. We have forgotten how to energize (feed) the body on light-energy, so we degenerate and die. Physician, heal thyself!"*

2009 4/30 – *"For centuries earnest seekers have been searching for victory over physical death. Deeply within, they all know it is possible. They have searched for the fountain of youth all over the earth. They are living in foreign mountain caves and ashrams in continual prayer and meditation. They are restricting their diets to only fresh and raw fruits, nuts, and vegetables. But, within 70 to 90 years they still die. You must lead them to the truth: Only light-energy ingestion will support continual physical body life. Tasting a bite of fruit, nuts or vegetables (after it is radiated with light-energy) from time to time just for joy and fellowship will not interfere with your body's health. The physical body can only live into multiple centuries by receiving its life-force from light-energy ingestion."*

2009 5/12 – *"Why have I waited so long to reveal the truth of light-energy ingestion to you? Would others believe a young man in perfect health telling them to fast and ingest light-energy for perfect health and longevity? No, they would not, and very few will believe a one hundred year old former heart patient who looks thirty years old and runs marathons; however, the few who do believe will lead the rest of humanity to life."*

2009 5/13 – *"During an extended fast, why radiate the morsel or taste of food that you decide to eat? The answer is that you are infusing the morsel of food with the real, basic food energy—light-energy. This is why the custom of blessing food was brought down through the ages. Originally, people knew the safety and nourishment of food came from the blessing (light-energy infusion) and not from the dead physical food product itself. Yes, even vegetables, fruits and nuts are dead food products and will eventually decompose (rot). Light-energy is the only continually-living food source for our bodies."*

2009 5/16 – *"There are four levels of food sources for the human body. The first level is direct light-energy ingestion. Light or divine spirit energy is everywhere. Even in total darkness, there is an abundance of divine light-energy. It is Father's life-force energy and is omnipresent in every corner of the universes, in every dimension, and saturates the void. It is always available. The second level of food source is the natural vegetable kingdom. This includes vegetables, fruits and nuts. This food source feeds directly light-energy and Earth energy. It therefore contains a great amount of light-energy and will sustain the body healthily for many years. The vegetable kingdom food source however, is diluted energy and is dead food when you eat it. The third level of food source is the herbivore animal flesh. God's do not eat animal flesh! The herbivore animal flesh foods are nourished from the second level food source—vegetables. Animals are not nourished by direct light ingestion as are vegetables, and, therefore, their life force is greatly diluted. The fourth level food source is carnivore animal flesh. This is the worst source of food for the human body and it carries very little life energy."*

2009 6/1 – *For any meaningful results, you must move light-energy into the situation. Remember I told you to 'Share the light. We are all light conduits.* (1999 2/25)

This is our command to send or infuse light-energy into other's needful situations. What else can we do? We don't know enough about their situation to make a rational judgment of what they need. They and our Father know; let them direct our light-energy to where it needs to be.

2009 6/9 – *"Jack, most of those near you will not believe your words on fasting until you prove them. When you prove the words, some very close to you will believe, begin a fast and miraculously heal their bodies through following your example in light ingestion and fasting. Others who have just read your book but don't know you, will also follow your* *example and be healed of miserable debilitations. Go for it, my son, for them and yourself."*

2009 6/9 – I asked, "Lord, how do I love habitual hunger back to a positive impulse?"

He answered, *"You have to remember these 'hunger impulses' are spirits, Jack. You have never fully understood or received this fact. You have, however, observed and acknowledged it in others, even in times past calling them demon spirits. Now, understand that gluttony is a spirit that needs to be loved back into a positive impulse. It wants to help and be faithful to you. Face this spirit entity with love. Love it and reprogram* (re-polarize) *it into a faithful helper in your quest for a lengthy fasting experience. It will help you on your quest to hold a fast indefinitely.* (See: 2003 8/1 on re-polarize)

2009 6/20 – I am now in the tenth day of my fast. Jonnie Ann and I have come up to our mountain house for the weekend. While walking up and down my steep driveway getting tools and material for a job my legs began to get weak. My pulse rate was no problem, since it was still at about 82, which is normal for me when exerting moderate physical energy at these altitudes, but the weakness was noticeable; I thought, "This is probably from fasting for ten days."

Someone said, *"Remember my exhortation to you, to pull more energy up from Mother Earth through your feet?"*

Look at the words on 1999 11/30. *"Don't neglect your feet. Pull my light-energy up through your feet too."*

I recalled also what had been said to me just this morning during meditation, and so with each step I took, I breathed in the red light-energy from my dear Mother Gaia. I brought light-energy up though the next foot touching the ground as I walked. The weakness disappeared immediately. I kept up this light-energy breath rhythm all the way up the driveway until I reached the top. The weakness did not return.

2009 6/20 – I have been made keenly aware today that when I just take a small taste of something for pleasure during a fast, I must stop eating with just that one taste. Any more than a taste will generate an appetite for more food. Light-energy ingestion is critical to eliminating hunger. It is the light-energy that satisfies my body's hunger, and not the physical food being tasted. This has always been true in this physical reality, but few have ever realized it.

> I remember the words given on 2000 11/9, *The Last Enemy:*
> "*The body is light-energy. It must feed on its source.*"

The words "keenly aware" are an understatement. I took a couple of mouthfuls at breakfast, and immediately found myself ravished by hunger. I ate more and realized the fast was over for this time, and that I would have to start all over again to experience a sustained fast. We live and learn, don't we? This was a lesson I needed to experience before I begin another fast. I must remember once and for all that JUST A TASTE WILL SATISIFY, BUT A MOUTHFULL WILL BREAK THE FAST. What I should have done when I was tempted to take another taste was pause and begin bringing in light-energy instead of a second bite—the fast would have continued.

2009 7/7 – "*Eating until full is food addiction. Eating animal flesh and animal products are addictive and this is harmful to your body. Look at the 'book of Enoch' for references to animal flesh addiction.*

The digestive system of the human species was designed for the processing of small amounts (tastes) of fruits, nuts and vegetables. Light-energy is your staple and essential food source."

Look at the size of most fruits and nuts. Most grow to the exact size for a good taste treat and enjoyment, but will not fill you up. Also, it is interesting that one nut, such as a pecan or walnut which is much smaller than most fruits, is big enough to give you the hunger satisfaction of feeling full, and it is rich in protein. Try it. Take one whole pecan, hold it in your hand and send light-energy radiation into it, eat it and drink some water. Your hunger will be satisfied, IF you have ingested light-energy first.

2009 9/13 – *"There is an order in fasting and light-energy ingestion. Ingest light-energy first. Fasting should follow when your body realizes it no longer requires physical nourishment. I did not tell you to fast first and then ingest light-energy. I said,* (2000 7/17):

> *'The truth you are now receiving about light-energy ingestion transcends the global thought-form about life sustenance. It may be the most difficult to learn and to prove, but you will prevail. It is crucial that you prove this light ingestion concept. Only by ingesting light-energy, can you sustain continual, vibrant, youthful, physical being.'"*

That is interesting. Notice: in the 2000 7/17 message, <u>fasting was never mentioned at all</u>. When we are ingesting light-energy, we are not fasting. We are feeding the body its basic life sustenance, light-energy. Maybe, if I ingest light-energy before meals, I won't be hungry and then not eat as much. Maybe I would eat less and less until I am eating very little or nothing at all but light-energy. Now I think I finally understand what He has been saying to me all along about light-energy ingestion.

HAVE A GOOD TIME WITH YOUR LIGHT-ENERGY ADVENTURE

Bibliography And Work Cited

Broyere, Rosalyn. _Wheels of Light_. Rockefeller Center, New York, N.Y.: Fireside, Simon and Schuster, Copyright © 1989, 1991, 1994. ISBN: 0671-79624-0

(Chakras locations and colors)

Emoto, Masaru. _The Power of Water_. Hillsboro, Oregon Beyond Words Publishing, Inc., Copyright © 2005 ISBN: 1-58270-128-8

(Emoto's discoveries of the consciousness of water)

Hawkins, David R. _Power v/s Force_. Carlsbad, California Axial Publishing Company. Copyright © 1995, 1998, 2992 ISBN: 1-56170-933-6

(Muscle testing and kinesiology)

Hawkins, Steven. _Steven Hawkins Universe,_ New York, N.Y. David Filkin Enterprises Ltd. Copyright © 1997 ISBN: 0-465-08199-1

(Present knowledge of the origin of the Universe)

Kelder, Peter. *Ancient Secret of the Fountain of Youth.* New York, N.Y
    Doubleday, A division of Random House, Inc. Copyright ©
    1999
    ISBN: 0-385-49167-0

    (Ancient Tibetan Rites of Rejuvenation)

Sitchin, Zecharia. *The Lost Book of Enki.* Rochester, Vermont
    Bear and Company. Copyright © 2002
    ISBN: 1-879181-83-5

    Note: All other Zecharia Sitchin Books are recommended.
    (Information: Translations of the ancient texts pertaining to our
    sister-Planet, Nibiru and its inhabitants, the Anunnaki)

Tuttle, Will. *The World Peace Diet,* New York, N.Y.
    Lantern Books. Copyright © 2005
    ISBN: 1-59056-083-3

    (Eating for Spiritual Health and Social Harmony)

Wolfe, David. *The Sunfood Diet Success System.* San Diego, California
    Sunfood Publishing. Copyright © 2008
    ISBN: 978-1-55643-749-6

    (Recommended Eating for Spiritual Health)

Yogananda, Paramahansa. *Autobiography of a Yogi,* Los Angeles,
California
    Self-Realization Fellowship. Copyright © 1946, 1974, 1981,
    1993, 1998
    ISBN: 0-87612-079-6

    (Studies on Enlightenment)

RECOMMENDED READING

Book Title: Galactic Alignment
Author: John Major Jenkins
Publisher: Bear and Company
ISBN: 978-187918184-7
Information: Studies on the 2012 galactic alignment

    Book Title: The Prana Program
    Author: Jasmuheen
    Publisher: Self Empowerment Academy
    ISBN: 978-1-84728-343-6
    Information: Studies on living on light-energy.

Book Title: God I Am
Author: Peter Erbe
Publisher: Buy at Amazon.com
ISBN: 0-646-05255-1
Information: One of the best books on *who we are*.

    Book Title: The World Peace Diet
    Author: Will Tuttle, Ph.D.
    Publisher: Lantern Books
    ISBN: 1-590-56-083-3
    Information: The right way to eat without animal flesh.

Book Title: Why Healing Happens
Author: O.T. Bonnett, M.D.
Publisher: Ozark Mountain Publishing
ISBN: 1-886940-93-2
Information: Great book on body/mind healing

    Book Title: The Fasting Path
    Author: Stephen Harrod Buhner
    Publisher: Penguin Group (USA) Inc.
    ISBN: 1-58333-170-0
    Information: Great work on fasting